GENERATION OF NARCISSUS

GENERATION
OF NARCISSUS
BY HENRY MALCOLM

With an introduction by

R. Buckminster Fuller

LITTLE, BROWN AND COMPANY

BOSTON / TORONTO

The quotation on page 144 is from Herbert Marcuse, *Eros and Civilization*. Copyright 1955, © 1966 by The Beacon Press, reprinted by permis-
sion of Beacon Press.

*Published simultaneously in Canada
by Little, Brown & Company (Canada) Limited*

PRINTED IN THE UNITED STATES OF AMERICA

To my wife, Angeline

CONTENTS

INTRODUCTION

Henry Malcolm is in synchronization with the thoughts and the drives of a very large portion of today's youth. He became synchronized with them not just by his senses and not just by his sympathetic heart but through extraordinarily important scholarly understanding. Malcolm's scholarly understanding derives from a broad spectrum of history, and particularly from his insights into the fundamental conceptioning of human behaviorism from which the Greek gods were evolved. I was struck by the similarity of Malcolm's thinking with that of a little-known preoccupation of my great-aunt, Margaret Fuller. In Boston, in the early nineteenth century, Margaret conducted a series of *conversations* on the subject of the "Greek Gods." She saw that great thinkers of early Greece differentiated out a hierarchy of unique human behaviors. Their discovered behaviors, as embodied in the character of the major and minor gods, disclosed a galaxy of nuances of understanding on the part of the Greek philosophers who categorized the human behaviors.

Margaret saw, as does Malcolm today, that the Greeks found it easy to gain understanding by their listeners, regarding the full range of human behaviorism, when they developed analogies. The analogies assumed the abstract existence of imperishable beings who coexisted invisibly with humanity. These gods dramatized clearly the unique behavioral characteristics which the great Greek thinkers had scientifically differentiated out from the complex of all known behaviors. Margaret realized that the Greek philosopher-psychologists had recourse to those imagined living models the better to explain scientifically generalizable, ergo eternally recurring, behavioral nuances. But she saw also that the Greek philosophers' listeners gradually tended to consider the fictitious characters only as special living case realities, either overlooking or never understanding, the completely abstract scientific concept of generalization.

Even today few people realize the abstract nature of scientific generalizations. Society is familiar with a literary generalization, which means covering too much territory too thinly to be persuasive. On the other hand, a scientific generalization is established only when a relationship is found that holds true in every known special case experience. Once an exception is discovered it can no longer be classified as a scientific generalization. The omnireliable, four-part, behavioral-complex relationship of the *lever, fulcrum, load,* and *working effort* and its mathematical proportionalities is an excellent example of an established, scientifically generalized principle. The mathematically predictable advantage ratios of the lever hold true whether the lever, or its fulcrum or its load, be of wood, steel, aluminum, fiber glass, or even of reinforced concrete.

If the distance from the load to the fulcrum is one foot and you go out on the lever arm ten feet, and you weigh two hundred pounds, you will be able to lift ten times your own weight, or exactly one ton, on the short end of the lever. With a ten-foot lever advantage, "little two-hundred-pound you" can lift one ton. The scientific generalizability or the lever consists in the fact that it doesn't *have* to be of wood. It can be of any kind of material, and it will work with the same mathematical ratios of advantage anywhere in the Universe. Whereas your personal experience with levers must always be with special-case levers — that is, with a ten-foot wooden one, or a twenty-

foot steel one, or with any special one. Only your mind com-
prehends the generalized principle of leverage and you can only
design your levers to be special-case, specifically dismensioned,
specifically materialized experiences.

That the mathematics and the principle can be separated out
from the gamut of special-case subjective or objective experiences is not popularly understood. So Margaret found the early
Greek thinkers to be discovering scientifically *generalized
principles* of human behavior, and using *special-case explanations* to illustrate them, with the listeners seizing upon only the
special-case explanations. That is why the Greek populace
thought in the terms of real — that is, special-case — gods. The
people thought of their gods as "realities" rather than thinking
of them as scientific generalizations and abstractions.

In the eighteenth and nineteenth centuries A.D., some two
thousand years after the Greek philosopher-scientists' conceptual development of scientific behaviors — which as we have
seen were popularly misinterpreted only as special-case realities
— electromagnetic scientists and electrical engineers evolved
a family of names to describe the unique family of generalized
behaviors manifest in complex electrical generating and con-
ducting systems. The behaviors of electromagnetics disclosed
conductance, inductance, resistance, impedance, reluctance, etc.
If we consider each and all of the known electrical behaviors,
we find those electromagnetic behavioral names neatly fitting the
Greek gods' behaviors. In fact, they seem to be the same phenomena as the unique behavioral characteristics displayed by
Zeus, Apollo, Hermes, etc. The dozen prime gods and the
dozen prime electrical behaviors seem to be identical. Because
the Greek philosopher-scientists developed their generalized
behavior concepts millennia before electrical engineering and
did so only from observing social behaviors of humans, it may
be inferred from all the foregoing that unbeknownst to the
social sciences, the same laws underlying electromagnetics may
underlie social behaviors. As yet unrewarded by discovery of
any scientific generalizations or laws governing social behaviors
the social scientists may be enlightened by Ohm's Law. While

Malcolm's employment of the Greek gods' behaviors does not derive from either Margaret Fuller's or from my own speculations, Henry Malcolm has performed an extraordinarily important favor for modern-day psychology by reconsidering these fundamental behaviors of humans today as those behaviors were originally understood by the great Greek thinkers. Having started with the Greeks, Henry Malcolm then moves forward several millennia to Freud and other contemporary psychologists. Malcolm explains changes in modern youth's behavior by combining the Greek god behaviorisms and those detected by Freud. He has not done this in a superficial, storybook way, but as a real scholar. I, personally, find his explanations of many of today's behaviors — in the terms of what he calls the "Generation of Narcissus" — to be valid. All of his thoughts are regenerative — they start you thinking as you have never before thought.

— R. Buckminster Fuller

PART 1
THE ADULT
ESTABLISHMENT:
THE TRIUMPHS AND FAILURES
OF A PROMETHEAN
GENERATION

1

AMERICAN MASS
CULTURE AND THE
ILLUSION OF PARADISE

The preeminent paradox of middle-class society is the contrast between the environment in which the young are raised — characterized by unprecedented affluence and ubiquitous technology — and the outside or "real" world, which is dominated by racism, poverty, bureaucracy, war, and pollution. In effect, we have revived, but altered, the ancient polarization between paradise and the pain-filled world. We prolong the child's stay in paradise before casting him full-grown into the world beyond. The biblical story of the Garden of Eden is in the process of being rewritten. Through unparalleled affluence, permissive child rearing, progressive education, changing family relationships, and the medium of television, we have unwittingly created the illusion of a world that can be possessed, enjoyed, and even manipulated at will. We have unfortunately failed to explain that this external world does not actually belong to those who perceive it from behind the television screen.

Most adults (pretelevision man) were reared to see the world beyond the home as the "real world." They regard the home as a sanctuary and they regard childhood as an all too short carefree experience which is suddenly ended by the imposing forces of the world outside. To contemporary adults, the realities of scarcity, rules and codes for behavior, and everyday demands for conformity and submission make the paradise of early childhood seem precious indeed. Today's children (posttelevision man), however, are reared to experience this external world in an entirely new way. With parents who are themselves confused as to what is appropriate personal behavior, an environment of immediate gratification, and heavy parental emphasis on the values of autonomy and self-motivation, these children experience the so-called real world from a unique vantage point. It is a world which seemingly extends outward from their own bodies and central nervous systems, gratifying at its core but hostile and confusing at its outer parameters. For the child, reality is one continuous experience which he understands from where he sits — gratified and fulfilled by the abundance made available to him. For the adult, reality is "out there" in the world he confronts daily.

Every adult over the age of thirty-five has seen the entrance of the television set into the house, not as another piece of furniture but as an ultimate source of information about the world beyond the home.

The vast majority of children, on the other hand, see the television set as part of the home environment — like beds, chairs, and record players. In this sense, the world is as much inside the home as it is outside. Many adults recall the television set in its early days as a reward for hard work — its cost made buying it almost like buying a new car. One sat for hours watching quiz shows, horse operas, and variety programs, never seeming to get enough of this remarkable source of pleasure at one's own personal command. Yet for today's children television has become only one of many sources of abundance, divorced from any reward value and taken as a matter of course. Like the freezer filled with Fudgsicles and an endless assortment of other orally gratifying objects, the television set — filled with information and fantasy — supplies an instant environment.

Even in a great many schools where children of the affluent

encounter a different view of the world beyond the immediate home, there is a remarkable attempt to remove traditional techniques of competition, emphasizing skill development geared to the pace of the individual child. Thus many of our more sophisticated approaches to education have the same effect as television: to place the child dead center in the universe, armed with technological and intellectual tools for manipulating "his" world. Even if he encounters serious conflicts within this kind of world — his parents fight or hate each other, his teacher rejects him through giving poor grades or some other, to him, meaningless set of demands — the child still remains substantially in control of his own world. The parents stay together — or arrange the details of their divorce — "for the child's sake"; the child finally moves to the next grade (leaving the teacher behind), and the potential ill effects of conflict are muted by the child's ability to manipulate things as he desires. He can turn violence, Vietnam, cartoons, sporting events, documentaries, ghost stories, and sex on and off; he receives what he needs and wants materially, while the most important adults in his life either regulate their own emotions for his sake or else disappear from his life as a program is changed from one channel to another. Thus, as he grows older, he may discover that adults have been playing games with him — his parents were dishonest about their true emotions, or the teacher was only following some predetermined mechanical curriculum and was not really interested in him — which inevitably turns these adults into "bad guys" but which does not displace him from the central place in his own world.

It is quite clear that much of what characterizes young people's perception of reality has its roots precisely in this kind of childhood experience. Our society has become a mass culture in the last twenty-five years because of the same forces of technology that have molded our children's attitudes and viewpoints. A mass culture, however, is unlike anything previous generations have known. It is not a culture in the traditional sense at all. It is a fabricated social system created by the centralizing forces of technology, geared to sell common goods, communicate the illusion of common attitudes, establish a universal and manageable society, and perpetuate an established political and economic system. As such, it is a society that does not act upon any explicit values or norms except its own survival. It is, more than anything else, a very large "system" of interlocking institutions constructed to perpetuate themselves indefinitely, responding to values and norms only as they appear as "feedback." In this sense, a mass culture is a "value-free" experimental society.

Without a doubt, young people rapidly discover this experimentation that is fostered by the abundance and technological aspects of the mass culture. Having learned at an early age that consumer products are endlessly changing, that many adults adhere to the most artificial norms of culture for the purpose of belonging to an identifiable and desirable group, and that many norms and customs are actually leftover values, these young people take experimentation extremely seriously. Adults, on the other hand, do not readily perceive the same option for experimentation that youngsters take for granted. The vast majority are locked into the institutional and professional structures that manage the mass culture. Consequently, they tend to experience the freedom of experimentation only as the young lead the way. While the adults conform to the institutional pressures and artificial norms of the mass culture, the young take their positions of economic and emotional liberation and use them as a basis for experimentation. Most adults could well do the same thing, but they deeply fear personal retribution and rejection by their own peers. Men cautiously let their sideburns grow longer and women endlessly debate the merits of leaving their bras at home. Their children, however, feel no such hesitation.

Individuals, as such, do have their own understanding of what constitutes the society's values and norms. As we shall see, one of the most fascinating attributes of this affluent mass culture is that, within certain political limits, it can absorb an incredible variety of values and life-styles. The upper middle class has reached the technological utopia Marx dreamed of:

they can do, materially, almost anything they want. But any value has meaning only when it is understood in the context of experiences that have determined it. The "generation gap" does exist, and it exists because of the divergent values and attitudes of adults and young people. And they are different because their experiences have been different.

We did not plan to create a mass culture. It was an accident of the economic, political, and technological forces of the past fifty years. And very few men have ever seriously anticipated the society that has come to pass. Even George Orwell's *1984* only remotely approximated what has happened and might yet happen. Obviously, what Orwell feared has taken place right on schedule. To put it simply, the values and beliefs of the present generation of adults have not kept pace with the effects that our mass culture's technology produces. Many of our most serious problems are caused by adults whose values were developed in the early decades of the twentieth century and who are now managing a late-twentieth-century mass culture. And because these adults assume that they know what they are doing, they continuously tend to read everything through the eyes of past experience. Affluence is viewed from the perspective of the Great Depression, education is seen as specialty training, war is understood in terms of victory or defeat, politics is rooted in party loyalty, and business is determined by the profit motive. As adults try to maintain control of the mass culture, they take on the character of Orwell's "big brother," using technology as a mechanism to ensure "law and order" — meaning by that troublesome phrase a society with which adults can identify.

At the same time, Orwell and other futurists did not fully appreciate the possibility that a new generation might evolve that would reject (indeed, not even comprehend) this older set of attitudes. In fact, most middle-class young people today seem to take our mass culture for what it is — namely, a non-culture, which by its very nature permits and fosters experimentation. Recognizing as they do that most of our major institutions in business, government, and education increasingly function on the most pragmatic, cost-effective means possible, that real values are inevitably subject to these more economic and political qualifications, they take the value void that is left as a signal to experiment. In this sense, a great many youngsters are far more candid and realistic about the way our society functions than are most adults, who seem to perceive the society as defined by the values and experiences of their own unique past.

Unfortunately, many adults, intuitively perceiving that the industrial Protestant culture is dead, frantically reassert what they believe to be its tried and tested values: a sure sign that the old culture is gone. These confused adults tolerate the mass culture only because they can't change it and because they have a deep need to believe in the illusions it fosters. (Note the use of American flag decals, Honor America Day, and the ready identification of the country with "Christian" virtues.) In fact, much of the value content that the mass culture seeks to communicate through its media is rooted in the past experience of adults. Old movies and television shows that avoid conflict with mid-American attitudes and propaganda and that inevitably reinforce the political, business, and educational establishment all typify adult attitudes toward the mass culture. Every time Bob Hope, Billy Graham, or John Wayne is used to represent something "American," the banality of it strikes the young far more readily than it does adults, for whom such figures represent identifiable past experiences. What these adults do not understand is the essential fact that the dynamics by which a mass culture functions are inevitably characterized by experimentation and continual change. And confusing these elements of the mass culture with the behavior of the young, they look for recognizable forces to blame. The truth of the matter is, everyone is a victim of the mass culture. The difference between so many adults and the young can be explained by the fact that the young only know the existing mass culture, while adults use the past as a standard by which to understand and condemn the present. The young are actually trying to adapt to what exists, while adults tend to regress into a more believable and knowable past.

In this sense, it is unfortunate that most young people have so little comprehension of what the early decades of this century were like. They do not understand the Great Depression, the First and Second World Wars, and the era of the twenties and thirties. As a matter of fact, there is among many young people a significant interest in previous generations (witness the popularity of *Bonnie and Clyde* and *Butch Cassidy and the Sundance Kid*). Too many parallels in dress style and attitude exist to ignore the fact that young people have taken a good look at their parents' earlier years. And if we consider the fact that most parents have given at least one lecture to their children on the significance of the Great Depression and the wars, in addition to the endless movies on television that give a partial image of the twenties and thirties, we realize that the young have had a fairly good education of the past. Nevertheless, what escapes them is the fact that their parents were the generation that inherited the twentieth century. Only in the vaguest manner does youth understand the gulf that existed between immigrant and Victorian parents of the late nineteenth century and their own parents. The struggles that took place in those decades remind most adults that the late nineteenth-century world and the world that evolved after the First World War were profoundly different. Prohibition, sexual freedom, women's rights, unionism, political reform, and mass education were the issues that signaled a new era for young people in those days. Now adult, they look upon the turmoil among contemporary youth as an old set of issues coming to surface once again — for example, they equate marijuana with illegal liquor. To them, it seems that history has come full circle.

But adults who make such judgments, and who assume that all adolescents must inevitably recapitulate the behavior of previous generations, do not realize that while the twenties and thirties heralded the end of the nineteenth century, the sixties and seventies proclaim the end of the twentieth century as we have known it. True, each of these two important periods had its own generation gap. But that is as far as the analogy goes. The simplest comparison between these two periods in American history reveals how enormously different they are. The "flapper" era was an obvious example of adolescent rebellion against Victorian morality, whereas the life-styles and attitudes of today's youth reveal more of an experimental approach to life. Liquor and beer during Prohibition were instruments of revolt against obvious Puritanism, but marijuana and LSD have become technological extensions of the television-oriented youth culture. When a youngster "turns on," he is using a channel on his mental TV that the manufacturers didn't put on the family's set. Whereas the Great Depression of the thirties put an end to most young people's childhood and rebellion, confronting them with the realities of economic scarcity and work, youngsters today have experienced what amounts to a guaranteed childhood. And whereas the Second World War created the need for a national mobilization, suddenly ending the adolescence of many youngsters, today's social, educational, and economic situation enables most young people to extend their adolescence, indefinitely postponing the limitations of adulthood.

Perhaps the real reason many adults draw analogies between their generation and that of their children is a deep desire to communicate to the young that they, too, have had important life experiences. After all, the world which existed prior to the fifties was an extremely important period in our national life. In fact, what happened in the early decades of this century could not have been anticipated, even as the events of recent years were unexpected. The naïve optimism of the Victorian era did not prepare this country for the great symbolic events of the first half of the twentieth century. The sinking of the *Titanic* and the burning of the *Hindenburg,* coupled with the pervasive horrors of depression and war, ushered in a new feeling of profound pessimism and basic distrust. In fact, the pre-Depression and prewar years are often looked back upon by adults as a brief childish fling, a kind of "acting out" in the psychological sense of the term. In Europe, where depression and war had an even more devastating effect, existentialism, atheism, communism, and fascism found fertile soil. In this country, when one considers how subtle and pervasive were the effects of economic collapse, social reform, and federal intervention, it is hard to overlook the fact that a new kind of realism evolved here as well. Young men and women caught up in the Second World War were much more cynical about the world than their parents, who had fought "a war to end all wars." Perhaps more than anyone else, the GIs had different expectations about their society than those of their parents. They wanted an education, professional training, a house in the suburbs, and a viable standard of living. For them romanticism was dead. The war had made existentialism, pragmatism, and skepticism far more realistic. For people born during the backwash of the First World War, weaned by the Depression, and thrown into an even more devastating war, these attitudes made a lot of sense. They knew precisely what Thomas Wolfe meant by the title of his book *You Can't Go Home Again*. The small-town rural mentality of the past century had finally been altered, and the whole world, albeit a battered one, had opened up to them.

Actually, enough cannot be said about the personal and social effects that the Second World War had on today's parents. No matter how these adults may recall those years, either as pain-filled and suffering or perhaps more romanticized, the fact remains that the war provided the social surgery necessary to create our present society. The conditions for the development of an experimental mass culture came into being only after the war mobilization turned the nation into a single manageable "system." Coupled with the values and attitudes many GIs and factory workers had acquired during the forties, the massive economic growth following the war years was entirely predictable. The war had given them a feeling for the nation, a kind of self-interested nationalism. With the GI Bill and the FHA benefits available, this particular form of self-serving nationalism paid off for hundreds of thousands of these young people. But the war did something else. It helped construct an interlocking political, industrial, labor, and educational establishment which, in part due to the Cold War, was not dismantled after 1945. The new adults' experience and training in the early forties, plus their co-opted support for this interlocking industrial and governmental system, made life in the fifties and sixties seem entirely consistent with their previous experience and values. They had become history's most highly trained and educated class of managers and professionals, and many of them have now become the corporate power of the nation. The GIs of the forties are today's establishment, and in more ways than one it is *their* establishment. Twenty-five years of economic boom, coupled with a large, educated class intent on both "getting ahead" and "fitting in," produced a generation with unprecedented corporate power. It was, and is, the most homogeneous generation in the nation's history.

And yet, almost in spite of this tidal wave of success, which so many have willingly ridden, it must be noted that many have also become history's most successful parents. They set out to provide for themselves and their children the most complete existence that money and education can provide. What most young critics of the adult world never seem to understand fully is that these same adults and parents have achieved most of their goals — and high on this list of goals was the rearing of aware, independent-minded offspring. During the late forties, the nation's campuses were overcrowded with older students, their wives, and their famous "war babies." Unlike their more youthful counterparts, these ex-GIs knew what they wanted out of life, they knew why they were in school. Their goals and aspirations were already determined. They wanted to possess the benefits that they felt society owed them. They believed that the future must provide them with what the thirties had denied. In the long run it would be their own children who would receive the ultimate rewards of economic and social fulfillment. The average youngster today, however, does not understand this kind of motivation. To him values have to do with immediate personal liberty, choice, and individuality, that is, the appropriate value issues of a mass culture. But to speak of values in terms of future expectations — involving property, education, economics, and social stability — seems meaningless to them. Just as their parents have taken scarcity, war, federal intervention, and education for granted, the young take affluence, peace, and self-determination for granted. And the irony of it is that the essentially economic values of one generation have fostered the more human values of another.

Had adults been more introspective during the forties and fifties, perhaps they might have foreseen today's developments. Perhaps they would have understood better that the successful pursuit of money and economic security inevitably leads to a reaction and to the pursuit of different values. They did know that a hungry man finds it difficult to be humanistic and idealistic. But they overlooked the fact that a man who is fulfilled economically may tend to become more interested in self-fulfillment. The society of competitive, struggling individuals is different from the society of those who have already achieved the means enabling them to wrestle with the more philosophical problems of life.

It goes without saying that economic affluence alone has not been responsible for today's revolution in behavior and values among the young. Those ex-GIs and their wives have had much to do with it as well. The real payoff from twenty-five years of economic growth has been the drive of these very parents to provide their children with a home environment and a type of education that they themselves never experienced. It is a commonplace that most people change their values when their economic conditions rise: they tend to become far more esteem conscious and to seek more autonomy. Inevitably, this change holds true very often for their attitudes toward children. They want their young to be gratified and fulfilled in the areas of personal growth that will enable them to rise above the conflict-ridden world of the lower middle class.

It is no accident, therefore, that these very parents — most of them successful professionals and executives — should now be despised by the working-class "silent majority." The New York longshoremen knew what they were doing when they refused to handle the boat owned by the permissive Dr. Spock. For hundreds of thousands who belong to the unions of this country, for those who still adhere to the values of fundamentalism and who guard with great vigor their place within the system, such parents seem weak and extremely irresponsible. It is a great mystery why those who have the most in this world should produce a generation that rejects all that the working class still strives to achieve.

What often disturbs these hard-working Americans, as they frantically search for someone to blame, is the very shift in values that has subtly taken place among the upper-middle-class adults themselves. They understand the esteem values of their leaders and managers, but they do not understand their bosses' tolerance of their children's autonomy and self-motivation. Criticizing the young for participating in some "communist" conspiracy, or calling them "bums" and spoiled brats, typifies the deep-seated anxiety these people feel. For example, while the affluent class insists that courses in sex education and drug addiction be taught in their schools, many working-class parents rise up in arms, sensing that a basic change is taking place. Practically every significant innovation in child rearing over the past fifty years has had its greatest impact among the affluent class. The theories of John Dewey, Maria Montessori, and A. S. Neill have had an enormous influence. The subtle and all-pervasive impact of Freudian psychology has also left its mark. Ironically, the lower-middle-class Americans are correct in their suspicions. A revolution is taking place. The affluent Americans have done precisely what they set out to do: they have liberated their children. They have given them the economic, technological, and psychological basis for self-determination.

Caught between the masses of Americans who still think and feel as previous generations have done for years and their own children who act so differently, these affluent parents mistake their success for failure. The values and attitudes that worked so well in the past, values acquired during the war and in the pursuit of economic security, don't seem to fit when applied to their children. Having taught their children to become autonomous and self-actualized, they suddenly discover that society rejects these qualities. For some of them, their own success and sophistication prevents them from returning to the older, simpler values of the past, and they find themselves identifying with their children. They see in their children the things they have wanted for themselves: freedom of self-expression, an experimental attitude toward life, a deep moral commitment, and an openness to new and different life-styles.

This unparalleled attention to the young is characteristic of a generation that never completed its own adolescence. The parents who identify with their children, the working-class and conservative people who feel threatened by them, and the establishment that hopes to manage them are all perfect examples of adults who have been forced to repress their own adolescent feelings. As adults, they think they understand the years between puberty and adulthood simply because they lived through them. But any comparison between the years of depression and war and those of the last decade only reveals that what passed for adolescent behavior in the past cannot be used as a standard today.

Adolescence as we know it is a very recent phenomenon. At most, adolescence in the past was that brief period of time between childhood and adulthood when the young learned the practices and expectations of the adult community. Social and economic realities being what they were, only the children of the aristocracy were permitted anything resembling a prolonged adolescence. The vast majority of human beings moved out of their home environment, got jobs, had babies, and fell into the same molds their parents had known. That is what the farms and sweatshops of the nineteenth century symbolized. There was no youth and not even much childhood as we have come to know it in the twentieth century. In fact, it probably wasn't until the child labor laws and the concept of public edu-

cation took effect that this nation even became aware of the
term "adolescence," and that wasn't until the turn of this century. In other words, the very first generation in human history ever to experience the beginnings of adolescent psychology were the adults of today, forty and fifty years ago. Even
that was a very limited adolescence, cramped between the First
World War and the Depression, and then again, between the
Depression and another war. The "flappers" and the "bobby
soxers" were this country's first adolescent generations. And
even then, neither lasted long enough for the young to have
any profound effect. Ironically, they had to wait for their own
children to do what the Second World War, the Cold War,
and now their own conformity and establishment would not
permit, namely, to challenge the existing "reality principle" —
basically, self-discipline and submission to authority.

Therefore, if permissiveness means anything at all, it has to
do with the widespread unconscious wish among many parents
that their own children would live out the fullness of adolescent testing and questioning in ways that they themselves
could not. But it is also true that these same good parents
belong to an establishment with no recourse but repression to
keep existing institutions intact. And that is where the young
are betrayed. Reared to be self-motivated, expressive, and autonomous, they soon discover that the world their parents live
in demands quite different attitudes. The tale of Paradise Lost is
retold every time a youngster is arrested for possession of
drugs, or for violently attacking the institutions of the establishment, or for resisting the draft. In other words, America's
parents have succeeded with their children but failed with
their own society.

To understand how this confusion in values and attitudes has
evolved, it is important to recall some of the psychological
themes of the fifties. It was an "age of anxiety" in which the
individual became reflective and raised questions of self-doubt.
Psychoanalysts were doing a booming business, and books like
The Man in the Gray Flannel Suit and *The Organization Man*
became best sellers, describing the personal price individuals

had to pay if they wanted to "make it" in the competitive world. David Riesman's *The Lonely Crowd* outlined the psychology of "other-directed man" and made it abundantly clear why personal autonomy and self-expression were such dangerous alternatives. In fact, about the only ones to challenge the system even slightly were the "beats" — Kerouac, Ginsberg, Ferlinghetti, and a few others. But like history's traditional Bohemians, they became more of a safety valve for the establishment than a real threat. They flaunted their personal rebellion but never challenged any of society's institutions. All that repressed adolescent energy, which the war and the establishment had bottled up in the forties and fifties, could only express itself in terms of anxiety, quiet criticism, and "safe" escapism.

As a result, there are a great many adults who still possess some of the same adolescent emotional problems that most young people normally resolve when given sufficient time and opportunity to do so. This is partly why there also exists among today's adult generation a deep and unresolved envy of the young, a kind of identification process in reverse. Unfortunately, it is an envy that results in deeper feelings of distrust, because these same adults also tend to project their own memories of adolescence upon the real adolescents of today. And in so doing they betray their ignorance of what it means to be young. For example, it is very common for adults to assume that all teen-agers are prone to fads and are often victims of naïve idealism, not having lived long enough to test their ideas against the limitations of society. Analogies are thus drawn between the fish-swallowing, hero-worshipping, panty-raid-type behavior of the past and the hippie-style protests and radicalled demonstrations of today. One frequently hears adults criticizing the young for not having a real investment in the way society functions, assuming that the young are not actual participants in the society but spectators awaiting their turn.

More realistically, however, the psychology of adolescence may be the only viable psychology for a mass culture like ours. If it is true that a mass culture functions more on the dynamics of experimentation than it does on established rules for conduct, then adolescent "reality testing" is the most logical perspective from which to view the world. According to psychological theory, adolescent reality testing is that normal phase during the years between puberty and adulthood when youngsters seek to test the limits of authority, question adult standards of behavior, experiment with sexual, personal, and emotional experiences, and seek to play out any number of roles for themselves, all in the pursuit of an acceptable self-image or ego. Under normal conditions in the past, this definition presupposed clear-cut distinctions between childhood, adolescence, and adulthood. And yet, no reputable psychologist would ever assume that any given individual achieves adulthood without a certain amount of childish and adolescent feeling remaining intact. Actually, adulthood is not a psychological category. Maturity is the term used to define the ultimate goal of human development. And it has been a commonplace for many years to assume that adulthood, in terms of a person's age, was no guarantee of maturity. A fifteen-year-old could well be more mature than a forty-five-year-old.

In this sense, reality testing seeks to keep the future open, to maintain options and alternatives, and to reserve the freedom to change. The degree to which a youngster's choices and actions result from a direct reaction to existing adult norms is the degree to which he has not found himself. He still uses the adult standard as his point of reaction. But when that youngster tests the reality of the world about him in such a way as to discover greater choices and alternatives for himself, it follows that he has begun to achieve an important degree of maturity. Consequently, if openness to change and experimentation is required, then all those who have patterned themselves on the basis of capitulation to group demands and submission to authority are the ones who suffer most in a mass culture.

If one examines the plight of public school education today, it soon becomes clear that a similar conflict is taking place there. Locked into the older priorities of having to meet the industrial manpower requirements of earlier decades, and now

confronted by the aims and goals of progressive education, the
modern school system ironically parallels the class conflict between the lower-middle-class workers and the upper-middle-
class affluent. With the majority of Americans still committed
to the industrial values of the past, and the richer class of professionals and managers seeking a more tailored education for
their young, the school system inevitably reflects the social and
economic environment in which it finds itself. Thus, for all
those who have participated in the upward mobile drive of the
past two decades, the aims of progressive education have become a normal part of their expectations from the school
system. In fact, progressive education has become all but universal in the more affluent communities.

But if this is the environment where the highest quality of
education is usually found, it is also the environment where the
young have been and are being reared to become autonomous
and individualistic. And it is no accident that such child-rearing
values suit the aims of progressive education perfectly. Competition is played down, and the attempt to give each child a
personalized education is far more successful than in schools
where the aim remains training-oriented. These progressive
techniques, the forces of affluence and technology, coupled
with the changing values of the upper middle class, have substantially reinforced the ability of many young people to
achieve an experimental approach to life.

Sensing the role in which this combination places them, a
great many young people have already taken upon themselves
the task of raising the value questions that must be answered. If
adults think the young are arrogant in assuming this role, let
them not forget that it is the logical extension of the kind of
childhood development that their parents have so persistently
provided. In fact, there is a very real value void produced by
this mass culture of ours. And it goes without saying that a
great many adults are willing to let the young assume this position in society. This is the point made by Margaret Mead in her
book *Culture and Commitment*. In her terms, we have become
a prefigurative culture, in which the young, who are un-

burdened by historical conditioning, now set the tone and raise the issues with which the society must deal. And since most of the youngsters who play this role for us are adolescents, it follows that adolescent reality testing has become the new norm for responsible citizenship. The older norms of capitulation to authority and surrender to postfigurative values are rapidly diminishing. For those who are threatened by this prospect, let them answer whether or not the adults who presently manage society provide a better standard.

Inevitably, all adults are forced to take the attitudes and behavior of the young quite seriously. And the more this happens, the more the young will become the cultural harbingers. Their life-styles; their experimentation with marriage, sex, and love; their music, dress, language, and other related barometers of culture cannot help but determine the issues with which we must deal from now on. The truly sad part in this whole *Alice in Wonderland* experience is that it is the young who must liberate the repressed adolescents whom we call "adults." The young, who are presently trying to lead the way, are forced to take all the risks and pay the personal price that an uncharted future presents. This, in fact, is much of what is involved in being young today.

Very few adults, of course, are ready to accept such a seemingly strange situation as this. It violates everything that their commonsense view of reality teaches them. The young are young, and it is not possible for them to take power away from those adults who guard it so dearly. And even if they could, it would still be wrong. But that is not the issue. No one in his right mind is talking about a youth revolt in which the teenage population suddenly inherits the controls of the world. Something far more subtle and important is involved in the effect that the young are having on this society, and it is something that has to do with the adults themselves, not to mention their attitudes toward the youth. To put it in psychological terms, we might say that it is a conflict between two generations and the way they have dealt with their own Oedipal feelings. Part of the problem stems from the deep-seated fear and distrust many adults have toward the adolescent population. Traditional Freudian psychology taught that the child must encounter his father with biologically determined feelings of rage. He wants to destroy his father and replace him in the affections of his mother. But the child soon discovers that he is no match for the father and so learns to repress his Oedipal rage, thus replacing the conscious rage with a new emotion, namely, that of identification with his father as his ego ideal. What follows this process is equally important, as Freud later discovered in his analysis of society. Society itself represents a giant family structure, filled with father surrogates, sibling rivals, mother-lover objects, and an enormous amount of socially determined repression. In other words, the Oedipal conflict is really nothing more than a conditioning process that the child needs in order to learn how to submit to the father surrogates that the society readily provides. Ultimately, of course, each and every son would eventually become a father himself, and the final reward for repression would result in a kind of secondary victory for the man. Or so the theory goes.

A great many adults today, however, have never really successfully resolved their basic Oedipal conflicts. The struggle with Puritanical prohibitions, the continued capitulation to institutional authority, the private ways in which one acts out his adolescent feelings, and the profoundly deep conditioning that the war and corporate power structure has had for them have all produced a generation of adults more prone to think and feel in terms of Oedipal psychology than their own children do. That is why so many adults see in the revolt by the young a kind of classic desire to destroy their fathers. But this attitude reveals how little they understand what the young themselves have experienced. Having remained more like sons and daughters to some giant paternal system in government, business, and education, adults cannot appreciate the degree to which that system long ago killed off the dominant fathers. Consequently, they view the young today as rebels against the very psychological system to which they have surrendered.

The most obvious examples of this phenomenon are adults

who have spent the last twenty-five years working in the military, governmental, and industrial bureaucracies. The so-called company man is the classic individual who represses his natural adolescent rage (or reality testing) and thus seeks to identify with the dominant father surrogate above him in the hierarchy. Like countless managers, middle executives, military officers, and bureaucrats, this faithful "company man" never quite achieves the role of dominant father figure himself. He is doomed to play out the role of a co-opted son in the vast institutional empire to which he belongs. Such a continued submission as this takes its toll in the most personal terms, and not having the power or authority that biology dictates should come to the father figure, he eventually begins to question the meaning of his own role as an adult male. If his ego is not strong enough, he may become pathological in his attitudes toward those "above" and "below" him in the institutional hierarchy. In most cases, however, the secondary gains of salary, prestige, and continued identification with the power structure help him to compensate. Ultimately, he opts out of the Oedipal struggle, never assumes the role of "father" or authority, and seeks to define himself solely in terms of his professional role.

For the young who have fathers like this, a very peculiar family life is predictable. Without question, they, too, go through the early stages of the classic Oedipal conflict. They want father out of the way, and they, too, want to achieve his apparent position of power. But when they reach adolescence, the reality of the world about them isn't what it was when their fathers were young. In fact, even before they reach adolescence, many of the effects of Oedipal submission and identification have been muted. Fatherhood is not really the same thing that traditional fathers symbolized. And with the forces of abundance, permissive rearing, progressive education, and television, a great many of these young people never really have strong father figures to test themselves against. The boundaries normally set by father-type authority are too easily transcended, while the ego ideal of father is quickly replaced by a more romanticized, albeit nonexistent father in the child's fantasy.

As a consequence, many young people today do not bring with them a well-developed and unresolved Oedipal psychology. Having experienced a world of instant gratification, having felt a certain control of their own perceived world, and having learned an endless number of ways to compensate for the absence of any powerful father authority in their lives, these young people have encountered an entirely different childhood than that their parents knew. In more ways than one, this explains why the young are not really rebelling against an authority figure as much as against a system of abstract controls — economic, social, and political. Their problems have far more to do with the legal and social mechanisms that limit what they consider to be their rightful options as individuals than with the more traditional images of paternal authority. As the young radicals put it, the "system" is the enemy of the people, not the ones who manage the system.

The political and ideological ramifications of this post-Oedipal psychology are truly remarkable, especially when viewed from the contrasting attitudes and assumptions of the adults and the young. And nothing is more characteristic of this difference than the divergent attitudes of adults and young people toward political liberalism. To a great many upper-middle-class parents, liberalism is the best adults have to offer the next generation. It is morally motivated, socially beneficial, and highly constructive. But to a countless number of youngsters, liberalism cannot be distinguished from any other political ideology that is used by adults to keep the controls over society firmly in the hands of the existing establishment. Thus, if young people consider themselves liberal at all, it certainly is not the same kind of liberalism most adults remember. There are too many hidden assumptions beneath what constitutes liberalism for either generation to be talking about the same thing. Liberalism has been identified since the twenties with unionism and social reform, federal programs for the poor, and most of the legislation that Roosevelt helped bring about during the thirties. To the young liberalism is the extension of the welfare state by the Kennedy administration — including civil rights, the war in Vietnam, and labor union reactionism. It is a mixed bag of progressive propaganda and the "guns and butter" programs of the sixties. If anything, liberalism as defined by most adults appears to the young to be a seriously qualified set of social ideals, inevitably limited by the vested interests of certain powerful institutions in government and industry. Somehow, there seems to be something inherent in the value judgments of most liberals that defeats all the liberal aims of this supposedly moral ideology.

As with so many other matters of historical significance, most young people haven't the vaguest idea of what liberalism has meant in the past. Viewing it from the sixties, in terms of the Kennedy dynasty, the Johnson administration, McCarthy's try for power, and the liberal coalition against the war in Indochina, they have a very distorted understanding of what liberalism looked like several decades ago. In any case, there remains something within the liberal ideology of so many adults that troubles them deeply. For example, how is it that a liberal administration involved us in the Vietnam War? And why should working-class people who seemed so liberal and progressive thirty and forty years ago, now seem so conservative? What is it within the historical tradition of twentieth-century liberalism that has led to greater federal centralism, the co-option of the universities, and the propagation of so many vested-interest groups?

To answer these questions for the young, it must be made clear that liberalism has always been the ideology of those adults who have fought against the "evil" paternalism of nineteenth-century capitalism, which was deeply rooted in the Victorian morality of their own parents' generation. In other words, most of the adults who have consistently considered themselves liberals throughout the years have been struggling against a particular kind of Calvinist fundamentalism, so characteristic of their fathers' world. That is why it is no accident that the "flapper" era and the rise in liberalism evolved at the same time in history. In fact, both the social rebellion of the twenties and the ideological revolt of liberalism represented much of today's adult generation's Oedipal struggle against self-righteous Puritanism. Thus, when that paternalism collapsed during the Great Depression and the good father image of Roosevelt came to power, many young people then felt the beginnings of power being handed over to their own generation.

Due to the enormous impact of the Second World War, the establishment of the military-industrial complex, the giant monopolies, and the supercorporation became the product of these young men and women, having been co-opted by the system. It was not conservatism that managed to construct this gigantic set of political and industrial institutions, it was the direct extension of the liberalism of the thirties, only now dominated by the massive war mobilization of the forties. In other words, the WPA projects, the TVA programs, and the invention of Social Security were all examples of federal intervention, which ultimately conditioned the country to accept the role of the federal government in the regional lives of the people. Consequently, the military bases, military- and space-dominated industries, and related federal institutions established around the country were really nothing new after the war was over. And whether or not individual liberals may have felt that the government had gone too far, the fact remains that the military-industrial complex has become the nation's largest welfare program. In effect, the postwar industrial growth, dominated by the continued military orientation of the Cold War, took the social and humanitarian thrust of the thirties away from liberalism.

Intellectually, of course, liberalism was much more than federal intervention to solve social problems. But it cannot be denied that most socialists and liberals in the twenties and thirties were predominantly concerned with the role the federal government should play in controlling the evils of industry. Actually, there have been two types of liberalism in the

American past. First, there was the liberalism of the nineteenth century, which believed in the perfectability of man. Rooted in laissez-faire capitalism, this particular brand of liberalism was dominant throughout Europe and the United States. After the First World War, however, a different style of liberalism arose. It had been conditioned by European existentialism, Freudian psychology, and Marxist socialism. It was the beginning of all modern theology. In political circles, it produced men like Reinhold Niebuhr, Walter Lippmann, Norman Thomas, C. Wright Mills, and Henry Wallace. And the enemy of this new style liberalism was twofold: nineteenth-century, capitalist liberalism and nineteenth-century Puritan conservatism. No longer could liberals speak of the perfectability of man, nor could pietism and belief in personal salvation be tolerated. Both the left and right wings of nineteenth-century political philosophy, which had been rooted in the traditions of economic liberalism and religious fundamentalism, were finally attacked by a neo-orthodoxy. The influence of Marx, Freud, the existentialists, and the logical positivists turned liberalism into an essentially pessimistic philosophy. Man is defined in terms of either economics, or instinctual aggression, or measurable quantities devoid of ultimate values.

The shift away from the traditional optimistic view of man and toward an emphasis on institutions became increasingly apparent, particularly during the forties and fifties, in the writings and influence of one very important man, Reinhold Niebuhr. Perhaps more than any other liberal intellectual, Niebuhr synthesized the various elements of the newer brand of American liberalism. In many university circles, among numerous labor leaders, and for a large number of civil libertarian members of the Democratic party, Niebuhr represented the perfect liberal intellectual.

What Niebuhr had done was to merge many of the most important elements of Calvinist thought with the more contemporary interpretations of existentialism, Freudian psychology, and socialism. To Niebuhr, the inherent values of pietism and fundamentalism, especially those beliefs that emphasized personal salvation at the expense of social morality, had to be corrected. The masses of workers in such a town as Detroit, where he had worked as a young pastor, had to cast off the rich Protestant establishment that wanted the working class to hold to a personalistic religion. As a theologian, Niebuhr knew that fundamentalism and pietism were bad theology. As a liberal reformer, he knew they were oppressive.

The very heart of Niebuhr's criticism, outlined in his major work, *The Nature and Destiny of Man*, became a neo-orthodoxy that emphasized Calvin's doctrine of sin and the Reformation's major teaching of "salvation by grace through faith." Instead of the Puritanical view of sin that addressed itself to personal morality, Niebuhr emphasized the "fallen nature of man," now seen, however, from the perspective of existentialist realism and Freudian insight. Rather than demanding a kind of self-flagellation, it was intended to help the individual understand the limits of human nature. There was a close parallel, which Paul Tillich also pointed out, between sin and neurosis — although they were not identical. Sin was the "human condition," which inevitably resulted in social problems of inequality, racism, and injustice. The old conservative religious views that taught unquestioning respect for authority, patience in the face of adversity, and personal salvation had to be replaced with a belief in the collective communities of man seeking power to gain for themselves what the older morality and power structure had denied them. Only rational self-interest among the working classes and disenfranchised groups, working through the political, economic, and social communities, reflected the existential reality of life. The attitude traditional among most industrialists and inherent in the fundamentalism of the people tended to equate successful entrepreneurs with the righteous, leaving the rest of men in the fallen condition of self-seeking sinners. Niebuhr's argument left no individual free from sin. In political terms, that meant that the real issues of justice could only be attacked from the perspective of men who knew the reality of power politics, interest groups, and enlightened liberalism.

As a perceptive social critic, Niebuhr fully understood that religion was being used as an opiate, especially as it tended to perpetuate notions that men have no right to expect justice, equality, and opportunity in this world. His own personal experience had led him to realize that the paternalistic structure of industry had fostered a very deep feeling of self-doubt among most working-class people. As long as workers saw themselves as unworthy of social expectations, and as long as religion could be relied upon to create an "other-worldly" set of dreams and aspirations, the management of industry was safe. But Niebuhr also knew that he could not judge management any more than he could judge labor. That was the weakness of Marxism. Somehow the relationship between the two had to be seen in the same moral light of shared self-interest. And in one of Niebuhr's most important books, *Moral Man and Immoral Society*, he defined the dilemma of the individual within such a system:

> As a generation we are therefore bound to feel harassed as well as disillusioned. In such a situation all the highest ideals and tenderest emotions which men have felt through the ages, when they became fully conscious of their heritage and possible destiny as human beings, will be seen from our perspective to be something of a luxury. They will be a moral disadvantage, because they appear as a luxury which only those are able to indulge who are comfortable enough to be comparatively oblivious to the desperate character of our contemporary situation. We live in an age in which personal moral idealism is easily accused of hypocrisy and frequently deserves it. It is an age in which honesty is possible only when it skirts the edges of cynicism. All this is rather tragic. For what the individual conscience feels when it lifts itself above the world of nature and the system of collective relationships in which the human spirit remains under the power of nature, is not a luxury but a necessity of the soul. Yet there is beauty in our tragedy. We are, at least, rid of some of our illusions. We can no longer buy the highest satisfactions of the individual life at the expense of social injustice. We cannot build our in-

dividual ladders to heaven and leave the total human enterprise unredeemed of its excesses and corruptions.

The thread throughout Niebuhr's liberalism, interwoven again and again, was his warning to both sides in the class struggle that no individual could remain content with his own ideals and "ladders" to heaven. The human condition demanded that the self-interest of both sides serve the greater self-interest of the collective. Society could not morally tolerate the tyranny of either the ruling or the working class. Individuals could no longer afford the "luxury" of high ideals and tender emotions in the face of the existential realities of life. And although this was a tragic loss to man as a human being, it was a reality to which everyone was forced to accommodate himself. It was at least a better condition than the one of unfulfilled hopes and unrealizable illusions.

Throughout the years during and after the war, such an argument was enormously appealing to most liberals and intellectuals. To many of the liberal leaders in the Democratic party, i.e., Stevenson, Humphrey, and Kennedy, Niebuhr had articulated the very essence of liberalism. Niebuhr struck a meaningful blow to the pietistic front of the Southern white power structure, the moralism of men like John Foster Dulles, and the neurotic patriotism of the Joe McCarthy obscurantists. But perhaps more than anything else, it gave a new sophistication to the floundering liberal Democrats. Thus, in 1961 when John F. Kennedy reached the White House, the realpolitik of modern liberalism finally had its day.

Unfortunately, the country was fast becoming a mass culture, and even the brightest liberals couldn't foresee what this might mean although they began to use its techniques. Kennedy introduced, via Robert McNamara, a new approach to problem solving and decision making. It was something called "cost-benefit analysis" or "the systems approach." In effect, it was a scientific methodology, often used in business, which seemingly freed one from the political methods of the past. Supposedly, it was a system whereby decisions could be made in the most efficient manner, discarding value-laden assumptions and taking all elements of "feedback" — or reactions — into account. But then, the issue of the nation's readiness for such an approach forced some systems analysts to question how strong the reaction of the public might be once the technique was applied, as the computer scientists say, in a "real time" situation. Were the American people ready for a "cost-benefit analysis" approach to wars of intervention, which, incidentally, had never been tried by Americans before? Obviously, the only answer was to try it out and see what happened. What followed was the Bay of Pigs disaster and the Vietnam War.

It seems clear now that what many planners and Pentagon aides had hoped for never actually materialized. The strategists in Washington during the early sixties assumed that students would remain apathetic, sophisticated business leaders would recognize the scientific rationality of their approach, and the rest of the country could be relied upon to remain appropriately patriotic. The only question in their system was the problem of Vietnam itself. No one really knew whether or not Ho Chi Minh would respond as he was supposed to. But as the sixties have taught us, they miscalculated on every issue except the patriotism of the lower-middle-class workingman — Mr. Nixon's "silent majority."

Actually, it has not been the techniques of cost-benefit analysis or the systems approach to problem solving that has alienated so many Americans, especially the youth, from a belief in their own political system. It has been, more than anything else, the values and attitudes of the adults (liberals and conservatives alike) that have been used to justify and reinforce the system. The realpolitik of modern liberalism, which tries to mimic the "self-interest" arguments of American business and labor; the appeal to confidence in the political values of liberalism; the sophisticated pessimism about human nature; and the alliance between government and the university, covered in the cloak of scientific objectivity, are meaningless, or worse, to the young. As value judgments they are too deeply rooted in the struggles of the past. The unfortunate result is that present reform programs are aimed not at today's problems but at those of twenty years ago. A new public philosophy is demanded, and liberalism doesn't seem able to fill the bill.

In the last analysis, there is no past value system that is meaningful to a mass culture. Just as the parents of today's younger generation rode the wave of technology and the gross national product, taking credit for it as their success story, so the young now take the existing mass culture for granted, congratulating themselves for their ability to adapt to it. We have a society created by the technology of instant communication whose most significant economic and political decisions are managed by a computer-type rationality that is utterly barren of unchanging moral values. What the young can't adapt to is adult society's tenacious insistence on justifying its standards of behavior and its control of the system with an outdated code of values.

The result is incredible confusion: the sale of American flags soars; but abortion laws fall. In a real sense, "the store doesn't need anyone to run it any more." Only those who understand the system believe in it and seek to use it for whatever priority demands exist. And because so many young people actually experience and understand society in this manner, it should not come as a surprise that they take the freedom to experiment with it seriously. After all, that is what a mass culture is all about.

The moral collapse of liberalism, characterized by the fiasco of the National Democratic Convention in Chicago in 1968, taught a great many young people something very significant. It made it clear, once and for all, that liberalism as defined in the twenties and thirties was no longer a value-oriented philosophy. The objective of helping the workingman (not altogether unachieved) or the blacks, or even of replacing the blatant vested interest of the rich, was no longer the major goal of liberalism. Like the repressed adolescent psychology of many adults, liberalism had always been a revolt against the Calvinist morality of the nineteenth century. At first impelled by moral intentions, liberalism, once it finally came to power, was more of an attempt to perpetuate its institutions than to confront serious issues. Perhaps it would be more accurate to say that many liberal adults have not been totally conscious of their long-range intentions. For no matter how deeply they may have been motivated to seek and to establish a more enlightened self-interest for all Americans, what they have actually done is to create the conditions for a "value-free" confrontation between the powerful and the powerless. Obviously, this is why countless numbers of academics who once saw themselves as liberal intellectuals have now become conservative defenders of the educational, governmental, and industrial establishment. They have discovered that they are not committed to taking seriously the value issues that confront us. Indeed, many of them deeply suspect all those who address themselves to questions of morality and ethics as being anti-intellectual. And if anything characterizes their attitudes toward young radicals and idealists today, it is this kind of criticism. The veil of moral intentions has been torn away from the bureaucratically devised power structure, leaving the young as the only ones to define the moral issue with which we must cope.

In summary, the adult middle-class society that has ridden the wave of economic and technological progress for the past twenty-five years has finally been forced by its own children to admit that this society belongs only to those who belong to its establishment. Under the guise of liberal and progressive goals, there has been an unconscious power play by all those ex-GIs to take over the society left them by their own naïve and blundering parents. And now that their own children, who take affluence and technology for granted, have grown up and demanded the right to change all those things their blundering parents have fostered, it has become a struggle for survival. So far, the young have only had an effect by "dropping out" and refusing to surrender to the system that belongs to the adults.

We have yet to experience what it will be like when they actually take over. But at least we have a much better vantage point than before — because the young have already given us a pretty good picture of what we can expect.

2

THE RESURRECTION OF NARCISSUS

Ever since Sigmund Freud developed the concept of "primary narcissism," relating the experience of the infant to the unconscious of man, showing how repression inevitably blocks out man's infantile sense of being unified with concrete reality, modern man has had a most powerful conceptual tool with which to understand himself. The history of civilization, unquestionably, has been the history of repression, especially repression of man's unconscious narcissism. In the simplest terms, narcissism is here defined as the way a newborn infant seems to experience the world around him. Everything is undifferentiated from the body and central nervous system of the infant. He experiences the world as an extension of himself. Without the symbolic language and the mental mechanisms he learns later in life, the infant is locked into a perception of reality whereby the external and immediate environment is not distinguished from the self.

Significantly, what is here outlined in the clinical language of psychology Western man has long only vaguely perceived in the language of mythology and religion. It is obvious, however, that much of that mythology has served the purposes of repression far more than the ends of health and sanity. The long and continuous struggle between the individual and the "civilized" community of men, typified by the institutional forces which manage and control the lives of people, has been the context within which these mythologies were understood. Those few intellectuals and artists, like Rousseau and Nietzsche, who have spoken out against the institutionalized forces of repression have always been considered perceptive but irrelevant. Western man simply has never been able to establish a culture wherein the elements of repression could be replaced with an acceptance of man's inherent desire for instant gratification. Traditionally, that would have meant total anarchy — incidentally, the very term adults most often use to describe the youth of today. And yet, much of what now characterizes our technological and affluent mass culture reveals a major shift away from this traditional and all-pervasive reality of repression. Repression remains with us, but the context of that repression has changed drastically. A new generation of young people, many having had permissive and liberal parents, and having experienced gratification of their wishes on a scale never before possible — while at the same time not having been prepared for the reality of repression as it now exists in modern form — are witnessing the return of the ancient conflict between the individual and society with a vengeance.

The traditional mythologies that have long been utilized by Western man to define this conflict are best remembered as the Greek and Hebrew tales of Prometheus, Sisyphus, and Adam, on the one hand; and Orpheus, Dionysius, and Narcissus on the other. Because the biological and psychological forces under which every infant is born and forced to live have always been affected by the conditions of society as they impinge upon the home, these and similar myths have served to orient the child to the established rationalizations of culture. Historically, the nature of child rearing has been determined by both the psychobiological and sociological facts of life. The reality of scarcity, the limits of technology, the inevitable patterns of work and procreation, as well as the proscribed rituals of worship and belief have all made life seem harsh and burdensome. Consequently, all mythologies that explain these realities have remained the mythologies of "common sense." The first set of myths (Prometheus and Adam) represented the plight of man as men knew it. In this sense, they were considered reasonable. The second type of myth (Orpheus and Narcissus) portrayed a different, dreamlike world, in which man seemed to live at peace with himself, his instincts, and the realm of nature.

In Hebrew thought, the story of Adam and his fall into sin represented the deep conviction that man has lost the world of innocence. Only God Himself could ever reconstruct the Garden of Eden, and even then many orthodox Jews never really believed that the idyllic realm of paradise would ever return. That was an interpretation that early Christianity took over. The ultimate resurrection by God of the original state of harmony was what Christ made possible by His death and resurrection. In Greek mythology, the dualism between pain and suffering versus the longed-for and long-forgotten realm of paradise was most often portrayed by two separate tales. Prometheus, who betrayed the will of Zeus by giving to man the secrets of the gods — namely, the fire of technology and the blind hope of children — represented a reality with which everyone could identify. The plight of man indeed seemed to merit some extraordinary gift from the gods. Otherwise man was doomed to continued suffering in the blindness of his ignorance. In the myth of Narcissus, however, the schism between man and cruel nature is overcome. There is no toil, no suffering, and no technology. Narcissus is in love with himself as he is extended outward into the elements. He pines away for the one he sees, not realizing that the image is his own. When he dies, he becomes a flower. Death is not really death as we know it, but the reincarnation of the self into another state of being — and that of the very essence of nature.

In the tale of Sisyphus, whom God punished for his arrogance, his plight was that of having to push a large rock up a mountain, never to succeed, but only to have it fall again and again. His punishment was the meaninglessness of life's tasks, endlessly demanding his toil and energy, but with no real reward in this life. To understand the contemporary nature of such a tale as this, consider Albert Camus's book *The Myth of Sisyphus.* To Camus, life poses the problem of frustration, courage, and the willingness to accept one's death in the face of meaninglessness. It is no accident, therefore, that this book is extremely popular among college students. While the original myth of Sisyphus simply portrays human existence as punishment for a kind of natural sinfulness, rendering man helpless before the frustrating inevitabilities of life, Camus and the young today analyze its meaning — not as previous generations might have thought, namely, that one has no recourse but to submit to such punishment. Rather, they raise the question; what meaning can be found when culture provides no meaning? What is there in the world that my parents have passed on to me that is worth dying for? Fighting and dying in Southeast Asia is too much like Sisyphus's punishment. It is pointless. To the older generation the punishment is accepted. The younger generation, on the other hand, refuses to accept the meaninglessness of it all.

And yet, more typical of these young people, perhaps, are the myths of Orpheus and Dionysius. Orpheus, like Narcissus, is in love with himself and nature. He plays his musical instrument to the beasts of the field, believing that the sounds of erotic melody can actually control all instinctual life. In fact, so narcissistic is Orpheus that he becomes more a homosexual than a socially determined heterosexual. Thus, according to one tradition, the women of Thrace, who are so taken with his beauty, are crazed by him and destroy him for his rejection of them. In the Dionysian myth, a similar theme is expressed. All the elements of suffering and toil are replaced with the libidinous activity of total abandonment. The fantasy life of the fallen descendants of Adam, the suffering sons of Prometheus, and the burdened children of Sisyphus is acted out by Narcissus, Orpheus, and Dionysius. Realism is thus challenged by the forces of infantile wish fulfillment.

In the book of Genesis, both of these mythological themes are played out by Adam. At first, God provides a paradise that is free from the limits of reality. The only condition is Adam's acceptance of continued ignorance of good and evil. His primal innocence, which is shared with Eve, is blind to the punishment of death, and this makes their decision to eat the forbidden fruit a kind of childish reaching out for divine knowledge. But once they disobey the prohibition of God, they discover their nakedness and crime and fall into a new state — that of sin. Interestingly enough, the punishments, "toil by the sweat of your brow" and the pain of childbirth, were directly related to sin. Obviously paradise knew neither of these conditions, and that is why Adam and Eve had to be expelled. As God said, "Behold, the man has become as one of us, to know good and evil; and now, lest he put forth his hand, and also take of the tree of life, and eat, and live forever . . ." In other words, as the Greeks spoke of two separate realms — romantic paradise where eros reigns and innocence characterizes its participants, and the real world where toil, punishment, and sin dominate — so the Bible speaks of paradise lost, followed by the reality of life as man knew it best. In both cases, the myths seemed to alleviate the painful burden that reality imposes by explaining it in cosmic terms, while on the other hand the dreams and aspirations of civilized man, typified by the myths of Narcissus, Orpheus, and Dionysius, have tended to turn the unreasonable nature of such images into a kind of divine truth that ultimately transcends the reality of everyday existence. None of these latter dream-myths has ever been considered valid enough to become a model for morality and behavior. They were "other-worldly" and served only as an opiate or spiritual drug to heighten the feelings of hope and expectation. Only children were free to have such fantasies, but childhood soon had to meet with adult reality. This, of course, meant that the Adam-Prometheus myths were models for morality, since they did give meaning to life as it was experienced.

It is important to note, however, that the Adam-Prometheus myths have carried within them a deep longing for the utopia that the Orpheus-Narcissus myths represented. For although Adam fell into sin, the promise was later made by God to reestablish the lost paradise. And similarly, in the words of Prometheus, "so, in his crashing fall shall Zeus discover how different are rule and slavery." The Jews saw God feeling sorry for man, thus giving him a hope in the latter days; while the Greeks resented Zeus and envisioned his downfall, resulting in the freedom of man from the rule of Zeus's heavy hand. In both cases there existed a great longing for the paradise Narcissus and Orpheus represented.

In the eighteenth and nineteenth centuries this same distinction between Promethean reality and Orphic fantasy characterized the attitudes of many reformers and radicals. The Promethean tale, which spoke of the fire of technology and blind hope, suited the optimism of nineteenth-century man perfectly. The industrial age had begun to fulfill that which Prometheus had promised. Paradoxically, however, it was a time when the "noble savage" captured the attention of the romantic naturalists. Industrialism deeply troubled the romantics, and the Promethean type of myth could not rationalize away the evils of continued toil and repression. The innate beauty of man's existence, so perfectly characterized by the newly discovered people of paradise in the South Seas, gave the romantics a feeling that industrialism had destroyed the essential meaning of life. Even Darwin's discoveries seemed to stand as a judgment against the mechanical and artificial views of civilized society. For Orpheus and Narcissus, nature was not an enemy to control and dominate but something of which man was a part. Industrialized man, however, had gone too far in his demands upon natural man. Man was becoming a part of the machine.

In spite of this conflict between the romantics and the Promethean industrialists who were beginning to change the face of the globe, the implicit longing for utopia that fallen Adam and suffering Prometheus held so dear paralleled nineteenth-century man's vision of the future. The blind hope that Prometheus gave to man was finally beginning to take substance. And in theology, the great debates centered around the new discoveries of Jesus as an eschatological figure. For the first

time in almost nineteen hundred years, biblical scholars had uncovered an entirely new Jesus, different from any that the
Church had taught before. By the term *eschatological* these
scholars meant that Jesus was one who taught about the "last
days." (Literally, eschatology means study of the last days, or
the final stage in history.) Paradoxically, these scholars didn't
quite know what to do with their findings. For far too long
Jesus had been seen through the eyes of credal statements, conventional philosophy, and established assumptions. As a first-
century eschatological figure, He seemed too primitive for
modern sophisticated man. Consequently, when at the turn of
the century Albert Schweitzer wrote his famous book *The
Quest for the Historical Jesus,* the only conclusion he could
make was that Jesus had been an unfortunate victim of his own
miscalculation. The world had not ended (as Jesus seems to
have predicted) and reality continued as before. In spite of the
romantics, most nineteenth-century men (including theologians) were disciples of Prometheus. The noble savage had to
be civilized and educated. Primitive man was ignorant of the
benefits that industry and Western culture could provide.
Only the romantics appreciated the simple Jesus with his longing for paradise on earth.

And yet, the discovery of the eschatological Jesus couldn't
have been more significant. It revealed how dominant the Pro-
methean-Adam type of reality has been for Western man
throughout the past two thousand years. No one except the
immediate followers of Jesus understood or accepted His
teachings about the imminently dawning Kingdom of God.
Thus, when biblical critics uncovered this startling picture of
Jesus, they couldn't explain Him. In fact, it has been only
within the last few decades that scholars have realized that this
newer image of Jesus is far more important than any previous
one. They discovered that Jesus's message and ministry were
revolutionary. He was calling for a particular attitude toward
the long-promised resurrection of paradise. This is what He
meant by saying that the Kingdom of God was "at hand." Morality, righteousness, obedience to the law, frugality, loyalty,

and all the other virtues of civilized man were not wanted. A
reaction to the dawning Kingdom was demanded. That is why
the rich and powerful went away sorrowful, and the righteous
could not understand him. But those who had the most to gain
by such an expectation of the immediate future, namely, the
prostitutes, children, and other "helpless" humans, found much
meaning in such a message.

Actually, what had happened to this original image and message of Jesus is most important to understand. The Church,
unable to maintain a belief in such an eschatological view of the
present, found it necessary to edit the sayings of Jesus in order
for them to fit the circumstances. The Kingdom had not arrived, and so the Church began to assume that they had misunderstood. Recalling the Old Testament saying, "A day with
the Lord is as a thousand years," they thought they had miscalculated. Perhaps death, they thought, will be the event that
opens the Kingdom for believers. Maybe the "Christian life" is
an interim period on this planet that serves as a testing ground
for heaven.

Even more vividly, the manner by which some of the most
radical sayings of Jesus were altered points up this very problem. The teachings that called for an end of poverty, hunger,
humiliation, and pride were interpreted by the writer of one
gospel to fit a less urgent situation. Not "Blessed are the poor"
but "Blessed are the poor in spirit." Not "Blessed are they that
hunger" but "Blessed are they that hunger after righteousness." Actually Jesus didn't have much patience with the righteous. To him, "The righteous have their reward." He wanted
all those who were open to the future, not those who had
learned how to master the existing system. Who knows, perhaps Matthew, who made these alterations in his gospel, had
the rich Joseph of Arimathea in his congregation and didn't
want his building program disturbed by alienating such a powerful man. (One mustn't be too harsh on the rich if one wants
to establish a Christian community for all! And, more important, how can one maintain a continued sense of urgency when
time goes on as it always has.)

To the leaders of the early Church, things had changed. It didn't take them very long to realize that they had to establish a theology and a morality that presupposed that the eschatological event was, indeed, a long way off. The very notion of the Church as an extension of Christ, with its sacraments and rituals, painted a very different picture of reality than the one Jesus saw. Old men were dying now, children were being born, and young people were reaching adulthood. The Church took this as a cue that it had now become the institution that was to manage this interim time until God saw fit finally to bring in his Kingdom. The prayer of the faithful shows the remnants of that original eschatology: "Thy Kingdom come, on earth, as it is in heaven." But no Christian in his right mind was expected to believe that such a prayer would really have the desired effect. Ironically, history has always had its "heretics" who have proclaimed the immediate return of Christ. The Anabaptists during the Reformation, who led the peasants in revolt, the Pilgrims, and certain sects within religious fundamentalism have all been eschatologically oriented. But established orthodoxy never accepted the eschatological message. Reality seemed to dictate otherwise.

In effect, Jesus was more like Narcissus and Orpheus in proclaiming the dawning of a new age but was interpreted by the Church to be more a Promethean figure. His role was that of savior from heaven, giving to man the principles by which he must now live. In truth, however, being more like Orpheus playing his music, Jesus's teachings of love violated everything rational man believed. Consequently, the inevitable result of the Church's institutionalized version of the last days, relating them to death and the day of judgment beyond the grave, was to inhibit the average believer from holding a truly radical openness toward the future. The real historical Jesus was lost, hidden beneath the theological and credal assumptions of the Church, while His message of radical urgency and expectation of paradise on earth was buried with Him.

Obviously, the orthodox mythology gained dominance not simply because of its inherent meaning but because it suited the social, institutional, and political realities of life. It could hardly be expected of the Church, much less of any other institution, that it would proclaim a message that ultimately meant the end of its own authority and power. Civilized man is institutionalized man. And that means that the individual has no alternative but to submit to that reality. Certainly, the Church set the tone for the rest of Western history in that regard. And with a Promethean Christ proclaiming man's ultimate victory over nature, the modern world could not have had a better conditioning than that which the Church provided.

As the role of technology and industry has increased over the past several hundred years, and especially in recent decades, the impact of these forces under the control of institutionalized man has also drastically increased. Inevitably, a very subtle transition has taken place that has gone relatively unnoticed by most individuals. Whereas in the past institutions like the Church, the state, and other influential bodies demanded the support and membership of individuals, thus teaching the values of institutional dependency, the traditional belief that history was in the hands of God has been slowly replaced with the belief that history is in the hands of the most technologically and scientifically powerful. (For those who still need a theological rationalization of this fact, it remains easy to say that such is God's will.) In other words, the role that the Church once played has finally been inherited by the secular powers of the state and its interlocking institutions. And faithful to the Promethean myth, theirs is now the power to bring Zeus down from his throne. The power of technology that Prometheus stole from the gods is no longer a feeble instrument. It has become the ultimate weapon over life and death. It can bring paradise on earth, or Armageddon.

The great paradox of this long history of confidence in the Promethean institutions of man is that now that many of the anticipated rewards are at hand, most adults still act as if the Promethean values of the past remain appropriate. They do not seem to understand that in the end, Prometheus and Adam are replaced by Narcissus and Christ. In fact, that is precisely what their own children are discovering. One cannot apply the value assumptions of the fallen Adam and the struggling Prometheus to a youngster who is living the life of an Orphic saint. And yet, strange as it may seem, a great many parents intuitively understand this as well. As adults, they themselves may give formal recognition to the values of hard work, performance, and submission to the artificial social norms, but many of them do not seem to insist that their children adhere to these same values. Like faithful Prometheans they do look to the technology and power of society's institutions to solve man's problems. But for their children, provided with the very environment that the myth of Narcissus proscribes, a new age has arrived.

In other words, today's affluent middle-class parents are caught up in a value conflict that is without recorded parallel. They do not know what values to teach their children. Consequently, they simply project their attitudes about the world as they see it. Obviously, the more troubles the society seems to develop (e.g., continued racism, pollution, the war in Asia), the more difficult it is for them to present a clear and positive picture of what they believe is sound and worthwhile. The result is that they give to their children a world of abundance, a high technology, and a guaranteed source of immediate gratification, but all of it in the midst of a value void. For those who have been critical of the society themselves, especially those who have been identified with liberalism, it now becomes impossible to make clear to their children that they are essentially supportive of the world in which they live. After all, for good or ill, it is their world.

As pointed out in the first chapter, however, many of these same parents and other adults who have lived through the past forty years have never really been permitted to have the kind of childhood and adolescence that their own youngsters now experience. For all those who once assumed, even a short time ago, that their children would grow up in a smooth generational process, the events of recent years have proved to be quite a shock. Like Orpheus and Narcissus, today's youngsters are arrogant. They cannot tolerate others who manipulate their world. Like the romantics of a hundred years ago, the young believe that industrial man destroys that which he seeks to control. The rule of civilization is now really at war with the rule of nature. And the rules that the young accept are taught by the experience of freedom, not the fears of chaos. It is no wonder, therefore, that the bard Orpheus should become a culture hero, resembling the endless array of rock musicians. With electric guitar in hand and the primitive beat of the drum, singing the erotic music of the natural realm, the musicians arouse and tame the animal within. As such, they represent in most vivid fashion the post-Promethean world of narcissistic pleasure. Theirs is not the beat of the drum that calls men into lockstep obedience, nor the music of the pied piper leading the blind masses to some unknown destiny, but the music of the body, uniting the physical with the emotional, the soul with the flesh.

Rock music, the television set, drugs, and all the other instruments of contemporary youth culture obviously do not create the constituent elements of utopia. But they do serve the purpose of many young people to express their longing for a world where beauty, love, eroticism, and nature become the dominant forces over repression, competition, and toil. Living the lives of Orphic gods in their childhood, they certainly are not interested in surrendering to some other reality when they finally approach adulthood. In the refusal to do so, there is a profoundly powerful wisdom. As Rousseau once put it, "When our natural tendencies have not been interfered with by human prejudice and human institutions, the happiness alike of children and of men consists in the enjoyment of their liberty." It is an illusion that men create who live their lives bound to institutions that the true peace and beauty of life results from submission to the power of institutions. And it matters not how democratic or benign the institutions claim to be. Institutions, be they Church, nation, school, or party, are all fabrications of men. They are not organic and natural communities created by the forces and laws of nature. Consequently, the morality, psychology, and even rationality of such institutional entities cannot possibly elicit from the young the same feelings and attitudes that have been expected of civilized men in the past. Institutional life has simply lost its magic, and to the young it is like a scene from some Kafka nightmare.

In its place we find today's youngsters, motivated by their own narcissistic morality, feeling that the world is an extension of their own bodies and being fundamentally antagonistic to the institutional powers that manage things. Unlike their parents and other adults who see such attitudes as destructive of the society, these young men and women understand their behavior to be a "harbinger" of things to come. Not unlike the eschatology of Christ, they demand an urgent sense of expectation, a calling for the "Kingdom of God" to come *on earth*. But instead of this expectation sounding like so much wishful thinking, as in the past, it seems to fit some of the actual conditions that scientists and technologists have created. In fact, the very nature of technology has caused the old idealistic dreams to appear increasingly realistic and possible. But the manner by which such possibilities are hindered from development, essentially due to the values and attitudes of those who control the economic power in society, forces young people to conclude that there is a kind of unconscious conspiracy among adults, coupled with a very real conscious conspiracy among those who refuse to permit such technological innovations to happen.

Obviously, there is a conspiracy within the institutional structures of society — not that everyone who manages institutions understands or even recognizes this fact. But as long as men are content to believe that what have evolved as the basic values of social order are the necessary and essential values for social stability (and survival), then such an attitude is bound to serve the interests of those who seek to perpetuate existing policies and practices. This is why the seeming paranoia of the young leftists is not so blind or empty of real significance. There is an adult conspiracy, but it is a conspiracy that has its base not simply in powerful governmental and industrial institutions but in the values and attitudes of those who feign help-lessness to do anything about the society's condition. We must not forget that the kind of narcissism we see among the young, which has been permitted to grow and develop, remains significantly repressed in most adults. Left with little more than a belief or hope that society's major institutions will ultimately make things right, they feel profoundly threatened by those youngsters who question and even take steps to challenge such institutions. But then, Orpheus and Narcissus have always had their enemies.

The true irony of this dilemma is that much of what appears as conscious narcissism among young people today also exists within the unconscious of all adults. Demands for instant gratification, feelings of oceanic, free-floating anxiety, megalomania, paranoia, and dreams of utopia are all common human experiences. Unfortunately, they are usually designated as pathology and neurosis. And since most adults have grown up within a reality of essentially practical and rational demands, their own feelings of narcissism are usually experienced as flights of fantasy and attempts to escape reality. That is why the traditional images of utopian visions (heaven, the Kingdom of God, or paradise) have always been seen as unrealistic and otherworldly.

For a great many young people, however, life in the latter half of the twentieth century is anything but rational and practical. The effects of television, the jet, space travel, the communication revolution, drugs, computer technology, and economic affluence cannot possibly help but reinforce one's narcissistic views of the world. How and by whom all these forces are managed matters very little to the developing child who receives a constant bombardment of their effects. To him, they are all different parts of his own singular selfhood extending his power of autonomy to the ends of the universe. This is why the limitations that society continues to impose on him are seen as irrational and meaningless.

For most adults who see all the economic and technological benefits as the result of long and hard years of struggle such

things are looked upon as "rewards." To take them for
granted, as many youngsters do, appears to be the height of
arrogance and pride. Even worse, it is to assume that such
benefits come naturally and without real pressures for performance and production. It is to forget that they can disappear just as quickly as they have arrived if the next generation
is not willing to continue the process of hard work and toil to
insure their perpetuity.

But this attitude, characteristic of so many adults, refuses to
recognize that there is no serious threat in sight to the real
continuation of necessary skills and talents. If anything, these
narcissistic youngsters are proving every day that they are
more than capable of doing the work required. They are
brighter, healthier, and far more creative than any generation
known to man. The fact that they take the benefits of society
for granted is nothing more than the natural tendency of all
young people to claim the inheritance of the world around
them. They have little need to appreciate what the years of
depression and world war cost their parents. They have other
needs, and most of those needs are directly related to the world
as it actually is. Beginning with their narcissism, their task is to
see how to use their talents constructively to insure a future
for themselves. This is why the utopian dreams of the past have
become the possibilities and the models for tomorrow. Orpheus and Narcissus have ceased to be the saints of unreality
and are fast becoming the models for a "brave new world."
Only this time, "big brother" is not going to be tolerated. The
very essence of this "brave new world" is the absence of "big
brother."

What must be understood by adults now is that the context
of traditional values and orthodox mythologies has changed.
Without an appreciation of this fact, it will remain impossible
to understand what is happening to the young. For example,
when the young turn to astrology, paganism, witchcraft, and
romanticism, it must not be assumed that this forebodes the
downfall of order and purpose in civilization. It simply means

that the older value rationalizations no longer reflect the essential value questions raised by our mass culture. *Prometheus Bound* cannot explain the ultimate meaning of life, because history has outlived the relevance of its message. The story of the fallen Adam cannot relate to the young who have yet to fall, who still have the garden of paradise open to them. Nor can the orthodox Christ of the Church speak with much power and significance, since the original Jesus (preinstitutionalized Christ) makes more sense, calling for openness to the immediate dawning of God's Kingdom. (Note the language: "It's happening," "The age of Aquarius" and the "now" generation.)

Actually, paganism, eschatology, and romanticism are quite appropriate frames of reference for our affluent, technological mass culture. They provide the individual with a wide range of interpretations for what he sees happening around him. They appeal to the dominant sense that one is living in the "last days," or perhaps in the dawning of a new age. And they replace the cold and emotionless rationality of previous attitudes with erotic, emotional, and inventive approaches. For example, if one were to talk with the young people living in some of the countless communes around the country, one might hear them speak of the human "aura." According to these young people, all humans are surrounded with a series of light or energy fields, especially about the head, which reveal the health or pathology of the individual. For those gifted enough to discern these auras, they can tell whether one is in harmony with the universe or suffering some kind of illness. In the language of science, one is either synergistic or entropic. At other times, one hears them speak of "vibrations," by which they seem to mean forces that have an emotional component, moving either toward some organic wholeness or else toward destruction and death. Then again, there are those who rely upon amulets and charms, often to ward off evil powers but more often as an outward display of their appreciation of the more animistic approach to religious truth.

What is so startling about these and other manifestations of paganism among the young is that they are characteristic of the most affluent and well educated. Obviously, there are many who come from poorer homes and for whom such behavior is really not much different than the religious fundamentalism of the lower middle class. (Perhaps the Charles Manson episode falls into this category.) But when young people who have been studying for graduate degrees in science or the humanities turn to what appears to be magic and fantasy, rational adults cannot help but wonder what has caused such a drastic change. How can one who has learned the ground rules for logic and rationality turn to the occult and the obscure?

Actually, as we have already stated, the answer has to do with the narcissism of the affluent younger generation. Having lived, as it were, at the center of their own personal universes, having experienced the control of their own immediate environment and learned that the adult world is hopelessly fragmented, competitive, and powerless to affect its own destiny, these youngsters continue to live out the narcissistic experience they had throughout their childhood. More often than not, however, this particular type of narcissism does not result in the conventional pathology that psychology dictates. They are not selfish and egocentric. In fact, "ego trips," as they like to call them, are considered illegitimate. Strangely enough, it is the kind of narcissistic development that consciously treats the needs and wants of others quite seriously. They share their goods and resources by treating the whole earth as one "system." The reason why paganism makes more sense to them than it does to their parents, therefore, is because paganism is the religion of narcissism. It is concerned with nature, its laws and rituals, and it presupposes that the individual is an inextricable part of nature. Promethean-Christian man has always seen himself as master of nature, not as a part of it. Pagan man sees himself indistinguishable from nature.

Obviously, the consequences of such an attitude as this cannot help but affect the entire fabric of society. For example, whereas our laws reflect the struggles and conflicts of Western civilization, many young people understand only that kind of law that permits personal freedom and is consistent with what they believe to be "natural law." If the law restricts nudity and sexual intercourse, then the young insist that nature reveals otherwise. If the law prohibits certain types of drug use, then the young insist that nature is filled with drugs, of which only the individual can avail himself or deprive himself. If the law dictates certain conditions for marriage, then the young insist that it is natural to experiment with many forms of male and female interrelatedness. In other words, the adult world is predicated upon the repression of narcissism. The morality that underlies our entire legal system makes this quite clear. But narcissism, as typified by so many young people, dictates a much different morality. Eventually, this will mean that a different set of laws will have to come into effect.

Unfortunately, there is nothing within the mass culture of today that teaches the young that respect for the law is a viable attitude. Everywhere they turn they witness rebellion against the law. In fact, about the only thing that most adults have to point to in this growing turmoil is their fear of the consequences of breaking the law. And yet all-white communities break the constitutional law. The President continues a war without the conventional justification of a declared war. The rich buy their way out of prosecution. And the minorities are forced to break the law in order to get it changed. To put it as clearly as possible, the law exists for those who have the most to lose. That is why the demand for "law and order" must inevitably be translated as a selfish expression of possessiveness and not an appeal to meaningful values or truly moral behavior.

Without realizing it, adults have forced the young to become society's "heretics." That is the real significance of the value crisis we now face. Promethean man was successful in his utopian pursuit, but he failed to prepare for his own triumph. His children take the world he provided them, and turn it into a Dionysian fantasy. And as we said earlier, one must not confuse or mix the two. Orpheus and Narcissus have played the role of "unrealistic" infantile dream figures for too long. Now it is their turn to set the stage, write the script, and perform the play. Old sinful Adam and old powerful Prometheus must take their seats in the audience, and let their strange progeny teach them a few new lessons.

3

THE DEATH OF DADDY

It is not without significance that within recent years one of the most seriously reviewed books on the subject of the "generation gap" defines the underlying cause of conflict in the terms of Freud's Oedipal theory. In his book *The Conflict of Generations,* Lewis S. Feuer describes the growing student rebellion around the world as an inevitable revolt by the young against the father figures who manage our political, military, and educational institutions. Actually, the appeal to Freudian theory is legitimate. One can hardly understand much contemporary literature in the Western world without an appreciation of the contributions made by Freudian theory. This theory is most useful because it finds so much support in the traditional conflict between the young and the adult world. Sons have always sought confrontations with their fathers. Such confrontation is, as we have already said, biologically determined and has its roots within the eternal triangle of mother, father, and child. And since everyone comes from some kind of Oedipal surrounding, having experienced a necessary struggle for power and self-determination, it is only reasonable to conclude that such a conflict will continue to play a role as the young inexorably move into the society beyond the family.

Historically, childhood has been experienced as the context wherein the instinctual drive for gratification has been met with a series of frustrating encounters. As the Oedipal theory defines it, the son is thus pitted against the one who usually acts as the major source of resistance, namely, the father. With mother as the main "loved object," the son's instinctual drive for narcissistic reunion with her is thwarted by the role which the father plays. The son, who desires access to mother similar to that he sees the father having, encounters a fundamental competition for mother's affection (affection that for all children is erotic and sensual). The son, predictably, loses the battle, since father must remain the authority over the family hierarchy. The son must resolve this defeat and save his ego in the process. Normally, this results in the son repressing his natural incestuous instinctual rage and replacing it with feelings of identification with the father. In any case, the son must learn that such feelings of rage are not acceptable to the adult world. Thus defeated, the son turns to his peer group for support and seeks to develop his own world of associations and relationships which will not recapitulate the same defeat. This is the beginning of the son's social competition for the role of self-defined adulthood. Consequently, as the son finally approaches puberty, his repressed erotic instincts reemerge, but this time they are directed at other females, hopefully satisfying his growing need for ego fulfillment. During the period of adolescence, however, those repressed emotions of rage and eroticism suddenly become socially important, owing to the simple fact that the son now approaches adulthood. He is capable of making a woman pregnant — strong enough actually to destroy father and the father-surrogates in society and thus begin the take-over of the adult world. At this point, he encounters the taboos and prohibitions of society, which earlier typified his own father's moral authority. Only this time they require a recapitulation to the father-surrogates beyond the family. Once again, the son must repress his instinctual demands for self-determined gratification and learn how to identify his wants and needs with the authority system which society provides. If the original Oedipal conflict is "resolved" in the home, between father and son, then one can be expected to resolve it once again as one encounters the larger Oedipal context of society.

But history is not simply a circular process of recapitulating events. There are definite discontinuities which have begun to occur, and these, in turn, make many historical points of view seem not to apply any longer. Most visibly, this applies to the Oedipal theory, especially within the United States in recent years. Not that people do not continue to experience Oedipal conflicts within the home, or that society is completely devoid of parental surrogates. But to assume that this society, or better yet this mass culture, is *characterized* by the older images of paternalism, authority, and Oedipal rebellion is to ignore certain fundamental changes which have begun to occur in recent years.

The major weakness of the Oedipal rebellion theory today is that it no longer reflects the common experience of a great many young people reared in affluent suburbs. If it applies anywhere, it is with the older generation in America and elsewhere, and perhaps with many young people around the world whose economic and technological cultures have not yet reached the level found in the United States. Obviously, most adults in America and most young people elsewhere in the industrialized world have far more in common with one another than they do with the young who have grown up in the surroundings of upper-middle-class America. The children reared in this country within the last twenty-five years can only be described as "postindustrial" people. And one of the chief characteristics of the Oedipal theory of rebellion, as defined in the past, has been the agricultural and industrial environment surrounding the home. The unquestionable need for the sons and daughters to inherit the same roles and functions which an agricultural or industrial culture requires heavily determines the continuing dynamics of Oedipal psychology. In a mass culture, however,

especially one that is the result of a successful industrial culture, the society encountered by the young as they leave home
has very little to do with the society their parents encountered
when they left home.

If one realizes that the model of the family Oedipal structure
has always played a more important role in European and Asian
cultures, then it becomes clear that much of what motivates
student and youthful unrest in those countries has its origin in
the Oedipal rebellion of the young. In this sense, Feuer's book
is most perceptive and useful. As the Minister of Education in
West Berlin recently said: "The young have only two alternatives. Either they kill the father or they learn to emulate him."
Certainly, such an attitude as this strikes very few adults as
novel or strange. It accurately reflects what many have long
believed to be the mark of mature wisdom concerning youthful behavior and adolescent dissatisfaction with the adult
world. Going back many centuries, such a view has traditionally been held by those adult leaders of society who felt that
they had to capture this youthful rebellion and use it for purposes of work and other means of fulfilling social responsibility.
Such men have long recognized that youthful energy had to be
put to "constructive" purposes if it was not to sour and turn
into violent rebellion. (In fact, a great many adults today make
this same argument. Note the conventional recruiting approach
used for the Boy Scouts, the Peace Corps, etc.) Such an attitude has always characterized the effective leadership of the
parental surrogates in society. The local football coach, the
honored military commander, the priest or pastor, the charismatic political leader, the boss on the job, and the loved teacher
have all been perfect examples of those who seemingly understood this vital dynamic of leading youth. They all had a
common task: co-opt the energies of the young and direct
them into channels of socially useful work and production.

And yet, had it not been for certain other factors which
have long characterized civilized communities, this particular
type of leadership could never have worked as effectively as it

has in the past. First, society had to have obvious parental sur-rogates, especially father-figures, which could relate the child's experience in the home with the authority figures in the soci-ety. Second, the society had to have visible means of release for the energies of the young. Work, performance, and skill requirements had to be in demand. And third, the young had to experience a normal amount of "repression" and Oedipal frus-tration in the home. In other words, they had to be pro-grammed for the dynamics of submission to authority. Not only did the society have to provide avenues for constructive adolescent release, but the home had to exert a certain restraint on childish wish-fulfillment in order for the child to look for-ward to his place within the social order of adults. Repression must have a reward somewhere later on in the life of the re-pressed. Traditionally, adulthood has represented that reward. One earned money, got one's own spouse, and established oneself as a member of the adult community.

One need only remember that it wasn't very long ago that these very same elements of adult wisdom applied to child rearing and adolescent control in this country. (For many in the lower middle class it still applies.) We had more parental surrogates in the leadership of our major social institutions than we knew what to do with. There were political heroes, aca-demic and scientific father-figures, famous theologians and phi-losophers, and an endless array of quoted intellectuals and au-thors. Young people looked forward to jobs and productive roles within the society. And the home provided all the neces-sary Oedipal conflicts. Father was a visible figure in the home, and the morality of the culture reflected the typical fears of erotic stimulation, undue gratification of wishful thinking, and aberrant searching after nonproductive pleasures. One took drugs to be able to function better, not feel better. Of course, society provided for a degree of adolescent rebellion in frater-nity rituals, panty raids, beach parties, and other examples of childish revolt, especially for the elite class of college students. Obviously, young people in those days could be permitted a degree of "sowing their wild oats," as long as they quietly promised to return to the acceptable patterns of adult responsibility.

Those in positions of leadership in government, business, education, labor, and the military understood that they must periodically provide for those under their control a degree of release from the constraints normally imposed. As in the religious season of Lent, when the believer is expected to submit to a kind of self-denial, the Church instituted means whereby the individual could have his childish "fling," a Mardi Gras or festival of erotic pleasure. Such has been the classic pattern of civilized mastery of the Oedipal conflict, manipulating the unconscious of the repressed individual, thus reinforcing his childish dependency upon the paternal authority of society's leadership.

Most adults in this country, not to mention elsewhere in the world, have permitted society (they had no choice) to structure their own repressed drives for gratification by capturing their loyalties, their energies, and their commitments. Not surprisingly, many of these same people have feelings for their country (homeland, fatherland, mother earth) and its institutions which are rooted in an unconscious identification with their Oedipal origins. To contemplate an honest feeling about father-surrogates is to risk the eruption of emotional anarchy, blindly striking out at the ones who are supposed to protect and provide security. In fact, this is exactly why so many intellectuals fear a revolt by the "silent majority" against the youth. They know full well that Oedipal rebellion and Oedipal submission are the most profound psychological experiences working people know.

Thus, insofar as this same dynamic is alive in this country, and in other cultures, orthodox Freudians insist that the young who revolt are actually striking back at their own fathers, usually through the visible father-figures who are in control. History makes it quite clear that such is the basis of revolution and rebellion. The Czarists in Russia blamed the revolt in 1918 on the young. Hitler blamed the threat of communism on the idealistic and anarchistic attitudes of the youth of the twenties. And a great many adults in this country today, J. Edgar Hoover included, deeply feel that young people in America are trying to destroy their father-authority figures.

Ironically, this argument is made precisely at a time when it no longer applies. Parental surrogates are increasingly invisible and powerless as individuals, due to factors such as "management without ownership" in most of our major social institutions. Prolonged education, the draft, and economic abundance have produced a new class of young adults whose participation in socially useful and constructive work has been perilously delayed. Meanwhile, the increased ability of the home to meet the needs and to gratify the wishes of the young, coupled with the moral abdication of fathers and the growing influence of mothers, results in a serious alteration of the Oedipal conflict. There are no strong figures to revolt against, and the rewards of power are available without a struggle. The classic adolescents are those who see in their nation a kind of "fatherland" which demands the adolescent feelings of respect and obedience. Not unlike children whose egos are threatened by serious identity problems, they attribute magical powers to the state, together with a conviction that "Daddy can do no wrong." And it is the adult population, not the young, who most nearly fit this definition.

Wherever men and women have had to suffer certain amounts of repression and submission to authority, the tendency to insist that the young who follow must do the same is significantly common. In many respects, this explains much of the conflict between faculty and students on our campuses today — not to mention middle-class attitudes toward the blacks and the problems of welfare reform. The demands which young people and minority groups are making appear to adults as shortcut steps into the mainstream of society. As such, they are often looked upon as childish requests for special attention and privilege. The academics who have "made it" are deeply resentful of the long years of hard work which they have suffered. They prefer to see the "contributions" they have made — usually magnified in importance by the little "domains" they have created around themselves — as the result of a faithful commitment to the better goals and directions of society. Why should an entire generation of youngsters be permitted to pass judgment on their performance? And why should this new generation expect to have an easier time in reaching similar heights of professional responsibility? But then, who has the greater Oedipal "hangup" in this conflict — the professors who protect their own realms from attack or the young students who demand a greater voice in determining university affairs? Could it not be that many of the faculty members are angry because they themselves had to submit to adult authority in the past and now are simply insisting that the next generation follow a similar pattern?

It certainly ought not escape anyone's attention that university life does tend to result in a rather deep-seated and prolonged adolescence. There are not many professional educators who have remained behind the skirts of "Alma Mater" (which means "stepmother") and have not been affected by the long years of striving for position and prestige. Their road to the adult standard of scholar and professor has been filled with submission to the petty and often irrelevant demands which their superiors have laid down. Consequently, it would be a rather important oversight for one who appeals to the Oedipal theory to ignore the degree to which many academics have accepted and perpetuated the psychology of such a theory in their own lives.

Nevertheless, what those who argue from the Oedipal theory today seem to ignore, is the enormous degree to which "father" is visibly absent from our major social institutions. In the universities, the concept of *in loco parentis* (the school as substitute parent) no longer has any serious relationship to the manner by which universities relate to students. If anything, the problems which administrators and faculty members face have far more to do with their own special areas of competence and responsibility than they do with providing students with paternal substitutes. The nature of the university has changed so drastically in recent years that the older images of "community" and "family" seem precious and beneath the dignity of university officials. This is why large universities hire counselors and psychologists to take care of the personal problems of students.

In government, especially federal and large urban government, the bureaucracy has evolved over the years into the worst kind of fragmentation and specialization. In some departments of the federal government, the Congressional and executive leadership is totally in the dark as to inner workings of contracts, research, and oftentimes budget. This has meant that the selection of very special types of men and women, skilled in technology, administration, and management, has created an interlocking set of agencies that only they can manage. Arthur Krock calls them "the Indians," and has demonstrated in detail how they subvert "the Chiefs." The old-fashioned father-figure (the "old man") is thus harder and harder to find — or, if found, less and less important — in such a maze of institutional structure. Given the common attitudes of most Americans toward the roles which these paternalistic types once played, especially such roles as President, Senator, and Mayor, it is hard to avoid the feeling that symbolic father-figures have all but disappeared. (It is difficult to see how Richard M. Nixon stands as a father-surrogate for many young people today.)

Even in business, that classic institution of the old-fashioned paternal entrepreneur, the role of the father-figure, has rapidly disappeared. In his place we find the faceless board of directors, who hold power but who, because of the complexity of modern management, must turn to their "technocratic" junior managers and specialists for information and direction. Consequently, the role of the parental surrogate is changed to fit the image of the executive. The executive holds the authority and power of the company, but he doesn't own the company and in the traditional sense he doesn't even run it. The management role of the top executive is more that of servant to the activities and personnel over which he has control. Like the modern father, the boss takes care of his people but rarely directs their activities. Until most recently, the Oedipal dynamics within most younger employees has worked to reinforce the normal ordering of authority. But that only applies to those younger men and women who bring a classic Oedipal unconscious to the job. In fact, one might say that much of the problem in training new managements today is complicated by the absence of visible father-figures. Ironically, junior managers who still turn their superiors into father-surrogates usually discover that their superiors see them as "dependents" who probably won't make good executives. (See Robert Townsend's book *Up The Organization*.) The decision-making process today requires only the shadow of Oedipal psychology.

Certainly, much of the turmoil which is taking place within the Church, especially among Roman Catholics, represents this same kind of decline of paternal control. In those countries where the economic and industrial levels of security have risen, many Catholics find it increasingly difficult to accept the directions of the Pope (the Holy Father) or the spiritual leadership of conservative bishops. Ironically, the Roman Catholic Church has long been history's greatest example of an institution patterned after the Oedipal dynamics of the family. No other institution so self-consciously uses family imagery to define the roles played by the members of the believing community. Priests are actually called "Father," the Church is labeled "Mother," thus perpetuating a maternal care for the individual believer from birth to death through the sacraments, and the believers themselves are often referred to as "children" of the Church or of God the Father. Thus, when young priests and nuns rebel, their revolt takes on all the signs of faithless youngsters standing up to the paternal system of authority. Significantly, the two major issues which reflect the most serious "disobedience" to the paternal rule of the Church have been celibacy and birth control. One might say that the revolution has started at the very place where the fathers of the Church have sought to control the deepest and most powerful emotions in man and woman, namely, those in marriage and childbirth.

Somehow the images of "spiritual" fatherhood, as elsewhere in society's institutions, no longer serve as the powerful dynamics of control they once did. A new feeling of independence and autonomy has begun to replace the old emotions of capitulation to the "father's" wishes. Another way to describe these signs of paternal decline is to say that the real psychological power behind the so-called death of God is the growing evidence that "daddy is dead." A new kind of social pattern seems to be developing which no longer requires that the Oedipal dynamics of the home be recapitulated in society. Such are its effects that the older forces of tribe and ritual dramatically lose their power to incorporate the individual within the institutions of culture. Relationships become rational, conscious, and contractual. And those who are the most prepared to make this kind of transition from home to society, without looking for home away from home, reinforce the mass culture mightily. (Today's youngster encounters the mass culture, through television, long before he even resolves his Oedipal struggle with father.) Increasingly, these people demand that their relationship to the society be based upon their skills, roles, and talents, but not on their psychological need to submit to a system of loyalty and patriotism.

In the writings of Freud, such a moment as this in history was never fully anticipated. According to his "horde theory" in *Totem and Taboo*, the original sons sought to destroy the father, take over his power, and thus gain access to mother and the other women of the family. This crime, however, threw the family into chaos and anarchy. No longer having a father to serve as leader, they had to "resurrect" him in the form of a totem and to establish laws or taboos which would prohibit them from recapitulating the primal crime. It is interesting that the nature of those taboos was such as to define morality in terms of what was *not* permitted rather than what was permitted. It was the incestuous instincts for gratification which Freud saw as the root cause of anarchy and revolt. Coupled with a universal condition of scarcity, the plight of precivilized man was greatly determined by a need for social order and meaningful hierarchy, with father at the top. This meant, then, that the very foundations of civilized behavior have been built upon a ritualization of feared chaos, and upon the perpetuation of the myth that what lies at the bottom of all civilized men's unconsciousness is a murderous wish against father and all father-surrogates.

Of course, Freud's theories would never have received the attention they have had they not so closely resembled civilized man's behavior. Having seen how potent the Oedipal conflict is within the unconscious of man, neither disciples nor critics of Freud have ever been able to challenge his theory. But then, no one has tried to understand what our mass culture, with its affluence and technology, does to the context which has always resulted in Oedipal rebellion. One must now explain why the young seek to destroy the father-figures of society, when in fact the father symbols are themselves so scarce. Could this mean, as some have suggested, that the young are actually searching for father-surrogates, that they are experiencing the anxiety of the original sons who found themselves leaderless after the primal crime? I hardly think so, especially if one recognizes that it is the irrelevant use of Oedipal symbols by adults, seeking to capture the loyalties of the young, which so profoundly disgusts them. Demands for loyalty, respect, submission to authority, patience with the institutional processes, and patriotism no longer elicit the kinds of feelings which adults want young people to have.

Perhaps the most obvious symbol of the death of daddy is the romantic manipulation of past events to justify the attitudes and values of the present generation of adults. In movies, television programs, newspapers, and other media controlled by adults seeking to gain the attention of the population, we find a standardization of past values. The Second World War is used as a source of countless movies and television plots, the early West is characterized as a setting "where men are men and women are women," government spies are made to seem superhuman and invulnerable, and even the futuristic images of space travel and technological innovation (which can't even stay ahead of real technological breakthroughs) are filled with culture-heroes who serve to take the place of the invisible father-figures in reality.

During the early forties it was quite a different thing for young boys and girls to attend a war movie or watch a serial and be propagandized about the heroes who represented the side of righteousness. Such a practice is as old as tribal indoctrination, and in the forties it still worked. But in a mass culture, to superimpose the image of the singular hero, supposedly representing the best and the most cherished images of manhood, is simpleminded, and the ends of propaganda become far more visible and artificial. A mass culture like ours is far too complex for the single values and patterns of any one previous culture to apply.

For young people, the artificial characteristics of values and symbols which the mass culture imposes become a source of amusement or real frustration. Having no roots in the past, where the dominant culture dictated the images of success, they find the values and attitudes used in the public media hollow and meaningless. The Spiro Agnew watch is a fine example. Agnew, playing a strong father-figure role, is humorously equated with Mickey Mouse — a *1930s* cartoon character. Yet that a man whose image is most precisely defined by a cartoon should have real power is, of course, enormously frustrating.

More important, young people realize that the prime concern of many of the institutional leaders of society is to evoke a predictable response from the masses. It is the very essence of the dilemma faced by politicians, administrators, and businessmen, and the war in Southeast Asia is the epitome of this type of problem. Instead of having a generation of youth motivated by the values and ideals of a tribal culture, which would serve the interests of those who involve us in wars, we have a large group oriented to the ways of mass culture, which sees the manipulation all too clearly. Older images of "Uncle Sam Needs You" become pop posters used to decorate apartments or dormitory rooms. Pictures which superimpose the face of

the President on an aggressive-looking member of a motor-
cycle gang, or identify the President and his wife with the
characters of Bonnie and Clyde, now replace the "pinups"
which used to hang on father's wall.

The more such responses become common among youngsters, the more we have evidence of the decline of the Oedipal
dynamics within society. To equate this behavior with traditional examples of adolescent humor or sacrilege is to mis-
understand how deep the rejection of adult authority really is
today. At the same time, the more adults seek to perpetuate the
father-son psychology of the past, the more the sons seek to
ridicule it. Rather than realizing that young people no longer
respond effectively to such classic patterns, the assumption is
made that all these signs of youthful revolt are natural adolescent forms of testing adult standards. Nothing could be farther
from the truth. They are examples, much to the chagrin of
many adults, of a social revolution similar to the tale of the
honest little boy who said, "The emperor has no clothes on!"

Of course, this forces us to ask about the nature of the Oedipal conflict within the affluent home, especially if it does not
seem to recapitulate the Oedipal struggle in society. Is it possible that the mass culture has completely altered the traditional family-society relationship? Has conventional society
actually become something alien to the patterns of child
rearing within the home? Insofar as the traditional values of
paternalism, adolescent revolt, and ultimate capitulation are
used to explain the behavior of society and its youth, the answer is yes. There is no greater illusion a mass culture can
harbor than the ridiculous notion that the real authorities of society are father-figures who seek only the best for their sons. It
has not always been true even in a tribalistic society. How
could it suddenly be true for a mass culture?

More striking, the homes of many young people today are
anything but models for conventional social behavior. In many
respects, a large number of them seem to be experimental communities where the young learn some of the most fundamental
revolutionary values known to civilized man. This is most true

of those where parents have insisted upon all the benefits of progressive education, permissive eroticism, and self-development. In the words of Sir Herbert Read: "Unless we can succeed in basing education on the *natural* (as opposed to 'social') instinct for order, education will remain powerless against the forces of destruction. The instinct for order is the only natural instinct that can control the instinct for destruction, the mortal instinct." * Obviously, Read is not appealing for "law and order" but for a progressive style of education which a growing number of parents desire for their children. The briefest visit to some of the schools, both public and private, around the more affluent suburbs of this country will quickly reveal how popular some of these ideals are. The concepts of Rousseau, Montessori, Dewey and the lessons learned from A. S. Neill's Summerhill school have not gone unnoticed in affluent America. For the first time, some of these "radical" ideas are beginning to be put to the test. Given the anxiety, bureaucracy, and ineptitude of most teachers and administrators, however they still have a long way to go.

Not surprisingly, therefore, the homes of many of these most fortunate youngsters are unique when compared to the ones most adults knew when they were children. Instead of the classic conditions of scarcity, managed by father's authority, resulting in the values of frugality, imposed orderliness, competition, and what the psychoanalysts call "the conspiracy of silence" around the subject of sex and the body, we find immediate gratification of many desires, creativity, self-expression, experimentation, and sexual honesty.

Add to this the popular attitudes and values which flourish around the youth culture in art, music, dress, language, and literature, and we can begin to see the outlines of a new moral and social system. What gives these developments so much significance is the fantastic degree to which the standards of youth culture become the popular standards for the masses. Even parents become profoundly influenced by the styles and

* Sir Herbert Read, "Art as a Unifying Principle in Education," pp. 34–35. *Child Art* (Berkeley, Calif.: Diablo Press).

attitudes of their children. Thus, it becomes far more difficult for the adults to provide symbolic and definitive examples of adult or mature behavior.

It is not an uncommon thing today for small children to begin to have their basic opinions concerning the world beyond the family formulated by many of these same mass culture, youth-standards. Consequently, the degree to which parents have direct influence on the establishment of their children's values is seriously circumscribed by the invasion of the youth culture into the home. So subtle and ubiquitous is this "progressive," permissive, and erotic influence upon children that it seems almost invisible and unnoticed.

This is not to say, of course, that the Oedipal conflict is totally nonexistent in homes such as these. It does exist, but what seems to happen, actually, is that the sons and daughters find that their conflicts with parents, especially those of the same sex, are substantially ameliorated by the parents' attempts to understand the child's problems. Also, the rewards which often serve as compensation, and a sense that the real aim they seek will ultimately be gratified, act to soften the Oedipal blow. Certainly, no child can escape a limited amount of repression. He does have instinctual drives which cannot be fully gratified under any conditions. He cannot have his mother (or daughter have her father) as his fantasy might demand. And insofar as these limitations exist, natually he has an Oedipal conflict.

But as any psychoanalyst knows, the point at which the Oedipal conflict becomes problematic is when the parents react neurotically. The child's natural desires are met with feelings of guilt and shame, which are then projected onto the child. Inevitably, every child is bound to feel a profound sense of inadequacy. His physical size, his intellectual ability and his emotional capacity are limited. All the child has to do is to compare himself with the adults around him and he immediately feels small and inadequate. As Karen Horney has taught us, such an experience cannot help but lead to certain neurotic patterns. But they need not become permanent patterns if the parents realize that the child also needs love, support, and a

flexible structure. If these things follow, then the repression of
the child's normal narcissistic wish for reunion with mother
can be made far less painful, and the child can move on to the
next stage of psychosexual development.

It ought to be obvious that there are a great many homes in
this society today in which the parents understand many of
these very problems. Not that we have suddenly turned the
entire mass culture into a utopian community where the parents are all completely healthy and well-adjusted individuals, or
that all their children are free from neurosis and conflict. That
much is not even necessary for the effects which I have outlined to exist. Each home is a unique community, and the
amount of sophistication and understanding which exists
within any one home is purely relative. But when one begins to
consider how many of these homes and communities are pro-
ducing young people who mature at an earlier age, who understand themselves and their society as well as they do, who do
not feel that they must forever reject their parents and who are
highly motivated to become self-developed young men and
women, we cannot escape the fact that many parents have been
doing an exceptionally good job in rearing their children.

The essence of this innovation, then, is really very simple.
The Oedipal conflict within the lives of countless young
people, remains an important factor, even as it has for centuries. But no longer does it become the conditioning factor
between home and the society. Almost accidentally, we are letting it take a more natural development. Thus, if anyone wants
to blame someone for the angry and autonomous young people
who are making their "demands" upon the society felt in almost every quarter, then don't blame the parents for failing,
blame them for having succeeded.

It is time we stop punishing ourselves for having provided
family contexts wherein the ancient dreams of man can begin
to be realized. The fact that society has not been able to keep
up with such developments is what ought to concern us. Perhaps the single most important factor which inhibits our culture from accommodating to this rapid advance within so

many families and homes is the fact that the society has not structured itself so that these young people can have a place within it. The adult population has become so big, works longer years, and maintains its roles (and control) into later life, and thus does not let the young move into the natural inheritance which is their due. Consequently, the young are forced into their own cultural groups, living together in schools and around our urban communities, and finding that the channels of access to the adult roles in society are closed to them.

Is it any wonder, then, that as these young men and women attend college and find problems which they share with their peers, they should decide that they have a collective interest in changing the society? What more logical place could they select to make their feelings and desires known than at college or university? Many of them can vote now, but, they cannot exert direct influence on government and industry, except as certain issues tend to mobilize public opinion. And they cannot use financial or capital control to get their way. They must rely on the one most important source of power they have, namely, their youth.

Interestingly enough, however, "student power" is not the basic issue involving young people in university and social reform. It is one of the lesser issues, because students are not truly interested in perpetuating themselves as a student class. Student power is a means to another end. What they want most is access to the resources of society which will enable them to change that society. And the university is one of those most important resources. As a very powerful source of information, knowledge, training, and research, the university is the prime target for getting at the rest of the society. Government and industry have known this for some time, and the invasion by agencies and interest groups from "outside" the university has only made the issue all the more clear. Universities are no longer isolated institutions of learning. Those who perpetuate such a myth are seeking to direct public attention away from the facts. Almost without society knowing it the university has gone through an enormous transformation over the years. The older images of a pastoral setting where young men and women prepare themselves for leadership in society no longer has any relationship to the facts. Nor do the illusions which define college life as an aristocratic community, standing apart from the world, apply to the modern institutions of higher education.

What clouds the picture of this newer reality are the myths and illusions which are commonly used to protect the university structures from serious political, social and economic control. To many students, the most visible flaw within this "ivory tower" syndrome is the problem of "power without responsibility." In a culture where the traditional values of paternal authority have been reinforced with visible signs of wealth, ownership, and direct management, modern universities appear to be something quite new. Like the corporate world of business or the bureaucratic agencies of government, the symbolic authority of father is totally absent. In its place we find the college dean or president, the executive or board member who has little or no power of his own; but corporately he wields enormous power and influence.

What troubles the student is that he cannot relate to any of these "individual" members of the institutional system of authority and seriously hope to obtain decisions or actions which will mobilize the institution to serve the needs of the individual. The individual administrator usually responds that he is "powerless" to do very much. In fact, he is powerless, if we understand that authority no longer has very much to do with traditional images of control and influence. This is why the criticism by the young radicals is quite accurate. It is not the individual administrator who is at fault. It is the "system."

It is amazing how few seem to appreciate how this affects the exercise of responsibility and authority in our society. Unfortunately, it means that we do not actually possess a value system which defines or describes the basis for leadership and adult responsibility. We know a lot about institutional authority and power; we have laws which protect the interests and concerns of institutions. We provide a kind of authority to those who manage these institutions, but we do not have a moral system which places authority in the hands of the management based upon their roles as "adults" or mature paternal figures. To do that would mean that every dynasty in business and industry would have to make the managements of those firms actual members of the original family who own the business. In universities, it would mean that administrators, trustees, and faculty would have to have an actual part in the "ownership" of the corporation.

Of course, such an archaic system of authority as this will never come back into existence. Society is far too complex for Oedipal dynamics to apply any longer. The fabricated system of "power without ownership," which so completely dominates our institutional structures, must begin to change. In its place, a system based upon authority of the people will have to evolve. Not communism or socialism, since these are nothing more than parallel bureaucracies to the corporate institutions in the West, but democratic institutions which exist to serve the interests of those who are most affected.

This, in turn, will mean that students will no longer be looked upon as passive recipients of knowledge or learning. They, too, will have to become members of the institutions, sharing in the decisions which govern them. Obviously, this will have a substantial effect on the ones who presently use universities for their own purposes. The domains of privilege which once protected scholars, scientists, business interests, and special groups will have to be opened to those who share the uses of higher education. But the reason why such an innovation must inevitably take place has little to do with political theory. It is an evolution which must be permitted to happen, simply because the society has finally created a "class" of people, young people, who have as much right to participate as anyone. The consequences of not permitting this evolution will inevitably be a terrible revolution. It will not be between fathers and sons but between those who seek to perpetuate their own interests and those who are trying to gain access to the resources of the society.

What is not understood by those who see a split in the ranks of young people on our campuses today is that they have far more in common than is usually appreciated. On the one hand, the radicals and revolutionaries make their demands for influence and control. On the other, the majority want to use the university so that they can begin to reap some of the benefits which a university degree and training will hopefully provide. The fear of many in the latter group has little to do with their love of authority or respect for university officials. They simply don't want the boat rocked while they face the realities of the world. Significantly, many of this group are from middle- and lower-middle-class homes. Like the blacks, they want the benefits of a university degree. Unlike the blacks, they are willing to tolerate the incipient racism which prohibits blacks from gaining access to such benefits. The radicals, on the other hand, usually come from affluent homes and communities. To them the degree is readily available anytime they choose to get it. Like the blacks, they know that they have to invade the structures of power to get what they want. Unlike the blacks, they are motivated by noneconomic and upper-middle-class values which reflect their disgust with how their own economic class has manipulated the university.

Very few of them, either the blacks, the radicals, the masses, or the indifferent, have feelings of devotion or respect for their elders. The images of adulthood have become so profoundly clouded as to be of little or no importance. Thus, we have constructed a society in which the sons of men leave home, never to return to the relationship of father and son. The glue which once used to hold man's institutions and communities together is beginning to lose its power to stick. And we haven't found a very good replacement for it yet.

4

THE DEATH OF DADDY
AND ITS EFFECT ON
GROUP PSYCHOLOGY

If the Oedipal rebellion theory no longer serves to explain the behavior of many adolescents, then what can be said to take the place of the traditional dynamics of group and institutional behavior? Assuming that we have become a mass culture, what are the psychological forces which enable groups to perform common tasks, serve specific goals, and elicit useful and necessary conduct from their members?

To answer these questions it is important to realize that many of Freud's theories were interpretations of Western civilization rather than scientific explanations of individual human behavior. The true merit of Freud's insight lay in his analysis of the behavior patterns, values, and internal (unconscious) dynamics of his own civilization. His lack of knowledge concerning such important matters as female psychology, non-Western cultures, and more recent anthropological findings about the origins of man is offset only by his genius in explaining the very things which have characterized Western man's behavior. To demand much more of Freud's theories would be to ask too much of one man. It would be much better to follow his own admonition. "Equal care must be given," he said, "to avoid two sources of error — the Scylla of underestimating the importance of the repressed unconscious, and the Charybdis of judging the normal entirely by the standards of the pathological."

In his book *Group Psychology and the Analysis of the Ego* we find the warning given, precisely because Freud realized that it is far too easy to apply psychoanalytic theory to all human behavior, concluding that it is all neurotic. Actually, his argument was with all those who refused to accept the repressed unconscious, those who defined man and everything he did in terms of a rational consciousness. The very nature of mass culture however, even more so than the industrialized culture, dictates the illusion that everything functions on a rational and conscious basis, when in fact what we are dealing with here is a very rapid transition from a Freudian industrial culture to a post-Freudian mass culture. And it is the adults who have lived in the Oedipal culture who now encumber the mass culture. This is the context in which many adults seek to maintain a feeling of continuity with their roots in a tribal past. What happens is that the values and myths which once seemed to have a kind of religious authority take on quasi-rational and objective characteristics. For example, if a tribalized man once fought or worked for his "fatherland" and its leaders, then it follows that he must translate those older values into more rational ones in order to replace the older system of motivation. He cannot live within a mass culture and be expected to serve its ends unless he can rationalize his responses to those demands. In a tribal culture such a response was obvious and binding. In a mass culture, it takes on the illusion of rationality.

Perhaps the most classic example of this in modern times is Germany during the years between the First and Second World Wars. As a country, Germany faced all of the traumatic experiences which war and depression had brought to the industrialized world. The attempt to develop a democratic society during those years failed miserably because Germany, like so many other countries, was making a rapid transition from small village communities to an industrialized society.

Had the First World War not been so devastating, and had the Depression not been so serious, it is possible that Germany might have made the transition rather smoothly.

As events turned out, however, industrialization increasingly elicited feelings of anxiety among the people with which they could not easily cope. Moving from a small-town Bavarian mentality to a national urban and industrial unity threatened many. It seemed that the very source of their values and attitudes was being destroyed. The more problems became rational and contractual, the more they longed for the simple rituals of preindustrial life. Hitler understood this very well, but he also knew that only an industrialized nation could readily solve Germany's problems. What was needed was a system which could take the feelings, myths, and values of the preindustrialized nation and use them to create a common, although fabricated, national purpose. Relying heavily on the ancient religious mythologies of pre-Christian culture, Hitler was able to instill in the masses a feeling of racial identity. With a pseudo science he attempted to prove that the Nordic race was superior to all other peoples. Appealing to astrology, Bavarian fairy tales, folk culture, and even certain lesser Christian teachings, he painted a picture of the superman, a race of industrious, loyal, aggressive, and courageous people. Even the German's love for Wagner went far beyond a devotion to good music. It became an important artistic instrument for creating the illusion that the German people were everything the old folk culture claimed them to be. In other words, Hitler created the illusion that the past was not lost by the development of a mass culture. In fact, he made a mass culture possible by using all the artifacts of a small-town folk culture, blowing them up to fit the scale of the entire nation.

The psychology which enabled Hitler to perform this seemingly impossible task was outlined in Freud's book only a few years before it was tested by the Third Reich. Not that Goebbels or any of Hitler's ministers had read Freud, but knowing something of the fears and deep-seated values of the German folk culture, they learned to manipulate an entire nation. They captured the powerful sense of devotion to paternalism, authority, order, and productivity. In Freud's terms, they used the Oedipal dynamics of the family which had for centuries been the major pattern for all social, political, and religious institutions. And they made them work for the purposes of creating a national culture.

Of course, there were certain other characteristics of German culture which had to be destroyed. Mostly, they were the literary, poetic, religious and political views which had made the German intellect so popular with the rest of the world. The youthful idealists who espoused the naturalism of Rousseau and the concepts of Fichte, Schelling, and Hegel, as well as the urban Germans who had long since lost their conscious ties to the Bavarian mentality of the peasant, all had to be put out of the way. Only those who identified with the Oedipal structure of the small-village folk culture were prime candidates for the superrace. The reason for this was obvious.

Hitler not only needed a common mythology, universal in the German folk culture, he also required a psychology which would facilitate the mobilization of the entire nation. Ironically, it was this very group psychology which Freud analyzed and made available to the world. Unfortunately, for most Germans it remained unconscious and therefore highly useful to the aims of Nazism. The values and attitudes which had been so deeply buried in the family and village traditions had all the psychological dynamics which could reinforce a national unity.

Rabbi Richard Rubenstein, author of *After Auschwitz*, saw this phenomenon quite clearly when he said, "The shock of defeat in World War I led Germany to attempt to reorganize society along the lines of a homogeneous Volk-culture. Insofar as super-culture was regarded by the Germans as the product of European liberalism and the French Revolution, there were important German advocates of a return to Volk-culture throughout the nineteenth century. The shock of national defeat added immensely to their significance."

Not surprisingly, the major elements of that Volk-culture

fitted perfectly with Hitler's anti-Semitic prejudice. In many ways the convergence of these two factors provided the mythic fuel for the righteous flames of hell which burned so deeply in many a good Christian's heart. The blond Siegfrieds and the heroic Fausts of ancient fame were to finally have their triumph over the forces of darkness. The Götterdämmerung of Wagner was to be "lived out" in all the glory which the Teutonic gods demanded. The Satanic Christ-murderers, the Jews, were to pay for their crime against God. And the righteous and faithful Germans were to bring in the Kingdom of God, under the proper reign of God's obedient children.

To many German intellectuals and scholars, this seemed like a psychotic dream. They could hardly believe, as they watched the parades and rallies, how blind the people seemed and how willing they were to act out this nightmare. Of course, the readiness of so many to participate, in the early years, was enormously fortified by all the classic Oedipal values of nationalism, pride, and devotion to authority. When Hitler began to establish his youth corps, it naturally seemed to serve all the traditional purposes of making men and women out of otherwise aimless children. In other words, it was civilization at its best. The state had abolished the Depression, production was increasing, children were given leadership, and the nation had a purpose.

In the beginning, not too many perceived the dawn of fascism or the consequences of another world war. Even the growing militarism seemed to be only another German way of solving its manpower problems. To many non-Germans, Germans always did seem to act like toy soldiers. But the real reason disaster was not anticipated by many in the rest of the world was that nothing seemed out of the ordinary. True, many non-Germans had their own suspicions of German belligerence and apparent love of war. But the orderliness of the people, their devotion to hard work, and their traditional spirit of compulsive behavior made them appear civilized, certainly not a threat to world order.

Freud recognized the power and danger of the unconscious,

and attempted to describe the dynamics which might be expected in all such traditional communities and groups. Having been reared in the European culture, he understood quite well the universal role which the father, and father-figure, played in the family and group dynamics of civilized man. He learned how important the system of authority was which was applied to almost every social, political, religious, educational, military, and industrial institution. This in turn led him to discover that there were certain forces at work within all such groups which serve the honored purposes of unity and cooperation. Reinforced by the beliefs and values of the past, which teach that the individual must submit to the superior authority of the group, these classic institutions served to provide Freud with living case studies.

In his book on group psychology and the individual ego, Freud outlined principles which seemed to govern the behavior of individuals as they participate in the life of groups. Three of the principles which he elaborated described what happens to the individual in such a context. First of all, there is a process, originating within the Oedipal conflict in the home, which dictates that the individual ego must be "split" in half, resulting in the creation of a "superego," or group consciousness. No longer is the individual a singular person with a unitary ego. In the place of his individuality, we find a developing group awareness. And at the pinnacle of the group's authority is the parent-figure, who becomes what Freud called the "ego-ideal." Consequently, the individual has a vital part of his own identity formed by the role which this ego-ideal plays in his life.

The second factor which characterizes the place of the individual within the dynamics of group psychology has to do with the level of emotional involvement of the individual member. Left to his own devices, the individual may feel his emotional energies to be either high or low. Wherever the power of the group is played down, either due to a dissipation of group function or a delay in the mobilization of group demands, the individual may experience a lessening of his group commitments. His emotional participation is then diminished.

But when the power of the group is imposed upon the individual, coupled with the demands made by the ego-ideal, or leader of the group, then the emotional level of the individual is greatly heightened. This assures his membership within the group and elicits a feeling commitment which extends far beyond his own love of self. His identity has thus been determined by the group, since his ego, or a part of it, has been captured by the ego-ideal with whom the individual emotionally identifies.

The third factor readily responds to the power of the other two forces. Not only does the ego-ideal capture the emotional loyalties and ego-identification of the individual, together with the power of the group's authority over the personal ego, they also control the individual's intellectual or rational capacity. As the dynamics of the group dictate, the level of rational criticism by the individual member may be more or less intense, in an inverse ratio to his emotional level. In other words, the greater the influence the group has on the individual, the more his intellectual capacity declines. Of course, this third principle does not mean that the individual experiences any feelings of antiintellectualism or irrationality. He simply surrenders his own autonomous critical judgment to the power of the group and its leadership. And reinforced by his mental identification with the group, his own rationality becomes circumscribed by the "wisdom" and authority of the group, usually defined by the leader.

The inherent logic of this group dynamic has been apparent throughout the history of civilization. Practically all the orthodox values and moral principles which have governed human behavior for centuries have defined the fundamental ground rules for sanity, integrity, and responsibility. For the individual to claim that his own ideas, values, feelings, or desires are superior to such group forces has traditionally been to espouse anarchy. To support the group, however, has been to serve the highest ends of civilized order.

This is not to say that Western man has had no appreciation for the deviant or the heretic. On the contrary, most of the creative and innovative ideas of the past have come from those who relied on their own perception, emotion, and intellectual abilities. The artists, philosophers, scientists, and thinkers have traditionally been the men who used their own intuitive and critical abilities to comprehend reality, while the soldiers, believers, citizens, laborers, and youth have been the ones most vulnerable to the morality of group behavior. Without the contributions of these individualists, it is unlikely that tribalized man would have developed beyond the primitive patterns of the ancient past. But without the continuity of group behavior, dictated by such forces as we have described above, it is inconceivable that the ideas of creative men would have even been tested. Paradoxically, the two have always relied upon one another for meaning and purpose.

Thus, the more the Nazis captured power and dictated the destiny of the nation, the more the German proclivity for submission to authority served their purposes. This is why it was not too difficult for many Germans to rationalize their feelings for autonomy, freedom, and individuality. Anyone who demanded such things was easily suspected of anarchist or communist sympathies. Only those who realized that unity, production, order, and strength were the true goals of society could rest assured that they were faithful Germans.

Perhaps the most obvious example of this classic group psychology was to be found at the Nuremberg rallies. With thousands of troops standing row on row shouting "Heil Hitler," feeling an emotional identity with the pure Teutonic race, surrendering their wills to the Führer, and having lost all serious traces of intellectual integrity, they represented a single force with which the world would have to deal. Paradoxically, at the end of the Second World War, during the Nuremberg trials one could still see the same psychology at work. As each Nazi was questioned about his role in the regime, almost to a man they insisted that they were innocent since it had been the Führer who was truly responsible. "I was only doing my job," became the standard reply. There was very little feeling of personal culpability among these men, because none of them had ever been taught that the one who follows commands takes any responsibility for his individual actions. Such concepts were liberal and sounded too much like the ideas which the romantics espoused. It was an idealism which had no relationship to the hard facts of life.

Such an attitude, however, is not a violation of civilized (read "repressed") standards for conduct. If the German nation was anything, it was civilized. The problem which Nazism brought to world consciousness was the inevitable consequence of thousands of years of tribalized group behavior. As long as one small tribe or state was fighting against another, such values and group dynamics could easily be rationalized as necessary to the survival of the group. But when one nation takes it upon itself to impose its own group values on the entire world, then civilized behavior suddenly becomes barbaric and dangerous. Traditional values and attitudes like loyalty, group pride, patriotism, and nationalism, when used by superpowers, become something far different than when used to instill within the young feelings of group identity. Being a Boy Scout is one thing, but being an SS storm trooper, or a modern technically trained instrument of world destruction, is entirely another. The psychology which worked so well on a much smaller scale suddenly becomes inappropriate in the world as it is today. As Hegel pointed out, quantitative differences, if they become great enough, produce qualitative changes.

Unfortunately, not many civilized men have done much to question these dynamics which have been so characteristic of groups and communities in the past. These dynamics have been taken for granted, because most of the major institutions of Western civilization have supported and even encouraged them. But Freud understood this, too. That is why he turned to the Church and the military as his prime examples for group study. Realizing, as he did, that both of these institutions are typical group structures which possess an internalized Oedipal dynamic, he sought to uncover the forces which made them so powerful over the centuries.

In the Church, the role played by the individual within the

believing community has always been greatly determined by the system of authority which was built into the institution. The very nature of worship was such as to instill in the believer a feeling of total dependency upon the "holy mother Church." With the power of God invested in the authority of the Church, in its Word, sacraments, and organization, the individual found himself engulfed within the group context from which it was most difficult to extricate oneself.

In the first place, the individual was expected to surrender his will to the ego-ideal of the "father God," Pope, priest, or pastor. Second, he had to have an emotional involvement with the believing community. He had to be a "good Catholic" or a "good Baptist" or just simply "saved." And third, it was essential that he not question too much, especially those doctrines or teachings which were grounded in "faith." In other words, his own critical faculties had to be qualified by the believing community, under the guidance of its theologians, priests, and authorities. And yet, even before Freud made his famous studies of group behavior, there were literary and intellectual critics of this very phenomenon. Men like Dostoevski understood it very well. That is why *The Brothers Karamazov*, especially the tale about the "Grand Inquisitor," has long been seen as an attack upon all institutional bureaucracies.

As the story goes, Christ returns to earth during the height of the Inquisition in Seville. But the leader of the Inquisition recognizes Him and has Him placed in prison. Late at night the old prelate comes to visit Him and seeks to teach Him about the mistakes He made when He was on earth the first time. According to the old man, Christ's greatest mistake occurred during the forty days in the wilderness. Having been confronted by Satan, He had an opportunity which He overlooked in His loyalty to God. Instead of turning the stones into bread, He insisted that man must live by the "bread of heaven." But the Church, as the old man knew, had learned the secret of feeding the hungry masses, thus teaching them who their true benefactor was. The second trial was equally important. Had He only permitted Himself to be saved by God's angels after having leaped from the pinnacle of the temple, He might have convinced thousands of His true mysterious powers. But He insisted once again that man should not "tempt God." The final test showed even more profoundly how Christ misunderstood the weakness of man. Had He responded more shrewdly, He might have claimed the political and military powers of the earth. But having invoked the First Commandment, He revealed how little He understood the poor peasant's need for authority and power in the hands of his masters.

After having lectured for several hours, in which Christ said nothing at all, the old man became enraged. But then, Christ moved toward him and kissed him. In frustration, the old man said, "Leave, and never return again." To him the spiritual struggle had been inherited by the Church, and Christ had no right to interfere with the wisdom of the Church, since it was the Church which now had the responsibility that God had given to those who would save man.

Like Freud, Dostoevski knew that the system of authority which the Church had evolved over the centuries reflected a profound pessimism about the nature of man. To follow Christ in faith, never seeking the security of miracle, mystery, or power, was a truly rare thing for man to achieve. Perhaps the saints were capable of it, but certainly not the simple peasant. He needed a structure which could give him the protection of a loving parent. But even more important, for one to teach others that such a thing was possible (Luther's notion of "salvation by Grace through faith") was to foment revolution. It was to give men a hope which would never replace the security which the Church could guarantee. It was to demand too much of the individual.

It is little wonder, then, that neither Freud nor Dostoevski has ever been popular in countries where the Oedipal structure of traditional group psychology has remained intact. It would hardly suit such cultures to recognize the forces which they unconsciously rely upon to keep "law and order." To shed the light of analysis and criticism on such people is to take the risk of rebellion. In that, the old prelate was quite correct. He has the weight of history on his side. But then such men intuitively realized what Prometheus meant when he said of Zeus, "So strong a wrestler [liberated man] Zeus is now equipping against himself, a monster hard to fight." Their only hope has always been that the peasants, slaves, children, and believers would someday thank them for their security. Unfortunately, there is little security for the father symbol as long as he must exercise his power and authority. This is because he never knows whether or not he has provided the conditions for revolution or social stability.

Of course, that is why the military, Freud's second example, remains the perfect model of an institution forever standing on the brink of mutiny. To place large numbers of men together in the ranks of military service, to force them into conditions where they must turn their aggression against the enemy, to risk their own deaths, and to obey orders without question is to create a most delicate human instrument. That is why the slightest sign of autonomy or disrespect traditionally is met with the harshest of measures. Every high command lives under the fear that revolution lies just beneath the surface of the enlisted man's automatic obedience. And every commander deeply believes that he must forever remain vigilant to the possible revenge he instills within the hearts of his own men. That is why the rewards are so precious, the memories of combat so delicious, the thoughts of victory so filled with the emotions of joy. For it to be otherwise is to face the potential condition of continuous revolt, to have an army of aristocrats, and to possess the conditions of perpetual disorder. Such is the mind of the military man, who has ultimately surrendered his will to the leader, emotionally lost himself in the ranks of obedience, and intellectually submerged himself in the wisdom of his superiors.

To argue that such a mentality as this has been limited to the very few, or that only the most militant possess these values and attitudes, is to overlook the effects of thousands of years of history. Freud's description of group life and Dostoevski's view of the institutionalized Church are far too accurate for anyone to insist that such traits have been rare or uncommon. They represent everything which is characterized as civilized behavior. They are the norms which have traditionally defined the relationship between the individual and the group, whether it be the Church, the state, the company, the school, or the team. To claim that one group may be more benign or permissive than another is certainly true. But to insist that any group has even existed which has not demanded of its members the submission of will, emotion, and intellect is to hypothesize an illusion.

That does not mean, however, that other models for group life are impossible or are unlikely ever to come into existence. The fact of the matter is that we seem to be in a period of transition, when an innovation in group psychology has become more than a mere possibility. Ironically, it appears to be happening to many of the very institutions which have been the most obvious examples of traditional group behavior: the government, universities, and business corporations. It is increasingly hard to locate the traditional sources of power and influence which used to serve the group dynamics that Freud made so explicit. We now find these forces veiled under the complex structures of bureaucracy, making the old ego-ideals or leaders invisible, placing increasing demands on the individual to intellectualize his role within the institution, and leaving his emotional ties to be defined by himself.

So artificial is the relationship between the individual and the major groups within which he lives that most of the psychological factors which motivate and prescribe his participation are increasingly left to the individual to determine. And this is precisely where the greatest difference can be found between the attitudes and values of the two generations reared over the past fifty years. The older individuals have experienced the classic group dynamics as a major part of their own psychic development. The affluent younger generation, however, has not had such an experience. The man whose life has been determined by ethnic or small-town morality understands the demands of classic group behavior. The youngster who has been reared within the culture of affluence, technology, and standardization has an entirely different orientation.

It is the effects of mass culture which have forced us to make these shifts in our patterns of behavior. But that does not mean that everyone has been able to make the transition. For a large number of adults, the old psychology which dictated what their responses must be continues to determine how they feel and react to the present institutional demands. For example, many businessmen in large corporations see themselves as servants to a corporate authority when, in fact, they share in the corporate power which ultimately determines the goals and results of institutional action. Perceiving themselves to have a certain amount of authority under certain roles and conditions, they expect those who report to them to respond appropriately. But when they are confronted with a higher authority, they themselves respond as typical group members. Consequently, they fall back on the older group psychology whenever the situation demands the "proper" response. In a great many situations, however, this means that the group psychology comes into play when the actual structure of group life no longer demands it. This results in the individual having to fabricate an Oedipal structure in his own mind. He has to create a leader to surrender his will to, psychologically establish a mental group image with which to identify, and then submit his own critical faculties to this illusory group. If all goes well, he may have spent an entire day having played several roles in his own mind, when in fact little in the external world demanded any such attitudes on his part. He played out a ritual, even though no one may have shared with him this personal drama.

It is hard to criticize people for outmoded psychological reactions to an artificial world when it is so easy to understand why they have them. One simply does not replace a traditional tribal structure with an enormous mass culture, filled with gigantic institutions, and expect the individuals to respond with a purely conscious and rational reaction. Even more important, one hardly expects such a transformation in conduct to take place so rapidly when even the culture itself continues to use the propaganda of tribalistic or group psychology. This is what Hitler understood all too well. It is far easier to appeal to the security of past morality than to demand that everyone adopt a newer, more rational attitude toward society. People respond to that which seems most familiar, even if it doesn't accurately reflect the visible facts.

Certainly, the dilemma of the Vietnam War reveals how common this phenomenon can be. Having experienced the Second World War as a major tribalization influence, unifying the nation into a singular military and industrial unit, there are millions of Americans who have been prepared to assume that world communism now forces them to continue the same old feelings for the country that characterized the days of the early forties. Submission to the federal government, emotional commitments to the military and industrial forces which demanded loyalty, and an uncritical spirit of devotion have served us well in war. But when used to serve explicit military and industrial pressures, under the increasingly transparent influence of pseudopolitical and economic requirements, the old system of group psychology becomes far more tenuous. Only those who have been conditioned in their youth by the traditional Oedipal psychology, who have permitted themselves to be co-opted by the group dynamics of the Church, state, military, university, and industry, can readily adopt the rationalizations which are used to further such practices. But for a growing number of young people, who have lived through the developments which have made us into a mass culture, such traditional demands appear all too weak and artificial. That is why it is difficult to elicit their loyalties when the methods are the same as those which have been used on their parents and grandparents. They are much too autonomous and individualistic. They challenge the group psychology of their adult leaders because they cannot understand why such outmoded thinking continues to be utilized in rationalizing the true intentions of those in power.

By contrast, in Germany during the thirties, most young men and women were grateful to the Führer for his leadership, which provided them with an opportunity for participation in the affairs of the Third Reich. But then, there was very little which could help these youngsters to understand the merits of individuality and personal autonomy. Similarly for a great many young people in this country during the Great Depression, the governmental programs of Roosevelt seemed sent from heaven. They could get jobs, help the family, and receive a degree of respect for their youthful energies and hard work. To demand anything more would have seemed the height of arrogance and selfishness.

Psychologically speaking, the regimentation of the youth corps in Nazi Germany, and the labor projects of the post-Depression years in this country tended to serve similar purposes. They both gave the individual a feeling of gratitude to the government, gave him a chance to benefit "constructively" from the opportunities of hard work, and provided him with a new relationship to his government. Ironically, both this democracy and fascistic Germany found similar ways to mobilize their respective nations. No longer would the regionalisms or small-town boundaries dictate the lives of the young. They had inherited an entire nation, and war coupled with industry provided them with a set of national values. The once-powerful family and community ties which had nurtured them in the past had become the basis for a larger community which demanded its own loyalties and commitments.

To assume, however, that this classic group psychology, which has worked so well for centuries, still applies to the group needs of a mass culture is a dangerous mistake. The only place it could possibly apply would be under conditions similar to the thirties and forties. But those conditions no longer exist for many Americans. Only those who recall such times as having been significant events in their lives confuse past reality with the present. For the rest, who have learned how to cope with mass culture, such a regression into the past is totally confusing. The circumstances, life-styles, values, and attitudes of the two periods are so dramatically different that they cannot easily be compared.

Of course, the principal reason why the demands of mass culture seem different from those of the past is its artificial nature. This, in turn, is because the very technology which is required to create such a culture relies heavily upon a process of standardization, resulting in the need for individuals to intellectualize, regularize, and rationalize their relationship to the institutions of mass culture. No longer are the traditional associations and contacts with the various groups of society on a direct personal basis. They become contractual, impersonal, and abstract.

Ironically, this leaves the individual a degree of autonomy as he is liberated from the restrictions of an earlier cultural system. Likewise, the various groups and institutions of the society must seek to "define" the individual as a part of the mass. Two distinct forces then come into play which make the older group psychology totally irrelevant. First of all, the individual has no meaningful relationship to the leaders of society, and second, he tends to experience the requirements and demands of those institutions as impersonal impositions upon his life. The result is that the older group dynamics may continue to be believed and applied by the older generation when the society no longer requires such an attitude. At the same time, the younger generation has little or no experience upon which to base an appreciation of such matters. Having lived in a time when the television set, the telephone, the jet, and the computer make the world much smaller, the old tribal loyalties increasingly seem out of place to them.

Paradoxically, the values which are required for life in a mass culture take on certain characteristics which when observed from the perspective of the past appear to many adults to be immoral, decadent, and chaotic, for example, permissiveness, pornography, narcissism. This is becoming clearest to those who have the responsibility for urban planning, ecological research, and environmental studies. As many of these men have discovered, the old pyramid model of authority, which traditionally has been taken from the Oedipal, religious, and military dynamics of the past, simply cannot apply any longer to the needs of this planet. New models of authority and a new definition of responsibility are required. Unfortunately, we in the Western world have no such model in our own past to fall back upon. We will have to take our cue from others, and that isn't going to be easy considering the peculiar forces which have influenced Western civilized man.

Perhaps the most dramatic set of values which reflects the changing life-styles of men and women within our urban mass culture is that which now characterizes the recent rash of demonstrations and protests around the issues of self-determination and local control. In the pluralistic society of just ten years ago, most individuals felt that their ethnic, political, religious, and social groups provided them with all the group authority and protection they needed. Regionalism served the needs of those who belonged to these various communities. Increasingly, however, more and more individuals have begun to sense that their own interests have not been served adequately by these traditional associations. In the place of these older groups we find large numbers of citizens turning to the more functional groups which serve the interests of individuals directly. For example, unions begin to protest against government, particularly local governments, representing the class and economic concerns of their members. Local control of education dominates the black and minority ghettos. Students find themselves, as students, in a separate class with special needs and demands. Consequently, there is a polarization of the individual and the society, which results in the individual seeking direct ways and means of self-expression. Feeling the mass culture to be leaderless, he discovers that his own individuality must become a resource. Those whose values and attitudes are more deeply rooted in the group psychology of the past feel such a condition to be terrifying and painful. They feel alienated, alone, and anonymous. Others, however, take the occasion as an opportunity to express themselves, their demands, and their special interests. Suddenly, the society appears to be populated by a mass of individuals all seeking to have their own concerns and demands met by the government, industry, the universities, and the unions.

Unanticipated or not, this is the inevitable result of a process of economic and social determinism so typical of the American governmental, industrial, and educational system in recent decades. You do not create a mass culture within a single generation's lifetime and expect the values and attitudes of the past to remain intact. The forces of centralism and standardization inevitably lead individuals to seek out their own life-styles and boundary lines. Such things simply cannot be dictated and prescribed by the establishment. It happened in Hitler's Germany because fascism made no room for the individual. But in this country the remnants of romantic and liberal beliefs about the individual, coupled with the economic and technological forces which impinge on the masses, have created conditions which even a Hitler could not manage.

The most obvious signs of this strange polarity between the individual and the society are found among the young people, especially the college-age and affluent ones. In contrast to their lower-middle-class counterparts, the autonomy and individuality of these young men and women appears unique in American history. This is especially true of their values, life-styles, and conduct, and it is most apparent in their group life. They simply do not seem to possess any of the classic attitudes toward leadership, responsibility, or organization. Phrases like "do your own thing" and "I don't like anyone telling me what to do" characterize their most precious values.

If one were to attend a meeting of student radicals, for example, one could not help but be struck by the obvious lack of leadership so necessary for most traditional political groups. Instead of the elected chairman dictating the policies and goals of the organization, one finds individuals taking the floor to articulate their own ideas and setting forth their own analyses of the appropriate issues. Whenever something like a consensus is arrived at, it usually is as the result of one who articulated others' points best, thus feeding the intuitive and subjective understanding of the majority. Those who seek to dominate the group with their own particular brands of ideology usually find themselves quickly rejected.

This was most obvious on one occasion at Columbia University in 1969, when the Students for a Democratic Society (SDS) held a meeting to discuss what should be done about the teachers' strike in the New York City schools. Not surprisingly, the vast majority of members identified with the concerns of the blacks in the ghetto who demanded local control of the school system. There were, however, a few old-line Marxists and progressive labor types who insisted that the political left has always supported the unions, or working class. To the majority who saw the issue of racism as the dominant problem, such a conventional leftist viewpoint seemed repressive and out of place. The working class in America, many thought, had become a conservative and even reactionary group of lower-middle-class supporters of the racists and the military establishment. To support unionism was tantamount to aiding and abetting the old group values of submission of authority, unquestioning loyalty, and blind obedience. Predictably, the leftist and conservative Marxists were expelled from the meeting. And now they find themselves having had to organize their own peculiar brand of radicalism, only one small part of SDS.

In conjunction with this, and at this particular stage in the life of the radical student movement, a most unfortunate thing has begun to happen which completely distorts the real character of the movement. Unhappily, it has to do with the reaction of the adult community to the disruptive aspects of recent events across the country. Most visibly, it is due to the manner by which the press and certain governmental and university officials have responded to the students. Assuming that the classic group dynamics of the past are still at work among those student activists and radicals, these representatives of the public media and other establishments have sought to single out the leaders and hopefully curtail the increasingly violent and forceful actions which seem to become an everyday occurrence. Strangely enough, the reaction to this particular tactic is that more and more students sympathize with the individual student who has been isolated, and in many cases prosecuted. Ironically, he is often prosecuted under a law which seeks to place the blame for massive action on the leaders. But as most college radicals and activists know, the so-called leader represents no one but himself. If he can be called a leader in any sense, it is usually due to the fact that he has served the group in a special capacity. But in no way can he be said to exercise any power over the group, apart from a certain degree of charisma. This is why the press usually misleads the public when they seek to pick out a symbolic representative of the radicals, question his views, and elicit some kind of common set of issues, ideas, and values which he supposedly shares with his group. There simply is no way to get a single representative of the whole. It is possible to find those who articulate some of the concerns which trouble a large number of young people. But it is impossible to find one who can speak for everyone, or even for any single political group such as SDS. And the reason for this is quite simple. They are not interested in developing a single political group which will replace the existing political groups in the country. If anything, they work in the opposite direction. They are trying to free as many people as they can from the political, economic, educational, and social controls which presently dominate the country. That's why the claim of anarchy is far more accurate than the notion of communist or socialist conspiracy. There is no existing model, past or present, for their various brands of social order. And anyone who thinks that such is the case totally misunderstands and continues to reinforce the hand of those who would like to use the Marxist models as their political reference.

   Much to the surprise of a great many adults, however, SDS plays a very small role in the lives of the vast majority of concerned college students. That does not mean that adults can hope to abolish these organizations without finding enormous numbers of students angrily rising to their support. That is where such groups gain their greatest influence, namely, under repression. Left to their own devices, most students find the ideology and tactics of the far left extreme. But what they share with them is a profound feeling that the society is sick, that the real problems which have to be solved are being avoided. And the manner by which such problems must inevitably be approached is by the dismantling of the military, economic, and social pressure groups which exist only to live off the plight of the middle and lower classes of society. In that sense, a very large number of young people are potential radicals. And it takes only a little blind repression to force many of them to become radical activists.

The adults who hope that these youngsters will someday adopt the values and attitudes of their parents and other adults, as they raise their own children, pay off mortgages, save their money, and do all the other things adults seem to feel are inevitable aspects of mature existence, had better do some more thinking about what characterizes adulthood. Frankly, there is no reason whatsoever to assume that the young radicals, hippies, and activists are ever going to arrive at the values and life-styles of their own parents. They may well have similar jobs one day and even live in communities not too dissimilar from the ones they grew up in. But one thing is certain, they will not see their jobs or their homes as places which ultimately dictate the boundaries of their lives.

But even more important, it is probably true that a great many institutions which will hire these young men and women will eventually choose to accommodate themselves to the youth, rather than seek to force them into some kind of company image. There is already a good deal of evidence that some companies have actually begun to make substantial innovations in the manner by which the younger employees are hired and managed. But then, American business often tends to be one of the more flexible sets of institutions in the country, especially when it comes to adjusting to public and social pressure. Their traditional conservative economic image has always veiled a profound proclivity to keeping up with the times. The average businessman is no ideologist. And sometimes that makes him the most obvious candidate for innovation.

That does not mean that such a pragmatic attitude is without serious problems. The so-called profit motive cannot excuse everything that American industry has done to this country on the other side of the ledger. Managed obsolescense, parasitic military production, industrial pollution, and technological innovation placed in the hands of the government cannot easily go unnoticed by the younger generation. All the arguments about pluralism, national responsibility, patriotism, and the now-sacred gross national product are not as potent as they might have been for the last generation. Whether businessmen like it or not, a new set of national priorities is going to dictate new markets, new problems, and different management strategies. But those companies which continue to elicit from their newer employees the old group psychology of submission to the company goals, loyalty to the boss, and emotional ties to the corporate power structure are going to have a most painful awakening.

Strangely enough, however, some of the innovations which have already begun to take place within certain industries pose both problems and solutions to this very issue about group behavior among the young. Most visibly, these new areas revolve around the "systems approach" to problem solving. In some respects this is exactly what the young are demanding. But in other ways it is one of the major causes of their deepest discontent. This is because the systems approach is one of the most potent and effective instruments of innovation and action that business and governmental institutions have ever been able to devise. It breaks away from the old-fashioned methods of hierarchy and pyramid management and uses the functional principle of "participatory democracy," which, ironically, is the watchword of the SDS. In the NASA space program, where this newer method has been most successfully applied, the task force approach to problem solving has produced fantastic results. With all the institutions working together on "task-oriented" teams, they are able to reach important decisions which no longer suffer from a top-heavy bureaucracy. Enormous responsibility is passed to lower levels of management, where the actual work is done. This results in a massive participation by countless numbers of scientists, researchers, planners, technicians, and all the other members of this systems operation. The result is that we have been able to place a man on the surface of the moon in less than a decade of persistent effort.

On the problem side of this newer innovation in decision making we find a most frightening prospect. No one really knows how to define the problem of responsibility in such an operation. When one of the Apollo space capsules burned, killing three astronauts, the officials of NASA had no easy answers as to who was ultimately responsible. A Senate hearing committee constantly sought to place the blame on someone, but the NASA officials persisted in their now famous response: "No one was actually to blame. It was the fault of the overall system." Unlike the Nazi officers during the Nuremberg trials, the NASA representatives could not place the blame on some Führer or absolute leader. The real responsibility lay with all those who worked together on the project, coupled with a few possible cases in which certain industrial representatives probably sought to cut corners by selling less than quality goods. Obviously, some older Senators and Congressmen assumed that since the military played a role in the space program, it would be rather simple to find the weak link in the chain of authority. But that only revealed how little such men understand the group dynamics of systems engineering. Even more dramatically, unfortunately, it shows something of the degree of discontinuity between the values and attitudes of many older and influential Americans and the actual methods which are increasingly being used to facilitate the ends of our enormous governmental and quasi-governmental agencies, not to mention the aims of big business.

To a very large number of students who are presently preparing themselves for a technological profession, such developments as these are extremely troublesome. On the one hand, most of them know that they will be given an enormous amount of responsibility as members of a task-oriented systems operation. Such an opportunity cannot but be pleasing and challenging. But on the other hand, they find that they cannot escape the question: "To what ends will I be working?" Will the overall result of our labors be for some constructive social good? Or must everything beneficial be defined in terms of "spin-off"? Must the primary work serve the interests of major governmental and industrial programs? Or can they be subjected to the overriding demands of a better life for everyone?

At the present time, most students do not witness any serious attempts to redirect the goals and priorities of this nation. That is why the most negative criticism by the radical left seems to possess more than a minimum of truth. Most young people can easily excuse the language, ideology, and even some of the tactics of the radicals when they are stacked up against the society's apparent unwillingness to solve its most pressing problems. Being the individualists that most of them are, they already have a deep-seated distrust of institutional self-interest. And it doesn't take very much to polarize them completely against such forces. This is because they are not, as one businessman worded it, "hungry enough to go along with the way things are." In other words (as we shall explain in a later chapter), the man whose narcissism has been checked by the reality of scarcity, repression, and power becomes the perfect candidate for institutional service. But the one whose narcissism has been gratified by the conditions of affluence, technology, and loving parents has no such motivation.

This brings to mind some of the concepts of psychologist Abraham H. Maslow concerning the levels of need which characterize each individual's emotional and value-laden attitudes. For the man, or the people, confronted with the most basic conditions of human *survival*, their values and attitudes inevitably must reflect their existential situation. What they believe must be in union with their needs. On the next level, the people who are primarily concerned with *security*, or a continuation of their survival, must have values that will mirror this reality as well. One more step up the scale, we find the group phenomenon coming into play, since the tribe, ethnic group, or company not only provides a degree of survival and security but also gives the individual something to which he can belong. Thus, *belonging* tends to result in the establishment of group norms, reinforced by the group dynamics of the classic pyramid structure. Following this up the developmental scale, we come to those within the *esteem* class, the leaders who are able to become motivated by more personal values. We finally arrive at the ultimate condition of those who are more driven by their needs for *self-actualization* and self-fulfillment. Thus, the evolutionary chart of growth reaches its highest point.

In the past, within any given developed civilization these various levels of personal and individual growth could be located on a similar scale. The poor and the most disenfranchised were obviously concerned with survival, with life and death. To the workers and slaves who had a degree of security based upon their roles within the system, there was a deep need to think in terms of protection and submission to the ruling class. As various civilizations began to evolve "folk cultures" and group values, the individual poor man or the worker had a higher level of motivation. His life depended upon the ability of his group to guarantee what he, as an individual, could not attain. On the other end of the group spectrum, however, the leaders of such groups often could afford to be guided by values which reflected their roles. Esteem and respect were essential factors which such men required not only for themselves but from the members of their groups who needed such leaders to govern their destinies. Finally, among the ruling class one found a few who were privileged enough to become concerned with their own spiritual, emotional, and intellectual faculties. Self-realization could become their primary goals in life.

Economically, socially, and politically, such a division of wealth and power has always dictated the class structure of any given culture. This meant that the old group dynamics of the past also reflected certain realities about life itself. The pyramid of authority, wealth and control was a rational system.

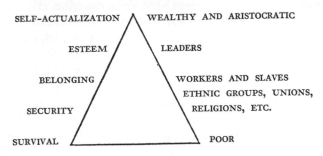

Strangely enough, however, if one were to try to apply this ancient model of society to the contemporary scene within this culture, he could not help but discover that the economic, technological, and social factors no longer parallel the traditional conditions of man. We still have people represented by all the various levels of development. But the majority are no longer on the bottom of the scale. And the number of individuals who traditionally have been at the very top has dramatically increased.

The result of this peculiar kind of economic revolution is that we have created a class system which is rapidly being turned upside-down. At the present juncture, the masses of working-class people are somewhere between the security and belonging levels. This is why they tend to be the conservative majority demanding "law and order." They don't want the boat to rock because they fear that the consequences will drop them back into conditions of deprivation. The very poor, however, along with a large number of those on the very top of the economic scale, find themselves sharing a common set of attitudes regarding the nature of repression, law, social pressures, and middle-class values. This is because the poor have always known that society discriminates against them, especially if it is reinforced by racial boundaries. The affluent young people, on the other hand, have no vested interest in the maintenance of existing power, since they have become motivated by more personal goals. This results in their having a much clearer perspective about the structure of power and authority within the society. Their parents, however, may share that same perspective, but since most of them have achieved their present positions by struggling through the previous conditions of group belonging, they find the values of the middle and lower class to be quite understandable (since that used to be their own situation). And being motivated more by esteem and leadership values, these parents are deeply troubled that their own children should not appreciate the plight of the middle class. Consequently, a value gap develops, polarizing the very poor, the blacks, and the youth on one side against the white majority of the working and management classes.

But how could such a peculiar division in social values and attitudes evolve? Hasn't the ruling aristocratic class always been divorced from the poor and working-class segments of society? Surprisingly, the answer is really very simple. We have become a mass culture, which in turn depletes the power of tribal or group dynamics, forces the individual (poor or wealthy) to stand against the institutions which hold the society's power, and places the authority in the hands of those who manage the society's major institutions. This means that the values of those who manage our government, our businesses, and our universities become the dominant values of the society. They dictate the morality and attitudes of those who control the news media (consciously or unconsciously), they prescribe the kinds of laws which are passed, the types of judicial decisions which are made, and the priorities which govern the major economic, political, scientific, and educational policies and practices which characterize our nation's life.

The leaders of our society, therefore, being motivated by esteem and public reputation, respond to two sets of influence, i.e., their older values, which have been molded by middle-class conditions in the past, and the concerns of the middle-class working people. Paradoxically, those who have also felt the potential liberation of self-actualization are deeply troubled at the blatant reactions or "backlash" of this lower-class conservatism. But they are also threatened by the young who develop life-styles and behavior patterns which do not directly serve the interests of the institutions which govern the society. Consequently, they take the path of least resistance. They regress into the values systems of their own past, identify with the lower middle class, and seek to manage society in terms of the industrial realities which once characterized society at an earlier stage. Consequently, there is a kind of schizophrenia in their lives. Personally, they may be highly influenced by certain self-developed goals. But institutionally, they are driven by esteem-seeking to please those whom they feel will be the most responsive and grateful. One thing they know — their youngsters are not very respectful or grateful, nor are the blacks or the radicals. But the hard-working middle- and lower-middle-class citizen, being the most group-conscious individual of all, can easily support the strong hand of management. Indeed, he demands it.

Thus, the question which confronts society as a whole, and not just its so-called leaders, is how such a society can be managed when so many of our future managers are not willing to lend their support to our institutional establishments. Paradoxically, we have a choice in this country. But it is not going to be an easy one to administer. Either we seek to develop a set of priorities which will result in a greater number of self-developed individuals, freed to make whatever contributions they wish, or we manage the existing priorities along the lines of more efficient repression and control, hoping that the middle class will be able to dictate a substantial balance between the forces of revolt and the pressures toward fascism.

If we select the first possibility, the chances are very good that we shall solve a great many of our most serious social problems, assuming that the middle class can be convinced that its security is not in danger. But if we choose the latter option, we cannot escape the day when countless homes will be hopelessly divided. Police not only will be invading campuses, they will be searching out those who violate "national emergency laws," and there will be no place to hide. Guerrilla war will be rampant, and the society will be completely vulnerable to a truly violent revolution. Both directions have their risks. Unfortunately, we seem already to have opted for the second solution.

5

PURITAN SECULARISM: THE AMERICAN VALUE SYSTEM

The essential causes of conflict between the generations today is the dramatic difference between the social, economic, and psychological forces which have influenced the two generations during two distinct periods of history. The Great Depression is contrasted by unparalleled economic affluence. The "righteous wars" of 1914 and 1939 had the effect of mobilizing the nation and influencing the values and attitudes of countless youths, who are today's adults, while the Vietnam War has alienated the youth of today, resulting in a profoundly deep suspicion and distrust among the young of their own government and its allies in higher education and industry. Even the traditional mythological and religious beliefs which have been unique to Western civilization have finally been polarized into the conservative values of established morality and the radical or utopian values of the young. Prometheus stands against Orpheus and Narcissus. Moses is contrasted with Christ, while modern Puritanism is confronted with naturalism, romanticism, and paganism. And to top it all off, the classic dynamic known to psychologists as the Oedipal conflict no longer serves to function as the group psychology, known to all men who have experienced that familiar role of institutional or group membership. We have become a mass culture without leadership; the word "system" best describes our interlocking institutions, and no one knows any longer where to place the responsibility for corporate and organizational action. In other words, a basic change has begun to take place which could not have been predicted only a few years ago. And it has come upon us with such speed that most Americans feel a profound sense of disorientation and confusion. Thus arises the tendency to criticize the young for all that seems to be happening, as though they were not themselves as much victims of these forces as anyone else.

Through the vision of hindsight, however, it is becoming increasingly clear why many of these problems have finally risen to the surface. In summary, one could say that the religious basis of our civilization has finally run its course, and we are now confronted with the form instead of its substance. This, too, is partly what the so-called "Death of God" theologians were trying to tell us. It is what those who have espoused a new kind of "religionless Christianity" have warned us of. And it is what presently threatens every major established denomination in the Western world, especially in this country. Indeed, one might even call it "Puritan secularism," or Calvinism gone to seed — a kind of religious frame of reference which no longer has anything to do with the meaning behind everyday life, but which continues to dictate an irrelevant morality, a prescribed belief, and a ritualized form, totally indistinguishable from middle-class existence.

Curiously, it has been Western religion, particularly Protestantism, that has provided the philosophical thrust that fostered the development of science and technology. Most scientists don't understand this and seem convinced that their roles and disciplines are what Daniel Bell has called "value-free." This is because they are scientific disciplines, committed to a supposed rationality, empiricism, and logic. The rational man is not supposed to become involved in questions of value and belief, or what has been called "the infinite regress of value questions." But all this seeming objectivity among the technical types is totally misleading, because there is a value system in the world of science and technology which comes directly from the most fundamental beliefs and assumptions of Western civilization. Unfortunately, twentieth-century man has tended to overlook most of these basic values, usually taking them for granted, and thus has allowed the scientists and technicians to conclude that they are free from the complicated questions of economics, religion, politics, and sociology.

Many scientists and technicians react to such arguments with indignation. They are convinced that science is, by its very nature, void of complicated value conflicts. Were it otherwise, many of them argue, it would not be true science. To men like these, each discipline is an entity of its own, with its own language, instruments of measurement, and scales of exactitude. For a scientist to condition his own use of science by questions of social, political, and philosophical significance, he would have to surrender his long-standing commitment to objectivity. But what these men continue to overlook is that even their so-called commitment to objectivity is a fundamental value assumption. By its very nature, it presupposes an entire system of related values about the nature of reality, which forces the scientist, whether he likes it or not, into the arena of value questions.

To place these hidden value assumptions in a historical perspective, it is best to realize that they have their roots deep in the traditions of Western religion. To the average scientist, this may come as a shock, since history reminds him only of the fundamental conflicts that science has had with religion. He recalls the confrontations of Copernicus and Galileo with the Catholic Church. He remembers, not too long ago, the "monkey trial" against the teaching of the theory of evolution in public schools in the South. And perhaps even more recently, he recalls the great debate over the problem of conscience in the making of the atom bomb. And he knows all too well that men like Oppenheimer are considered rebels and idealists, while men like Teller remain faithful to the discipline of scientific empiricism. But no matter what qualities he may feel characterize the truest scientist, he cannot escape from his own value assumption — that science dictates its own demands for truth. And where did science acquire that assumption? Wasn't it Archimedes, Aristotle, Bacon, or Einstein who taught that science was governed by its own laws of truth? But had it not been for the overriding value-assumptions of their civilizations, it is hard to see how these men would have been free to act upon their belief. For the fact remains that science and technology have flourished only in those cultures where the basic value system of the people tolerated them. And one cannot avoid the fact that Western civilization has provided such an environment.

In fact, three basic beliefs, characteristic of the Jewish and Christian traditions, have been essential to modern science. Although there have also been many parallel concepts over the long haul of history, these three notions have continued to remain orthodox assumptions to Western thought, especially American Protestantism. In biblical terms, they are (1) God is not a part of creation; (2) all reality must be understood in terms of history; and (3) one must understand the present in terms of the "last days," or what the prophets called "the Kingdom of God." As such, these three beliefs provide the essential basis for all biblical religion. But even more important, they have become, over the centuries, the roots of Western man's understanding of reality. Of course, they have not remained in their pure biblical form, especially in modern times. A great deal of what certain theologians called "demythologizing" has occurred, leaving, in most cases, the kernel of truth without the religious or theological form.

Interpreting these three concepts, however, we find how distinctively American they seem to be. For example, if God is not a part of the created order — He created the world but is not part of it — it follows that the fundamental nature of all creation is "secular." If we were to contrast this with many other values or beliefs — say, from the animistic religions of Africa, Latin America, and Asia — we would discover that most other peoples of the world believe that the universe is filled with sacred and divine power. This means, therefore, that certain places are immutable and untransgressable to man. In biblical religion, however, God may intervene on occasion into the world of creation, but He can never be understood to be natural to it or be seen as a part of it. He may reside on the "holy mountain," the burning bush, or even in the person of Jesus Christ. But He cannot become "created." This means, therefore, that the universe which God has created cannot possess places or space which "contain," in their natural state, the Being of God. Only that which God Himself chooses to invade may possess the Divine presence.

In recent years, however, the demythologized version of this very same belief served the scientist and technician quite well. For it means that he has a universe available to him which is free from the animistic and sacred prohibitions of religion. He is therefore free to measure, label, manipulate, and alter that universe, limited only by the boundaries of his skill and resources. In this sense, the modern scientist (and all those who willingly support his work) is a secularist of the highest rank. Indeed, he is quite free to "think the unthinkable," to plan the total destruction of the earth, to contemplate various means of controlling the human organism's brain, nervous system, and bodily functions, or to create the very future itself, if the need and priority demands it. As one psychologist who works for the government has put it, "Modern science refuses to accept value limitations in the quest for more knowledge." Indeed it does.

But if the first assumption provides us with a secular universe, the second does something equally important. It turns time into history, and linear history at that. In other words, whereas most other religions of this planet follow a naturalistic view of time, understanding it to be nothing more than the cycle of seasons, the biblical view persisted in the belief that time is that period on earth, known as man's "lot," between the poles of creation and the final day of judgment and reconciliation. Obviously, it was the Hebrews who gave us this concept. In fact, the word *Hebrew* itself means "wanderer." And

coupled with the prophetic writings and the eschatological periods of later Jewish Scripture, we discover that the Hebrews
never completely lost sight of the ultimate goal of the coming
"day of the Lord." Thus, they could never be completely at
home with their Canaanite neighbors, who readily worshipped
the earth gods and the ever-recurring seasons of time. Consequently, as Christianity came onto the scene, with its enormous
emphasis on the imminent end of the world and the establishment of the Kingdom of God, this linear view of time and
history received a major endorsement. For almost two thousand years Christianity has pursued this view, looking upon
itself as the people of God who must lead the world in the
interim period between the event of Christ and the day of judgment. And whenever the Church has tended to lose sight of
this task, reformers and critics have risen to put the Church
back on the path.

As a result of this particular assumption, Western man has
inherited a view of reality which perfectly suits the needs of
science and technology. It turns the past into the facts and the
future into the unknown. It makes for a world wherein the
principle of change is paramount, building upon the past or
rejecting it, as the case may be, for the purpose of extending
the present into the future. In those areas of the world, however, where certain customs and traditions reflect the closed
cycle of nature, where time almost literally "stands still," science and technology are replaced with ritual, because there is
no such thing as change. There is only that which is, that
which is mystery, and that which is not.

Coupled with this notion of Western man, however, is the
firm belief that man himself is not truly a part of this universe.
Unlike the primitive peoples of the world, Western man prides
himself in his mastery of nature. And since he has a concept of
linear time to aid him in his quest to expand his authority and
power over nature, he becomes the world's chief manipulator,
never content until he has tampered with everything, measured
everything, and ultimately mastered everything. Indeed, so important is this belief to Western man that he even measures

time itself, turning it into a quantity that can be measured economically (time is money), thus quantifying his very life into various stages and segments. Consequently, his view of linear time has become absolutely essential to almost everything that matters to him, for example, education, work, science. He is completely conditioned by linear time, in spite of the fact that it is an invention of his own civilization. Unfortunately, most Westerners never learn how to escape linear time. For without it Western civilization would die and ultimately return to the laws of nature by which time is on an organic and biological scale.

And yet, if secularism and linear history have proved to be so essential to Western man, it must not be overlooked that the third belief we have referred to plays an even more important role in his thinking. Concern with the future, or "last days" as the theologians word it, has made Western civilization, and especially the United States, the most eschatological-minded culture on earth. In the Bible, if time meant linear history, then the end or fulfillment of that history must possess great meaning and power. It was the dominant teaching of the so-called prophetic years and meant everything to the faithful Jews who were waiting for the promised day, when God would establish His people forever. But if it was so meaningful to the Jews, it became even more important to the early Christians. In fact, Jesus's entire ministry and preaching were eschatological, pointing to the imminent dawn of the Kingdom of God. And as biblical theologians have known for quite some time now, it was Jesus's eschatology which fundamentally characterized His entire ministry.

Unfortunately, the established Church (as we have shown in Chapter 2) has never completely understood this phenomenon and thus has tended to turn the radical sayings and teachings of Jesus into rules and laws for behavior, as though Jesus the eschatologist was only a minor subject of interest. Even the early Church had trouble with Jesus's eschatology and therefore sought to play down the futuristic elements, by emphasizing the so-called timeless meaning of His wisdom. And when the Church had finally become established as the dominant religion of Western civilization, only a few sects and heretical groups continued to preach the radical views of Jesus about the immediate dawn of God's Kingdom. This fact alone explains why it was not until the late nineteenth century that biblical scholars rediscovered the true nature of Jesus's ministry and teachings. It was too difficult to "get at" the historical Jesus through the pages of the New Testament. Nevertheless, it remains true that the various sects, especially the Anabaptists and certain Calvinist groups, remained true to the eschatological emphasis. In their simple reading of Holy Scripture, they couldn't escape the large number of sayings and teachings which referred to the imminent day of judgment. Consequently, their lives were tremendously affected by this attitude toward the immediate future.

Interestingly enough, however, it was such sects and groups as these which first came to this country. And the influence which the Puritan and Calvinistic denominations have had upon this country is incalculable. It suited our frontier mentality perfectly, and continued even into the nineteenth century as the one distinctive religious belief of the majority of Protestants. Over the last hundred years, however, it has become clear to a number of social critics that the experimental or tenuous nature of social order in this country has been largely due to the national preoccupation with the future. Being a people without a true tradition, or even a common past, the future has always served as the major source of spiritual motivation. It is the very essence of the Horatio Alger myth. And it reinforces all the values about success, achievement, and personal gain, so common in American life.

And yet, perhaps even more important is the significance of this futurism for the world of science and technology. For with the implicit blessing of secularism and linear history, this futurism opens an unlimited view of innovation for science. But the nature of our religious beliefs being what it is, science has finally become the means whereby we shall achieve that eschatological future. And the way this thought seems to work its way into the beliefs of so many Americans is through that strange kind of syncretistic thinking which characterizes the average citizen. First of all, he assumes that the inherited values of Christianity are all but synonymous with our national goals, especially in the areas of industry, science, and education. Second, he calls upon his God to bless those goals, as they increasingly take us into some realization of their end. And finally, he makes a slight leap of faith, from belief in the providential power of God to belief in the innovative power of science and technology, concluding that they are one and the same force. Thus, science has about as perfect a social climate as could be desired. It has an open-ended future, the potential blessing of the people's Deity, and an almost complete endorsement from the financial and economic forces which righteously have the most to gain from the pursuit of those unlimited goals. The most obvious example is the flights of Apollo to the moon — the American people prayed to their Christian God, an astronaut read from the Bible and one took Holy Communion, while the space industry made a fortune from the federal treasury.

Underneath this most interesting type of futurism, however, lies an even more significant innovation. In its purest form, those who work in the Pentagon and its allied "think tanks" call it "game theory." But far from being an unpracticed theory, it has become something characteristic of the scientist's world-view as he confronts problems which must be tested "in the field" before hard conclusions can be made. Indeed, it is a vital link in the so-called scientific method otherwise known as testing, development, and deployment. For example, one invents an instrument, a drug, or a weapon which then must be put to the test. If however, it happens to be a theory strategy or concept about certain matters which involve large-scale military, political, or international problems, then one must stage a test of such a problem to see what the potential results will be. Without a doubt, this type of thinking played a strong role in the early stages of the Vietnam War, not to mention the other minor interventions in the Dominican Republic, the Bay of

Pigs, and Guatemala. As one argument goes, we had to develop a strategy whereby the military could test its ability in a limited war, thus avoiding the "horns of the dilemma" of all-out nuclear war or capitulation in the face of wars of national liberation. Indeed, so respected is this type of thinking that the Russians claimed, after they invaded Czechoslovakia, that they were only reacting to a plan, developed by Herman Kahn, to turn the Czechs into a buffer zone compatible with the interests of the West. Propaganda or not, it was clear that the Russians appreciated the new role that this game theory plays in our military-industrial view of the world around us.

Intricately linked to this game theory, however, is the systems approach to problem solving we have mentioned earlier. And insofar as the systems approach has moved beyond the older methods of decision making, characterized by pyramid or hierarchical methods, it is increasingly difficult (and in most cases impossible) to find out who is responsible for the end results of such a method when put to the test. Consequently, if one cannot easily put his finger on some authority or person who seems to be the major link in this process, then he must turn to the implicit values which seem to govern the systems actions. And that is where the three values we have been analyzing profoundly come into play. With a secular universe, the games theorist is completely free to tamper with any subject, measure it in any way necessary, and even test it under certain "cost-effectiveness standards," thus playing the role of God. Also, with a linear view of time and history at his disposal, he is completely free to contemplate any innovation, event, or direction that meets his purposes. And with an eschatological or futurist frame of reference, he is free to "create the future," unhampered by tradition, custom, or human values.

Of course, any number of academics, scientists, and technicians would insist that I have overstated the argument, that there are still fundamental human values which guide the choices and directions of science and technology in this country. But the fundamental values and assumptions we have outlined here are themselves characteristic of our way of life.

They are not rationalizations after the fact. It is the persistent application of such value assumptions as these which has finally created a condition in society in which contrary values appear as primitive, pagan, and unsophisticated. For example, to believe, as many young people do, in a universe filled with sacred and divine powers seems to many adults foreign and fundamentally contrary to our cultural beliefs. Or to insist that time is really a natural cycle, conditioned by forces we do not yet understand, is to challenge the very basis of social order and the values of "progress." And most certainly, to become more interested in the present than in the future is to undercut the very basis of the nation's optimism and hope. And yet, these are some of the most important value conflicts which have recently risen to the surface.

Perhaps the best way fully to appreciate this growing conflict in values, however, is not simply to point out how secularism, "value-free" science, and technology have turned our lives into categories, statistics, and quantities, but to understand that we have no existing options within our own historical value heritage. We are not secularists simply because we have outgrown or matured beyond believing in spirits and supernatural powers. Nor is it true that the peculiar religious and cultic beliefs of young hippies and radicals are antiintellectual. Quite to the contrary, the secularism of the academic and intellectual establishment, and the youthful reaction to it, are the logical consequences of our historical values once they have been permitted to run their course. In this sense, the impact of science, technology, mass culture, institutionalization, and all the rest of our modern elements of existence continues to result from a very few persistent beliefs handed down over the centuries. In this manner, the secularism, linear history, and futurism which have endorsed fantastic strides in science and technology have their roots in Western religion. And in this country, that means a kind of "Puritan secularism."

We must call it Puritan, because the life-styles of most adults are directly in line with that tradition. And we must also call it secular, because that is precisely what Puritan Protestantism emphasized the most, when it affirmed a universe freed from pagan spirits, committed to a linear history of God's predestined will, and continuously searching for that future day when God's judgment would finally triumph. Admittedly, it was a theological and cultural secularism if compared with the established religions of Europe, especially Roman Catholicism. But far more significant, it provided the nation with a moral basis from which to develop. And although any of our Puritan forebears would be shocked at the technology, customs, and practices which presently characterize our society, it would be only the "externals" which would trouble him. For the "internal" morality which went hand and glove with Puritanism hasn't changed that much over the years. Frugality is still a virtue. Modesty, orderliness, and respect for authority still remain an ideal for most adults. Unfortunately or not, Puritanism seems to have run its course. The best example of this fact is the behavior and values of countless young people who are beginning to inject a paganism into our culture, never before seen except perhaps among the American Indians. For instead of the morality suited to our Puritan-secularist culture, we are finding large numbers of young people rejecting the fundamental Puritan values, emphasizing the values of naturalism and romanticism, and totally condemning the secularism and value-free methods of science and technology.

One value which has lasted over the years, for most adults, is the virtue of making money. Apart from being at the heart of our so-called free enterprise system, it is a belief which is about as old as the industrial revolution, which made it possible for large numbers of simple peasants and citizens to earn a "living." The power of currency has made it possible for people to live their lives in an increasingly noncommunal mode of existence. Whereas the community of the past was a total structure of people, living in direct and interwoven relationships, for the purposes of survival and security, the role of currency has tended to isolate the individual family from the community, and has replaced it with abstract relationships of a contractual and rational nature. By and large, however, the role of wealth in this country has become something far more complicated than the mere earning and possession of money. Indeed, it can almost be said that the more affluent families and individuals have become the most isolated from the community, while the poorest remain bound to their communities, extended families, and localities. Beyond the simple economics of this rather obvious phenomenon lies the effect which this has upon those who have been freed from the previously necessary bounds of community.

Certainly, with the innovations of the automobile, radio, telephone, jet travel, and finally the television set, this isolation from the communal existence of previous decades has meant that adults can have both worlds at the same time. Communication makes the community of the past a continued possibility, but now one of choice rather than of biological, vocational, and geographic necessity. Significantly, however, the basis of this freedom rests on the level of affluence possessed by the individual families. Thus, countless numbers of middle- and upper-middle-class families across the country have become small islands, isolated in one sense and yet tied to one another by a ubiquitous interlocking technology. Ironically, however, because this newfound autonomy has become such a desirable possession for most American middle-class adults, the means for achieving and maintaining it has become a value in its own right. Thus, the role of money has taken on a new dimension far beyond the needs of survival and security once provided by smaller interdependent communities. As a value, consequently, it has become one of the chief secularizing forces in American life. For insofar as it has been the means by which countless adults have freed themselves from the family ties and social limitations of their childhoods, it has become the instrument whereby they are free to dictate much of their own life-styles, goals, and modes of existence.

Characteristic of each of these small islands of autonomy and independence, however, is a fabricated value system inherited from the Puritan past. It is a fabrication in most cases, because our modern contractual and technological existence uses such a value system in order to maintain a particular set of norms and customs suited to the organizational structures of our mass culture. And it is Puritan only in form, since the true substance of Puritanism was in the social structure of common believers who adhered to their particular values and beliefs as a self-defining community. This quasi Puritanism of many modern urban and suburban families, however, is not an authentic life-form or value system. It is only the best one suited to reinforce the type of values our mass culture finds manageable and suitable. It does not essentially conflict with our existing goals and national priorities. It fits in perfectly with the institutional needs of industry and government. And it provides a relatively common set of norms by which to make laws, judgments, and opinions about social behavior.

Consequently, for most adults who have been striving over the past two decades to achieve the economic freedom to establish their private little islands of autonomy, the acceptance of this pseudo Puritanism is only a minor limitation on their lives. Indeed, a great many adults personally challenge and even violate some of the assumed Puritan values, but insofar as they represent a national standard, or a social norm, they are not only tolerated, they are implicitly supported and defended. This is especially true of the more external values of cleanliness, orderliness, frugality, work, and submission to authority. The internal Puritan ethic, however, which calls for belief in the absolute power and authority of God, the predestined life, and the total commitment of one's life to God's will has been secularized. It has been replaced with belief in the right to obtain more money — thereby gaining freedom to govern one's own private life and destiny — provided that one does so by submitting to those forces which are in one's own self-interest: the new God, our national institutions. Thus the adults' plea to their children to change or reform whatever they wish to, provided that these activities are accomplished "within the system."

As a result, middle-class families are models of the artificial national standards. Most adults easily tolerate, and even accept, violations of the moral norm, as long as they are kept personal and out of sight. This is especially true of the more urbanized and sophisticated families. But when violations challenge the national myth or conventional system by which the society is governed and managed, then they take on the aspect of real danger. This is because society has constructed a conventional morality in which no one is really expected to believe, but which it is assumed that everyone will pretend to respect and follow. Indeed, nothing could be more secularist than this peculiar duality about moral and ethical behavior. It is not the conventional duality of ideals against actual behavior; it is the distinction between stated and real values.

But far more important is the significance of this common conventionality for the management of the nation as a people and as a group of institutions. It makes language, dress, style, custom, and behavior fit into a predictable norm. Thus, individuals are supposed to move into the society, predetermined to conform. As a result, the individual adult can identify with almost any other adult who lives by a similar standard of living. The astronauts are "all-American" men. The soldiers in Vietnam are "our boys." And business leaders and government officials are interchangeable figures of respectability, predictably committed to similar goals. Thus, to challenge the business, government, or related institutions is tantamount to challenging every adult who would do the same thing under the same conditions.

In the United States the family model is a totally hypothetical phenomenon — a kind of self-propagandized mythology linking the family with an image of the supposed national standard. In those cultures where the religious and ethical values of the family are recapitulated by the society's laws and customs, it can readily be understood why the family-society relationship is so interwoven. In this country, however, the relationship is strongly conditioned by the so-called national customs, primarily due to the organizational and structural pressures the society places upon the home. The family does not dictate what the standards will be; it simply responds to whatever pressures dictate conformity. In fact, this is the major reason why traditional ethnic and religious behavior characteristics have long since been lost to the universalizing Puritan value system. Eastern European families, Latin, Asian, and other traditional ethnic subcultures, once having adopted this country, have all been strongly influenced by this "American" standard. And wherever these subcultures also have had within their traditions particular values and customs which parallel our Puritan tradition, they have tended to emphasize that aspect of their culture in order to fit in more readily. Consequently, the true success, if we can call it that, of the "melting pot" view of America is almost completely based upon the ability of any other culture to take on the artificial moral and social standards which have been inherited from our Puritan past. Because it is so pragmatic and artificial a value system, it doesn't essentially conflict with other traditional values and customs that can be maintained within these families; that is, until the next generation adopts the hypothetical standard as a means of liberating itself from the older family and religious ties. One may cease to be a Jew or a Catholic or even a Southern Baptist, as the case may be, but he becomes a Puritan secularist as he adopts a conventional mode of behavior. But what he as a person becomes in his own eyes, is an aspect of his own personal self-understanding.

As a result of this phenomenon, a great many young men and women have long been free to adopt or accept almost any standard for behavior and values that suits their taste. Until the last few years, however, that freedom was heavily conditioned by the economic, political, social, and educational limitations of the culture. But in more recent years that freedom has begun to backfire on the home and the society. For with the almost unqualified license that secularity, mechanical morality, institutionalized norms, and linear-futuristic thinking has imposed upon the society, the young have begun to experience their own independence within the context of an artificial public morality. On the other hand, a great many adults are convinced that this distinction between social and personal morality is a fundamental breakthrough for them, for it means that the external morality which is prescribed by the institutional and social pressures around them is finally divorced from the values which really mean something to the individual personally. And one of the most characteristic examples of this distinction can be found in the businessman or professional who comes home in the evening, or on the weekend, and puts on his false beard or sideburns and colorful clothes, perhaps takes a little "pot," adopts the language of his adolescent children, and thus seeks to find those little experiences which can express his own choice of self-understanding. Also, without too much disorientation, he can easily return to the norms of his peers on Monday morning, fitting into the order that he has come to accept as the fundamental structure upon which the society's institutions function. He submits because he has learned to believe that the rewards have provided him with the means whereby he can also possess his own private and personal existence. And as long as he doesn't confuse the two worlds, he can maintain his balance.

Not surprisingly, many of these same adults are convinced that the quasi-Puritan morality which indirectly endorses secularity, progressiveness, and systems-thinking must never be subjected to direct moral questions. That would seem to place the nation back in time to the days when conventional morality placed serious limits upon not only personal behavior but also social, institutional, and scientific innovation. Somehow the air of "value-free" innovation, discovery, and expansion must be protected from the potential controls of value questions which might ultimately threaten the functioning of society's institutional bodies. Indeed, this very argument is often used when the young raise value questions about the society. For in the memory of most adults, direct intervention by those who would raise complicated questions of human values has always resulted in the establishment of a controlling morality, which fundamentally limits the growth and development of any given society. For example, to label the Vietnam War as immoral is to overlook the true factors which got us involved in the first place: experimentation, testing, innovation and rationality. To have placed a moral judgment on the action before the fact would have severely limited the nation's ability to learn from such an experience.

And yet, all such rational arguments as these, no matter how Machiavellian they may seem to some, grow directly out of the traditional Western assumption that the universe is open to man's experimentation. And experimentation is the historical frame of reference of all those who have sought to free the mind from the bonds of traditional moral confusion, thus opening the possibility of a civilization where innovation, invention, and discovery create their own questions, and not the other way around. Nevertheless, one of the chief characteristics of this way of thinking in modern times is that peculiar schizophrenia which turns morality into something personal and thus leaves the problems of social, institutional, and organizational behavior all but devoid of such limitations. But this is where the Puritan-secularist influence is so perfect for institutional purposes. It takes on the appearance of austere self-limitation, reaching out to control the lives of all who live under its rubrics while providing a seemingly traditional moral explanation for growth, development, and innovation. Thus, anyone who would seek to question such actions publicly — private behavior doesn't count and isn't strictly regulated — must inevitably be attacking from his own personal and therefore highly subjective, even antisocial world view.

To a great many young people all this is something of a mystery, because most of them have never really confronted a consistent moralism like that of the late nineteenth century, or its various forms in the early decades of this century. To them morality is not a fierce grandfather imposing his will upon his patriarchal tribe. Morality is a set of values which teaches the wisdom of love, compassion, peace, and honesty. But to most of their parents morality dictates laws about sex, pleasure, violence, freedom, and instinctual gratification. To the young morality is not limitations placed upon the individual by official "blue noses" committed to some prescribed ethic; it is the discovery that love is better than hate, peace is more natural than war, pleasure is the essence of life, and honesty is the rule for all interpersonal relationships. Unfortunately, to most adults all these latter values, though they are of higher significance, cannot possibly become the context for human beings in the world as it is. Reality contradicts all such "idealistic" values when put to the test. For to adults, man seems disposed to violence, aggression, chaotic instinctual gratification and total license. That is why the established rituals of Puritan secularism are far more liberating, since they control man's behavior in those precise areas where he can do the most damage, namely, in society's institutions. Otherwise, in his own private life, he can remain free to affirm the ideals, gratify his wishes, believe in peace and freedom, and conduct his affairs under his own guidance. It is a perfect harmony for a society that would otherwise crumble if the two worlds were to become mixed.

At the same time, however, it is rapidly becoming clear to a great many people, both young and old, that the ultimate consequences of an applied Puritan secularism to a society's large institutional structures would be an anarchy that would have made Adam Smith's head spin. For whereas it appeared only a few years ago as an endorsement of growth and development, it is fast becoming a kind of nihilism which all but condones total destruction of the earth in the name of growth and innovation. And to retreat behind the common belief that there are some "experts" somewhere in government, industry, and the universities who are ultimately motivated by basic human values, and who are really in control of this gigantic process, is the worst kind of neurotic fantasy. The fact of the matter is that we really do not know how society would function if we were to presuppose that love, honesty, pleasure, and peace are the true characteristics of man. It has never been tested on a large enough scale. But we do know now that the opposite assumptions about man, when programmed into the society's laws, priorities, and practices, become much more than a self-fulfilling prophecy. They fundamentally cause such behavior to follow.

Let us take three minor examples to emphasize the point: the problems of pornography, violence, and submission to authority. In the case of pornography, it is most significant that those who react with shock and guilt are usually the very ones who have the deepest voyeuristic and/or exhibitionistic tendencies. In fact, it is one of the cardinal principles among pushers of "hard-core" pornography that sex and eroticism must be linked with appeals to guilt and shame if they are to continue to capture the attention of those who frequent their shops. Similarly, if one seeks to unravel the rationality behind those who seek to curtail pornography, inevitably they believe that children and other "vulnerable" individuals will become conditioned to erotic pleasures and gratification, and thus will not "learn" how to put sex in its socially beneficial place. They will suffer the fate of psychopaths, continually feeling bombarded by instinctual desires for gratification, thus destroying their truer values of love, work, patience, law, and order.

And yet, everything we know about human psychology tells us that ignorance and repression of sexual and erotic matters inevitably lead to one of two reactions. Either an obsessive-compulsive reaction takes over, forever directing one's unconscious libidinal energies into "acceptable" directions, else they come out in pure form; or a kind of addiction to that which is forbidden takes over, driving the individual to seek greater levels of stimulation, rising from one level of guilt-oriented pleasure to another, always stimulated by the guilt-associative wishes or actions. On the other hand, whenever sex and the erotic are handled as natural phenomena, unrelated to guilt and shame, the individual tends to organize his life in such a way as to have periodic enjoyment of sex, and thus uses his libidinal energies to eroticize the world around him, developing a wide variety of meanings and feelings for the artifacts that make up his universe.

In any society where sexuality is repressed, and thus human energies are directed toward what psychiatrists call "secondary gains," the mechanism of guilt or shame becomes a neurotic device creating the underlying value definitions for the culture. But in those other cultures where sexuality and eroticism are condoned and ritualized by the culture, guilt and shame regarding sexuality are almost unknown. Instead, the entire society is grounded in the erotic interplay of man and nature. Sex becomes less "functional" and more a part of all human, emotional, and physical contact with the world, and there is no such thing as sexual pornography. But if one considers war, pain, suffering, and related matters as pornography, it would have to be accepted that whatever stimulates the repressed unconscious is pornographic. For if one were to take these latter factors as true elements of pornography, it would have to be said that we are a totally pornographic society.

Related to this, obviously, is the significance of violence and aggression. As many anthropologists and psychologists have told us, man is a creature of aggression. Or to put it in more accurate terms, he possesses enormous reserves of psychic energy which are greatly affected by such things as survival, security, meaning, identity, and esteem. If any of these elements are threatened, his psychic energies turn into fear, anxiety, or hostility. Of course, it is a very complicated phenomenon because it is not always clear if a threat is real or apparent. Sometimes it is fantasized or imagined. But the reactions can be just as real. Consequently, this psychic energy can result in almost any behavior, given certain conditioning factors, both conscious and unconscious.

In Western civilization a very high priority has traditionally been placed upon the assumption that man's basic drives are predisposed at birth to be evil and destructive. As a result, most moral notions in the West presuppose that man must be "conditioned" to respond, learn, and behave in ways acceptable to the society. He will not naturally do so because his drives will force him into competition for scarce goods and pleasures, and thus will leave him in some imagined "jungle"-like existence. In other words, the territorial imperative not only determines how fish and animals live, it also determines what man feels and does about his space and property. If threatened, he can and will fight to the death (in spite of the fact that most animals

never kill one another in this regard). But even more important, this same energy which can become rage and violence is
also used by Western man (and others as well) for the purposes of production, work, and sex. It is a redirection, or what
psychiatrists call cathexis of the libidinal energies toward ends
that are prescribed by the logic of the social order. Thus, the
worker learns to invest in his job, machine, or task a part of
that energy. But if he takes that same psychic energy and subjects it to his own choices, pleasures, and expressions, then he
potentially threatens the social order which is established upon
the principle of dictating the ends toward which that energy
must be directed. Consequently, there is a perennial fear within
Western civilization that man's natural instinctual life will rise
to the surface and cause a fundamental disruption of order,
production, and social stability.

Western man, however, has never known a civilization
predicated on the notion that instinctual freedom and self-
expression can become their own order. Somehow it has been
assumed for too many years that repression of the instinctual
life is the only logical way to achieve an ordered culture of
prosperity. And yet, in spite of this age-old assumption, some
of the concepts in modern education and child rearing presuppose exactly the opposite. Indeed, experiments in self-directed
learning, permissive attitudes, learning by association, and
body-oriented contact with the world of objects make a very
strong argument for believing that every child has an inherent
order and logic which predisposes him to master the world
around him far more skillfully and happily than his forebears,
under the effects of traditional education, were ever capable of.
As a matter of fact, the self-directing child is far more capable
of setting limits upon himself when he discovers the merits of
doing so than any other child who "learns" by incorporating
the wishes, ideas, and information of adults.

Significantly, most of the children who have been permitted
to learn in this "modern" fashion are almost always much freer
to learn the futility of aggression and violence. In fact, most of
them seem inevitably to associate it with childish feelings that

must be replaced with rewarding and fulfilling feelings and actions. And in those cases where this is the situation, they find it most difficult to appreciate the formal and socially acceptable uses of aggression in such matters as the military, racial hatred, and male-female sexual hostility. Consequently, they find it difficult to tolerate the pressures which adults normally place upon them to compete, fight, or otherwise act out their unconscious aggression. And because childhood and adolescence has been a period for most adults of competition, aggression, and periodic violence, it seems wrong that such children should avoid or ignore these traditional experiences. As a matter of fact, this is precisely why so many of the bright young people from our more affluent homes today are the least interested in those conventional values of adolescence such as military service, competitive sports, business vocations, college spirit, fraternities, and other so-called youthful pursuits and activities. They all presuppose an aggressive experience, predicated upon the repressed but socially acceptable modes of behavior. Those who have been encouraged to be self-directing, autonomous, and individualistic, as many young people from our "better" homes have been, mature on a biological scale, suited to their own needs, and not on some prescribed social scale which presupposes a certain amount of repressed aggression and violence. As a result, they tend to possess a maturity which most adults, being repressed adolescents themselves, have never really achieved.

Inevitably, this leads us to the third problem of respect for authority. For in any civilization where authority is based upon the power, role, and wealth of the few, those who must live out their lives in submission to that power find respect and surrender to be logical and necessary feelings and attitudes. Not to nurture such feelings would thus lead to the more conscious emotions of hatred, rage, and violence. Consequently, in such a civilized order, it must be assumed that this necessary repression of hostility and rage demands respect for authority, else the society would crumble under an inevitable revolution of those most repressed.

It is no accident, therefore, that the types of young men who normally select the military, the police, competitive business, sports, manual labor, and similar vocations are men with higher levels of repressed hostility, protected by a need to submit to some form of authority, and not surprisingly, they also tend to come from middle- and lower-middle-class homes; while those who choose vocations in which they can remain individualistic and autonomous in their minds and bodies reserve their hostility for the occasions when society attempts to invade their lives. Thus, they resist authority, believing that it is illegitimate unless it has something to do with their own needs to affirm themselves. For example, the good parents, teachers, or bosses who respond supportively to the individual's independence are acceptable authority figures precisely because they accept the individual as being self-determining, creative, and responsible. And rather than seeking to "manage" his unconscious hostility for ends beyond what the individual himself might want, they become good authority seeking to help the individual find those expressions and modes of being that fulfill the individual as a person.

Strangely enough, we have long praised those adults who seek to instill and nurture self-expression in the young. At the same time, however, we have relied upon the assumption that everyone will remain repressed enough for those authority figures within society to be able to mold and manage the energies of the masses for the purposes of social order. The fact of the matter is, however, that we have finally begun to rear an entire generation of young men and women who have experienced enough self-expression and independence for them to recognize forms of repression, manipulation, and control as unnecessary and blatantly authoritarian. Ironically, to many of the adults who find themselves representing forms of authority, especially in those areas which directly touch the lives of young men and women, i.e., university administrators, draft boards, and so forth, the various reactions of these autonomous and self-directing youngsters come as quite a shock. They find it hard to understand why individuality should take on more value for the young than the traditional values of competition, group pride, nationalism, social climbing, and related adolescent emotions. But what truly confounds them is their inability to recognize the evolutionary changes in both individual behavior and institutional order. The chaos which seems to be increasing is far more real in institutional expansionism than it could ever be among young people seeking meaning and fulfillment for their lives. And the more the society's institutions attempt to protect themselves with self-limitation or what is worse, governmental and social controls, the more individuals will be manipulated by the managers of these institutions for the purpose of protecting and supporting these institutions. Thus, all of those young people who have been taught from birth that it was best to become self-determining and independent must inevitably reject authority which seeks to capture their freedom for ends that go beyond their own choices.

Consequently, if one were to ask many youngsters how they felt about pornography, violence, and authority, they would tend to respond that they feel pornography is a problem more for adults than for children, violence is an established value among adults (as long as it serves the appropriate social ends), and authority is a problem for the most repressed and those who claim to possess it. But if one were to ask the same question of many adults, the answers would be: pornography is dangerous because it undermines acceptable forms of sexual behavior, violence exists only for those who are too selfish to learn how to live within the given boundaries of society, and authority is essential for any civilization to maintain continuity and order.

In spite of this, young people are having a much more profound effect upon adults and the entire social structure than is the reverse. And that is what causes so many adults to question what is happening to the society. The behavior and values of the most articulate and independent youngsters are raising questions for the society which adults cannot easily answer. One might even say that the young are leading the way into the future, and it is the adults who are kicking and screaming as they are carried into an uncertain social climate. In spite of the fears, repression, and controls which many adults are capable of expressing, the values and modes of behavior which must inevitably win out will be those set by the most autonomous and independent among the young. Consequently, pornography, violence, and authority will remain only so long as the society is predicated upon repression, guilt, and submission. Ironically, parents and teachers are doing too good a job in seeking to instill independence and autonomy among the young. And as a result, the entire society is laying the groundwork for its own social revolution. The adults couldn't quite do it for themselves. But their children can do it. And the consequences are quite predictable. In fact, we can expect to see the following changes occur within the next few decades:

1. The values of Puritan secularism will rapidly be exchanged for a conscious set of values which predicate human problems, human priorities, and human needs. Thus, more and more, individual modes of self-expression will be accepted and even encouraged as being necessary for maintaining sanity and health within society's institutions. The only alternative to this is a kind of technological and bureaucratic fascism, much of which we presently possess, but which cannot remain unless fathers and mothers are willing to see their children shot in the streets, placed in prison, sent to endless wars, or simply placed within detention camps for indefinite periods of time.

2. The present adolescent practice of sexual experimentation will increasingly become a norm for adults seeking to find themselves. Marriage will thus be governed by a kind of situational monogamy, as complete and fulfilling as the two people are willing to make it, then terminated as the two seek other relationships to give variety and fulfillment to themselves in the rest of their lives. (This, of course, will not mean that many, if not most, will not be able or willing to live out their lives together. It only predicates the condition that choice and the freedom of choice will be far more of a value than is presently the case.)

3. The social values which have long dictated what an individual can and cannot do with his own mind and body will rapidly be re-

placed with the value that only the individual can determine what he wishes to make of himself, feel, experience, or tolerate. This, in turn, will force the society to condone a variety of activities governed by "consenting" individuals. As a result, the age level of consent which will be tolerable for the society will be lowered to the early teens.

4. Emotions which presently come under the category of social acceptability — such as chauvinistic nationalism, male aggression, double sexual standard, competition, self-denial, guilt about sex, and related "civilized" feelings and attitudes — will become antisocial and labeled as pathology.

5. And finally, as a result of these types of innovations, politics, industry, labor, education, and religion will inevitably evolve into a much more individual-oriented system, seeking to express not the commonality of society's norms but the variety of society's beliefs. Industry will be forced to manage its production and marketing, geared to the needs of society, under the direct influence of consumer-protected guidelines. Labor will cease to be a political or social force; instead, it will take on a shared role in management. Education will be of two distinct types: (a) skill training, and (b) self-determined learning within self-limited communities. And religion will rediscover ritual, seeking to provide a more conscious opportunity for individuals to share their own needs for "infantile regression in the service of the ego" — a kind of therapeutic play-acting similar to the Esalen Institute and sensitivity-training programs in use now.

Consequently, as innovations of this magnitude begin to take place, many adults will experience a deeper anxiety about society's directions, but a much greater freedom to determine what those directions are will also be present. Freedom is not without its emotional price. If the anxiety level can be tolerated for the next few years, the outcome will be much brighter than presently appears. If it cannot be tolerated, the result can easily be total disaster. It goes without saying, however, that all these innovations in behavior and values will not take place without some profound conflict, turmoil, and disruption. Conventionality, artificial or not, will not easily give way to such enormous changes. But the very nature of the changes, rooted, as they are, in the demands by more and more individuals to determine their own life-styles, cannot help but eventually win the day. And to understand why this is the case it is essential to understand just how dramatic the behavioral and value revolution really is which the young have fomented.

PART 2
THE GENERATION
OF NARCISSUS:
HARBINGER OF THINGS
TO COME

6

NARCISSISM AS A WAY OF LIFE

One of the things which is beginning to cause a minor revolution within the disciplines of psychiatry, clinical psychology, and psychoanalysis is the problem of adequately defining what is meant by the "reality principle." Back in the days of orthodox Freudian psychoanalysis, reality was not a complicated problem. Adulthood and childhood were clearly distinguishable; power, wealth, authority, and position were obvious; change was slow; and scarcity dominated the lives of most people. And yet, over the past few years it has become clear that a good many therapists and psychoanalysts have so strongly emphasized the need for the patient to "test" reality for himself that such hallowed reality concepts as monogamy, inevitable frustration about infantile gratification, attitudes toward so-called acting-out and even assumptions about various forms of antisocial behavior have all been seriously altered. With an increased emphasis on one's freedom to test the limits of one's ego boundaries, to define one's own self in a world of artificial limits and standards, the result has been that concepts of personal growth and maturity, once assumed, are now subject to profound questions. Only the individual can make tentative claims about his maturity. Fundamentally, it means that the individual must accept the risks involved in life to achieve what he wants out of life. No longer does the old Freudian dictum hold true that one must achieve health at the price of an inevitable frustration about gratifying one's wants and needs.

But if this is true of those disciplines which are supposed to orient us to reality when we cry out for help, then it is quite clear that applied psychology today is far more than a process which provides the individual with a clearly defined reality, reinforced by a supposed real world. If anything, it is becoming an almost revolutionary discipline. It serves the needs of the individual, enabling him to seek ways to make reality into something that he wants, and not the other way around. Wishes for nudity, sexual experimentation, drugs, extramarital affairs, and even homosexuality are no longer considered classic examples of exhibitionism, instinctual chaos, flights of fantasy, acting out, and simple deviancy; they are becoming modes of experience which may have pathological qualities but which only the individual himself can conclude are insufficient to meet his needs. In any case, he must be free to test for himself whether or not life can give to him what he wants. And for the therapist to assume that any of these and other forms of behavior are totally pathological, and to communicate such to the patient, is to violate that increasingly sacred responsibility of letting the patient discover reality for himself.

As a consequence of this innovation in defining and understanding the "reality principle," a growing number of Americans are dealing with problems of conflict, disorientation, and personal growth as though they were totally governed by the individual's choice. Somehow, the norms which once seemed to invade even the psychoanalyst's office, under the guise of clinical judgments about pathology, no longer carry the weight of social judgment, much less the paternal criticism of the therapist. The question is asked: "Is this what you really want?" And instead of the classic assumption being communicated — that this obviously is not what any sane, healthy person would desire for himself — the responsibility for one's behavior (conscious and unconscious) is left to the individual.

Of course, many practicing psychiatrists, psychoanalysts, and therapists have long handled their patients in this manner. But the communication of this method of treatment to the outside world as a general theory applicable to all individuals, leaving them completely responsible for their own behavior (unable to blame environment, parents, or related circumstances), is to inject into the society a clinical truth which cannot help but stand in judgment of society's norms and practices. Thus, a radical kind of individualism is endorsed by the psychological "healing profession" which refuses to permit moral standards, religious teachings, and conventional beliefs to dictate final definitions of "normal" behavior. Of course, most Americans are still unaware that such an attitude is shared by many therapists, counselors, and analysts. They continue to assume that psychological "help" means "getting the individual functioning within society again." To learn, however, that individuals have to "experience" life on their own, that they have to "act out" some things to find themselves, or that only the individual can determine for himself what he wants and needs, is tantamount to an espousal of moral anarchy.

Anarchy or not, what has finally begun to happen is that the old Freudian notion that civilization inevitably breeds neurosis is now being accepted throughout the clinical profession. And beyond that, it is beginning to become the hallmark of all those who have discovered that the process of finding themselves involves as much "unlearning" and correcting of the "remembered" past as learning new and better ways of being. And as a result, one can readily find an increasing number of individuals who consider most social norms and standards to be neurotic and destructive. Consequently, they must test for themselves the things which they believe are necessary for them and reject all that is repressive, conformist, and constricting.

In the last few years, this assumption has finally reached far beyond the private confines of the therapist's office. Across the country, small groups have been formed which seek to confront the individual with his socially ritualized modes of being, feeling, and thinking. Instead of the group's helping the individual to become oriented to the so-called norms of society, emphasis is placed upon the individual's learning to be free from such norms in order for him to discover his lost energy, his personhood, his sexual abilities, and his emotional freedom. In the sense that William C. Schutz of the Esalen Institute uses the term, such groups are seeking to help people rediscover the "joy" which society took from them shortly after infanthood. And as a young coed worded it on a national TV network program dealing with the subject of the generation gap: "Most adults have forgotten what it means to be children."

Even the business world has not been spared some of this same point of view. In fact, one of the most successful experiments in modern business and management training has been the use of T-groups or confrontation groups, enabling a growing number of businessmen to rediscover much of what their society and their professions have denied them, namely, the freedom to be honest and open about their feelings. And for many married adults, the experience of sitting down together in groups, speaking the truth for the first time in their marriage, has revolutionized the concepts of marital love and conjugal fidelity. Even most universities and colleges across the country are establishing small groups of students, some of them including faculty and even a few administrators, which seek to help the individual members learn how to express their feelings, fears, and desires without experiencing the sudden silence of society's rejection.

Parallel to such experiences as these is the rapidly changing world of women and teen-agers. With the now ubiquitous contraceptive devices, husbands are discovering that their wives and daughters are independent human beings, free to express their own sexual and emotional desires, even as men have supposedly been for centuries. One no longer simply leaves the home as father and husband safe in the paternalistic assumption that his women will remain extensions of *his* needs and desires. Many women have begun to discover that they have their own lives, and the burden or the freedom which choice now gives them is beginning to change the traditional ways in which women once regarded themselves. Among teen-agers, this same discovery is even more apparent. It can be found in their dress, language, attitudes toward sex and love, interpersonal relations, and countless other factors which make up the newer forms of adolescent self-expression today.

But quite apart from the potential liberating effects of "the pill," progressive attitudes, and increasing desires for self-expression is the growing belief that one's own life is sacred territory. In almost all traditional societies such an attitude would be considered selfish, scandalous, and antisocial. But inherent in the American tradition is that peculiar notion, which served the frontiersmen quite well, that each individual had to "take care of himself." In more ways than one, it was reflected in the Jeffersonian view of democracy, which incidentally means a great deal to many young radicals today. The concept that an individual is a self-motivating, self-determining person, bound to society only by choice, is at least as old as the Republic itself. But one hundred years of industrialization and institutionalization have made such a value seem precious and highly impractical. Consequently, much of what has passed for liberalism and conservatism in the last few decades has been more in line with the industrial facts of life than with the more romantic but very American concept of radical individuality. The very fact, however, that we are becoming a leisure-oriented society, has made our political ideologies more and more irrelevant in adequately defining the reality within which we live. To argue that man must be a social creature before he is an individual makes sense only in a culture where social identity is absolutely necessary for survival. But to insist that a youngster whose world is composed of a television-oriented education (almost from birth), jet travel, advanced education, sexual and emotional experimentation, and a host of related experiences, is somehow supposed to be oriented to the existing norms, policies, and standards of behavior would be like saying that individuality is antisocial. Unfortunately, that is precisely what many adults are saying, especially about their own teen-agers. These adults tend to resist the idea that individuality is a prerequisite for health in this society. We do not have a tribe or culture which can do for the individual what most other tribalistic cultures can. We are an artificial society, a mass culture which depends totally upon the ability of the individual to find meaning and purpose in his own life. And though Jefferson didn't have this kind of society in mind when he spoke of democracy, his emphasis on individuality couldn't be more relevant today. The only difference is that individuality has become essential to personal health and well-being.

Leading in this growing affirmation of individuality, autonomy, and self-actualization, however, are the behavior and values of a segment of society which is primarily composed of young adults, adolescents, and even children. Not that there aren't any older adults who fall into this same category; there are many. But for most of them, all this has been a long struggle over the years, and their individuality as adults has been bought at the price of realizing that most of their lives have been a surrender to society's pressures and norms. Consequently, self-affirmation for them means something very special when contrasted with that of so many young people. This is why the younger generation can serve as a kind of model for many adults in seeking to test that reality on the "outside" world, where sexual, emotional, personal, and existential experiences await them. In a sense, the adult reaction to the younger generation is both an exciting rediscovery of all that has been repressed and forgotten and a paralyzing fear that such freedom will eventually destroy us all. It is the repressed adolescence within most adults which responds to the true adolescents all around us. The young have opened Pandora's box for us. And many adults see the dark forces of chaos being released upon the world, while some are slowly coming to believe that the guardians of Pandora's box were afraid that we might find life itself. But whether we like it or not, the box is open. And no one will be able to close it again, except at a price that no one in his right mind will be willing to pay.

If we take a long hard look at what has been released upon the world, however, I think we will discover that it is life, not death, which has been set free. But each individual will have to make up his own mind. As for me, I think I can see the outlines of a new mode of being for civilized man. In any case, I do know part of what this mode may entail for years to come. In brief, we have finally begun to reach that point in human evolution at which the reality of the child's world-view is becoming more powerful than the world-view of the traditionally defined "adult." The narcissism of infanthood is beginning to replace the rewards for delayed gratification. The freedom of the individual to remain secure at the center of his own universe, supported by incredible affluence, a new kind of matriarchy, and a very popular acceptance of personal freedom, is now making it possible for human beings to take the idealism of the past far more seriously than ever before.

Is it really possible for the infant's narcissistic world-view to become a realistic, ordered, and meaningful context for man and his communities? We do not know the answer to that question. But we can rest assured that this world-view is beginning to stand in judgment against the reality we have inherited from the past. Our own success in providing a world where countless numbers of individuals can receive immediate and real gratification of their narcissistic drives will not permit us to turn back. It will only mean that we shall have to learn to understand and appreciate infantile narcissism as a conscious and powerful force in setting new rules for human behavior. In fact, it is conceivable that the entire society will one day, in the not too distant future, become structured like a "Brave New World." But because the change will probably come about not as a sudden revolution led by the charismatic few but as a revolution led by individuals setting their own boundary lines, we shall only dimly perceive its occurrence. This time the revolution will not be the changing of the guard or the enthronement of different authorities over us, it will be a reconstruction of society around the needs, wants, and choices of individuals.

Let us now turn to the forces, innovations, and factors which seem to make such a prediction more than a mere fantasy. In other words, let's take a good look at the behavior and

values of the younger generation and see if some of these
changes have not already begun to take place. One of the most
inescapable characteristics of large numbers of young people
today is the degree to which infantile narcissism — or, as the
psychoanalysts call it, "primary narcissism" — dominates their
lives. But before we get into that, we must try to define what
we mean by "primary narcissism."

Sigmund Freud has provided modern man with several concepts which have since become everyday jargon. When we
speak of someone being narcissistic, we usually mean that he is
in love with himself and is unable to establish meaningful relationships with other people. Or we make a distinction between
fantasy and reality, normally concluding that fantasy is unreal
and pleasurable, while reality is inescapable and unpleasurable.
In the same regard, we also speak of reality as that necessary
context in which one is forced by circumstances to delay one's
wish for immediate gratification and thus sublimate the libido
into socially useful forms of action and behavior. In other
words, the narcissism of the infant cannot possibly remain as a
"realistic" way of dealing with external reality. One must repress narcissism and replace it with a different kind of ego-
functioning, namely, love of others, cathexis of that reality
which is outside one's self. Unfortunately, even Freud was not
clear about the meanings of narcissism, ego, delay of gratification, and related concepts. As a result, psychoanalysis has remained in something of a turmoil. Several years ago, Heintz
Hartmann, in his book *Essays on Ego Psychology,* and more
recently, Reuben Fine, in his book *Freud,* both admitted that
there remains a certain amount of confusion over the most
adequate definitions of these terms. In his earlier writings,
Freud seemed to feel that every infant experienced an invasion
by the outside world of reality which forced him either to repress his narcissism or to replace his narcissistic and pleasure-
oriented ego with a "reality-ego." In Freud's later years, however, especially as he gave more thought to the nature of the
individual's mental structure, he seemed to change his mind and
conclude that perhaps the individual infant adopts external

reality as a kind of extension of his narcissistic ego and thus seeks to make reality into a pleasure-gratifying phenomenon. Thus, whenever the individual child experiences external reality as repressive, painful, and hostile, he returns his libido (erotic love) to himself. But when he can gratify his ego with higher levels of satisfaction, his narcissism and external reality tend to merge as extensions of one another. He knows that the world is not himself, because his mastery of language, his body, and his nervous system make that evident to him, but he breaks off his cathexis of that world only when it ceases to gratify his ego. As a result, the healthy child (as well as the healthy adult) participates in turning the world into what he wants it to be. At times, the helpless infant and the neurotic person feel incapable of changing external reality and thus return their cathexis to themselves and seek to live under the rule of what Freud called "secondary narcissism" — in other words, real "selfishness."

Consequently, when therapists understand this latter view of ego development, their approach with patients tends to be that of enabling them to "test themselves" in the real world, eventually to develop enough experiences in making reality work for them, and thus to feel themselves capable of affirming what amounts to their own narcissistic selfhood. Narcissism, in this sense, is interpreted not as selfish withdrawal from reality but rather as affirmation of the self through the ego-oriented drive toward pleasure and fulfillment. Not surprisingly, many adults who learned their Freud in the thirties and forties got a heavy dose of his earlier view: Life is difficult, and narcissism is escape from reality; therefore, health is that inevitably unhappy condition of repressed narcissism rewarded by the end results of hard work, performance, and loving others.

However, the more Freud's own change of mind carried him into what scholars call his "ego-psychology" phase, and the more his disciples and followers sought to keep up with him, the more his later view of narcissism and ego development caused confusion. Unfortunately, not many patients or even interested observers noted the full significance of his change of mind.

This is what Herbert Marcuse sought to convey in his book *Eros and Civilization*. Behind Freud's thought that it may well be possible that narcissism and infantile ego have their own reality-defining capability lay the fantastic assumption that it might even be possible that narcissism never truly becomes repressed, except in those who see external reality as alien or foreign to their own wishes for gratification. Consequently, one is forced to raise the question: "Is it possible that primary narcissism, repressed throughout the centuries, is the true human force which makes meaning out of the external world?" In the words of Marcuse:

> The concept of primary narcissism implies what is made explicit in the opening chapter of *Civilization and Its Discontents* — that narcissism survives not only as a neurotic symptom but also as a constitutive element in the construction of the reality, coexisting with the mature reality ego. Freud describes the "ideational content" of the surviving primary ego-feeling as "limitless extension and oneness with the universe" (oceanic feeling). And, later in the same chapter, he suggests that the oceanic feeling seeks to reinstate "limitless narcissisms." The striking paradox that narcissism, usually understood as egotistic withdrawal from reality, here is connected with oneness with the universe, reveals the new depth of the conception; beyond all immature autoeroticism, narcissism denotes a fundamental relatedness to reality, which may generate a comprehensive existential order. In other words, narcissism may contain the germ of a different reality principle: a libidinal cathexis of the ego (one's own body) may become the source and reservoir for a new libidinal cathexis of the objective world — transforming this world into a new mode of being.

Significantly, it has been men like Marcuse who have had the greatest impact on large numbers of college students in recent years. For example, not only has Marcuse helped to give them an intellectual frame of reference for understanding the world around them, he has also provided a rational context to explain why their own wishes and desires for a different reality are not simply immature struggles against an inevitable foe. In other words, narcissism is not simply childish rebellion against adult reality. It can also be a new force which challenges and even eventually changes the reality by which adults have lived for centuries.

Since Marcuse wrote this book in the early fifties, it is hardly likely that he thought he would ever have such a receptive audience. But we are witnessing an entire generation of young men and women whose lives closely parallel what he asserted as a possibility. In hindsight, Marcuse couldn't have been more of a prophet. Primary narcissism is, in fact, the context out of which many youngsters from affluent backgrounds are now making their values, ideas, and beliefs known. It dominates the entire "hippie" world-view. It fits in perfectly with the manner by which drugs are used and experienced. It relates to the newer attitudes toward sex and eroticism. It characterizes the newer modes of dress, language, dance, and music. And it underlies the political, educational, and social aims of countless young radicals who haven't quite learned how to make narcissism into a theory for government, education, or society.

Of course, it would be foolish to assume that the younger generation today is totally characterized by the Freudian notion of infantile narcissism. For whenever they are capable of thinking, feeling, and acting like the generations which have preceded them, they are no different. But when we examine certain elements in their psychological, spiritual, and social development, it simply cannot be ignored that some fundamental changes have taken place within the last twenty-five years. Significantly, they are the types of changes which relate directly to the vicissitudes of primary narcissism in childhood development. For example, it goes without saying that the phenomenon of economic affluence provides a profoundly different context for early childhood and adolescence than has been the case in previous history. And if we add to this the effects of technology, making the world more available to the individual, in some cases instantaneously, the affirmative effects upon narcissism cannot help but be witnessed.

Let us take the effects of television, for example. Most adults have the tendency to look upon television, as Marshall McLuhan has shown, as an extension of previous forms of information processing and communication. The book defined the movie, and the radio has defined the uses of television. Also, the traditional use of any new technology for economic purposes determines what television programming will be. And most adults accept this fact, or at least tolerate it, because they cannot imagine that television could well be used in entirely different ways. Children, however, see television quite differently. For them, it is a window on the universe, with a "handle" (the channel changer) that gives them a world which they can create with the simple turn of the wrist. To most children, the thought that there is somebody "out there" who determines what programs, commercials, and subjects will be shown, seldom occurs. Thus, they can easily become "wrapped up" in what they are seeing, as though it were a part of their lives. It is, in a profound sense, *their* world which is happening. Not a world under somebody else's management. In other words, they are actually "participating" in the world, not by surrendering their narcissism to someone who dictates the rules for their participation, but by their own choice of what they want to participate in. Unlike the movies, which are, as McLuhan has said, finished products, with identifiable "stars," plots that are complete, and packages which can be produced for total consumption, television is a ubiquitous extension of the narcissistic ego (the body), enlarging the body to encompass a world far beyond the physical limits of the individual organism.

The way this works is most significant. Every child is born a total narcissist. There are two modes of experience for this narcissism — either godlike, giving to the little magician a world available to him at the slightest demand, or totally helpless and powerless, causing frustration and anger. Most children have loving mothers who gratify their omnipresent narcissism by meeting their needs and wants with continual care and love. And where this is the case, most of these children grow up with at least a vestige of self-confidence. What happens to them after the world takes mother away is another problem. If her leaving is handled with concern for the infant's feelings, then most infants can tolerate the separation as long as it is compensated by her return, or at least by someone else to take her place. If, however, the child is left by himself, then the narcissistic world has been broken. That which the infant thought was a part of himself, namely, mother, has suddenly been detached. And if his magical cries don't bring her running, then he must begin to accept a different reality, one where he is powerless and frustrated.

The fluctuation throughout life from feelings of omnipotence (making the world do as one wants it to) to impotence (feeling that one is a victim of the world's reality) has its roots in the vicissitudes of primary narcissism in early childhood. Normally, the healthy individual has received enough affirmative experiences of his primary narcissistic omnipotence for him to believe that life is at least partially subject to his own attempts to make it do what he wants it to; whereas the neurotic individual has never been truly free to experience his own narcissistic ego as an instrument affecting external reality. In fact, he is so completely convinced of the radical distinction between himself and external reality that he feels himself to be "alienated" from reality. As a result, most neurotics have been perfect candidates for the classic group psychology which has dominated human communities for thousands of years. A neurotic, i.e., a repressed narcissist, believes that his identity, security, and even survival, are dependent upon his membership within tribal, social, political, or religious groups. And whatever narcissistic gratification he can receive, he must inevitably receive from these groups. He cannot take the risk of affirming his narcissism on his own. For it has been the group which has defined external reality, as well as the group which has made it possible for him to receive a partial gratification of his narcissistic ego through identification with the leaders and representatives of the group.

In most modern examples of neurosis, the dominant syndrome which occurs again and again is the cyclical emotions of elation and depression, variations on the theme of manic-depressive personalities. This is why so many people today experience "highs" and "lows" as a normal part of everyday existence. It goes hand in glove with our modern posttribal mass culture. The more artificial society becomes, the more the individual is thrown back upon his own narcissistic ego. And the more that narcissistic ego has been experienced as weak and victimized by external reality, the more the depression of failure, defeat, and loss rise to the surface. Such an individual is forever looking for an "ego ideal" or father figure, to support his own weak narcissistic ego. Thus, he becomes a "superpatriot," a "company man," or a good "member of the team." Everything depends upon his receiving, from outside himself, a confirmation of his ego. In other words, he is "hooked" on his need for the esteem of his superiors and peers. His own self-affirmation is totally dependent upon what others think of him.

On the other hand, when such an individual experiences his "highs," they are almost inevitably when he has been praised, rewarded, and supported by those within the group which mean the most to him. On his own, he fluctuates between elation and depression, depending upon others' evaluation of him at the moment. Consequently, if such a person were to seek out a therapist, the long-range goal for his therapy would be to enable him to experience life as a singular narcissistic ego, testing external reality and trying to make it work for him. Of course, this would involve a certain period of time when the patient would want his wishes and fantasies magically to change external reality. But as the therapist continually points out the difference between fantasy and reality, the patient would learn that his actual testing of reality is far more rewarding than his wishing for it to change. As a result, the success of such a therapy would be in the individual's rediscovery of his primary narcissism, reeducated by a more realistic view of himself and external reality, and finally aimed at consciously making the external world into an extension of his own needs and wants.

In his later years, Freud often speculated about the possibil-

ity of the development of a society which would not have to
presuppose inevitable repression but rather would seek to
affirm each individual, thus unleashing upon the world a whole
race of healthy, spontaneous, and creative people. Freud was
rather pessimistic about such an eventuality, but, as Herbert
Marcuse has shown, he did leave the door open to further spec-
ulation about the subject. And that possibility is confronting us
today as never before in history. For whether or not our
society has set out to create the conditions whereby infantile
narcissism is confirmed and supported, the convergence of affluence and technology have all but set the stage for such a condition. But if this is so, what then are some of the characteristics
of our contemporary culture which seem to confirm this
reality?

To begin with, one of the most commonly shared values
among parents in our more affluent suburbs is the wish for
their younger children to become self-directing in their ways of
relating to external reality. The impact of Dr. Spock and the
rapidly increasing popularity of "modern" methods of education are teaching parents that children are born with deep desires to experience reality, examine it, play with it, change it,
and make it work for them. Instead of the traditional attempts
to invade the child's world with some supposed wisdom or
knowledge about reality, many parents are learning that it is
best to let the child discover many things for himself and that
the real task of parents is to help children expand their abilities
to affect the world around them, rather than simply learn how
to fit in, as the case used to be. But when it comes to their
feelings about their teen-agers, parents tend to forget that they
fostered autonomy and self-direction when these "rebels" were
children.

Quite apart from this fundamental change in values and attitudes among parents are the direct effects which television,
travel, education, music, dance, language, abundance of food,
sweets, drink, and other sensations of immediate gratification
have upon the psychic development of the young. Without the
traditional structure whereby rewards are held up at the end of

a demand for performance, work, or repression, such rewards have become immediately available to the growing child. To put it in a radical way, many young people do not have to look upon adulthood as that time in life when they will be able to get what they want. Much of it is available now, even without having to ask for it. Consequently, when youngsters contemplate what adulthood will bring them, they certainly are not interested in "working" for those very things which they have come to take for granted in childhood. Nor are they willing to submit themselves to an external reality which dictates the limits of their freedom and defines their option. Nothing could be more of a violation of what they have come to believe about themselves — namely, that the world exists for them, an option which they can choose, determine, or reject.

In most traditional cultures of scarcity, like those most adults have experienced in their childhoods, the replacement of infantile narcissism with what psychiatrists call the "reality ego" was a predictable and necessary transition. The child was made to accept the "world out there" and to reject the world of his own wishes and fantasies. In a culture of abundance, however, the tendency to do the exact opposite is also predictable and inevitable — that is, unless the parents consciously deprive, invade, and seek to mold the narcissism of the child. But no matter how traditional the parents may be in the process of orienting the child to the external world, the very existence of television as a surrogate parent which is almost perpetually available to the child alters the ability of the parent to be very successful in this task. The direct confirmation of the child's infantile narcissism, unconsciously condoned by the parents who permit the child to watch TV, serves to short-circuit the parents' attempts to "civilize" the child.

Now if we add to this another characteristic of modern urban and suburban life, we find that many parents not only permit their children to watch television, they use it as a kind of baby-sitter. Thus, the child has an experience of learning about reality under the controls of his own will. He can change the channel and — extremely important — walk away from the TV or sit in front of it for hours, play with it and use it in any way that suits his purposes. The degree to which this confirms his narcissistic ego, strengthening it as an instrument for making external reality do what he wants, is very important. Instead of being thrown into a conflict in which his ego is continually under attack from the outside world, he progressively develops a strong ego aimed at affecting the world around him. Consequently, he looks upon traditional demands for social conformity, group psychology, and tribalistic pressure as illegitimate attempts to invade his own universe.

As the child begins to get older, his narcissistic ego takes on a few of the characteristics of a "reality ego," but now it is not an ego easily subject to the inevitable pressures coming from the external world. Instead, it is the narcissistic ego seeking ways by which it can cope with that reality to achieve its desired goals. Ironically, this is precisely what any patient in therapy seeks to achieve in his own personal growth and maturity. But when we see it in a teen-ager or young adult, we call it arrogance and pride. And yet this is precisely what must happen for the healthy narcissistic ego to feel that its goals and aims are honest and legitimate. One must test his narcissistic ego in the real world in order to make the necessary qualifications and changes he needs to achieve his ends.

In other words, television serves to do something for the state of primary narcissism that all the romantics, idealists, and lovers of the "noble savage" have never been able to achieve. A substantial part of the life of the normally narcissistic child is reinforced, totally apart from the immediate controls, repressions, and forces of the "outside world." Thus, as the average child increasingly confronts the world around him, he carries with him a much stronger narcissistic ego and a much different potential for developing a "reality ego." Now, however, his reality ego is not only determined by his having to accept an external reality, it is more closely related to his narcissism, seeking to make reality conform to his needs and wants, than the other way around. But far from turning the average child into a potential chaos demon or instinct ridden egotist, this simply means that he is far more capable of relating to the world in terms of his own defined needs and wants than those who let others dictate to them some socially approved definition of their needs and wants.

Of course, television by itself, without a loving, abundant, and accessible environment, cannot have the total effect we have seemingly attributed to it. The effects of television within a ghetto, for example, may have quite different results on the development of children. If a small child sees one world on his television screen and then is forced to contrast it with his immediate surroundings, this causes a serious conflict with his narcissistic wish for that television world to be more real than the one in which he lives. As such, television for the small child is an immensely important experience. That is part of how ghetto children are seriously cheated in their formative years — they are confronted with a contradictory world. They want the television world to be their world, but external reality forbids it. Most middle- and upper-middle-class children do not experience such a clear-cut dichotomy. External reality seems more in line with their television and narcissistic world than is possible for the ghetto child. The affluent child can have almost anything that is advertised. The people look like him, they do things he can do or anticipates doing someday, and the world which the television presents seems homogeneous and available. In other words, television lets the child "participate" in the world around him long before he has to master the necessary skills that are required for him actually to do so. This means, then, that many children today are led to assume that there is no serious distinction between the world of their own narcissistic egos and the actual outside world. And when parents seek to make the transition from infantile narcissism to socially conscious membership in society an easy and smooth process for their children, they only succeed in strengthening their children's narcissism rather than repressing it.

Without a doubt, the results of this kind of childhood development cannot help but lead to serious conflicts for most of these children when they begin to reach adulthood. In fact, this is why so much of what characterizes adolescence today is typified by a kind of narcissistic revolt against authority, poverty, racism, war, and bureaucracy. Suddenly, teen-agers realize that there is somebody out there in television land who really wants to manipulate their wishes, control their choices, and manage their pleasures. And what a shock this revelation is; all along they assumed that it was their world, open and exciting, immediately available to them. But then it hits them that it really belongs to someone else, someone invisible, who only wants them to continue to believe their illusions and remain happy with the world as it is. But that's where the manipulators of "feedback" have made a terrible mistake. You can't rear an entire generation convinced that the world is theirs and suddenly expect them to accept the fact that others really manage it, own it, and control it. Either the society prepares itself for the next generation of autonomous individuals or it continues the classic pattern of reaching the narcissistic infant before he has a chance to trust his own primary ego feelings. To support his narcissism in childhood and early adolescence and then suddenly confront him with the world as it is, to breed an entire generation of angry aristocrats who must eventually be dethroned from their kingdoms. Because this is what we do, all the behavior, violent and self-destructive, honest and devious, aggressive and obvious, that we have been witnessing over the past few years cannot help but increase.

This is also why so much of the youthful behavior we presently concern ourselves with is deeply troublesome and frightening. Much of it has become pathological, because it is almost impossible for a child with a narcissistically gratifying background to accept the world as it is presently structured without experiencing a profound attack upon himself. And no matter how creative, resourceful, and original he may be in his attempts to fight back, he experiences an emotional wound that cannot be shared with most adults, who have long since learned how to tolerate "the real world." Even the average neurotic patient, who finally learns to affirm his narcissism, is better oriented to the facts of life than the child whose narcissism has never really been subject to such forces. In fact, it may well be that the only way to help those adolescents who seek therapy as a relief from the real world will be to teach them a kind of neurosis as a way of coping with the real world. I am sure that many therapists have often considered this as an option when dealing with young hippies, whose "hangups" involve not their sexual and emotional problems but their inability to find a place for themselves in society. For the truth is that this society is not ready for healthy people. We still seem to function on the assumption that a little repression, a little guilt, and a little submission to authority makes for a more stable society. But if that is true, then we had better pass the word to mom and dad in modern affluent America. Either throw out your books by Dr. Spock, or else elect him to the White House.

But then, Dr. Spock, Dr. Menninger, and all the father figures of modern psychology never told us that rearing healthy children would eventually mean that a confrontation with society was inevitable. Somehow we assumed that healthy, self-motivating, and aggressive young people would make a better world than we were capable of passing on to them. What we forgot was the fact that we haven't really been interested in turning the world over to our children. We have not only trapped our children, even tricked them, we have deluded ourselves that we could provide a happy childhood for our offspring while deferring the truth about the way things really are. And many young people can't forgive us for that basic failure. We have given to them, and continue to give to them, a childhood of which history has deprived us. When it comes to letting them join our world, and eventually inherit it from us, however, we feign helplessness and powerlessness. No wonder they take over our offices, reject our norms, despise our authority, and ignore our warnings.

It goes without saying, therefore, that many young people today possess a true mixture of emotional health and deeply pathological conflicts. This is why it is so difficult to label any one aspect of their subculture as sick, utopian, idealistic, or healthy, mature, and creative. It is a complete mixture of all these elements, and more. The fact that most of them seem to be living out a continued adolescence, as Kenneth Kenniston has defined it, is because they cannot see how it is possible to make the shift from childhood to adulthood without losing something of themselves that is very precious — namely, their need to see the world as an extension of their own bodies, minds, and emotions. They know all too well that most adults live in a fragmented and artificial world, happy with what little private experiences, possessions, and comforts they can acquire. But that is not an existence most young people want. They want an adulthood in which the individual can have clearcut powers to determine his own choices, do with his life as he chooses, and make contributions to society that will have an immediate effect. And because this is true, many young people are quite willing to remain adolescents, alive to their feelings, bodies, and minds, instead of having to capitulate to an "adult" existence which seems all too mechanical.

The fact that so many adults continue to feel that attitudes like this disqualify the young from inheriting adult responsibility only clouds the picture all the more. For there is nothing in the behavior or values of the young today which disables them from assuming a truly mature role in society. The real problems have to do with the interpretations we give to adulthood. In the most profound sense, many so-called adults today are far less mature than their own adolescent children. This is why the usual designations of submission to authority, hard work, social conformity, and orderliness have very little to do with the real marks of adulthood. If anything, these are the qualities which adults have imposed upon the young traditionally in order for society to become a managed community. And this is also why the Freudian notion of Oedipal conflict refers more to the psychology of adults than it does to young people today. Social organization in the past has always relied heavily upon the repressed child within all men and women simply for the purpose of maintaining group life along the lines of family-tribal communities. The fact that our artificial mass culture no longer requires Oedipal dynamics for individuals to fit in to social organizations makes all such values and attitudes of the past irrelevant and obscurantist. The so-called adult who continues to "need" an alterego or father figure in his social life is far more a child than the teen-ager who seeks to define for himself what he wants out of life.

It is completely misleading to use conventional labels to define what we mean by adulthood and adolescence. If an adult really has in mind a set of values and a list of behavioral norms which seek to keep one's childlike feelings and thoughts repressed, then he really isn't using viable standards for adulthood; he is preoccupied with all the inherited fears about human nature, inevitable scarcity, instinctual chaos, and good old-fashioned sin. In fact, it may well be that all the things he usually assumes characterize adulthood are really little more than feelings he has never been free to test for himself. Is adulthood independence or dependence? Is it freedom, self-expression, and autonomy, or is it structure, conformity, and group membership? And adolescence — is it really an extension of childhood, oriented only to peer values, competition, self-doubt, and continual attempts to test one's boundaries? Or could it be that adolescence is the first stage of real adulthood, mastering the skills of self-expression, testing the fullness of emotional involvement, defining one's basic values and goals for life, and preparing to make a viable contribution to the human community? Without a doubt, there is much confusion in the minds of many adults, as well as young people, regarding the true characteristics of adulthood. Whether or not many young people today are prepared to understand what those qualities are cannot be confused with most adults' fears and suspicions that the young are doing nothing but making blind mistakes. The young inevitably are making mistakes. There really isn't much of a model for them to follow.

7

SEX: THE COURAGE OF INNOCENCE

For most young people today, sex stands as the primary area within one's life in which social values, prohibitions, and conventions have no right to intervene. What one does with his or her own body is the business of no one but those involved. This is a major belief among growing numbers of teen-agers and young adults in their twenties and thirties. A kind of private sanctuary has been staked out by these people, and they consistently refuse to let society interfere with their personal worlds.

Before examining this attitude, we must dispel some of the faulty assumptions that many adults hold regarding sexuality among the young. It simply is not true that most young people today are more experienced or more adept for their age than adults once were. It just so happens that most initial acts of sexual involvement are examples of sexual testing. Both male and female try to learn from doing. Adolescence is the time when one tests reality to find out about one's self, and this applies to sex as much as to any other activity. For this reason, much of today's sexual context is determined by two people willingly being together, on a situational basis, committed only to the relationship for the moment. This kind of behavior strikes adults, locked into their conception of sex and marriage, as cynical; and they equate cynicism with sophistication and experience.

The only significant innovation is in the attitude of girls and young women, in that they are increasingly more willing to have such experiences but no longer seem preoccupied with making the relationship a step toward marriage. In other words, many girls are beginning to discover that sex is a vital aspect of being a woman, and that it is not always related to the feelings and desires of getting married and having children. Like many boys and young men, girls are coming to realize that sex can be a liberating experience, related to one's own self-expression and identity. It is not a part of life that has meaning and purpose only under the rubrics of marriage and family.

Another misconception that many adults seem to hold is that young people are preoccupied with sexual intercourse. The fact is that adolescence and young adulthood have always been periods in life when the genital drives of expression and release have been intense. Quite simply, this period in life is the best time for men and women to have children. A young woman is stronger and a young man is more physically capable of carrying out the traditional tasks of working, fighting, hunting, and providing for the family. The fact that society is no longer organized to reflect these biological realities only makes genital sexuality a luxury instead of a necessity for communal survival. And, of course, now it is no longer necessary for women to have as many children as possible. As a result, sex has become more of an experience of choice, not simply a biological event.

If we add to this the obvious fact that genital sex is intensely pleasurable, then the older psychology of condoned sex only after marriage inevitably takes a back seat to the wish to have such an experience whenever it seems most appealing. It simply is not true, however, as certain psychologists, educators, and parents have assumed, that genital sex is more common among today's youth. What is different is the availability of choice in the matter of sexuality. This fact alone explains why the young have had to invent their own social and communal rituals in order to give meaning to their natural biological drives. They do not have intercourse at every occasion. In fact, there is a very clear economy in the manner by which most youngsters experience sexuality, organizing their time and lives in such a way as to add to the experience, rather than seeking ways to become sexually involved under the complete domination of their instinctual desires. This is partly why sex in the back seat of the car is rapidly being replaced with sex in the girl's bedroom, or in a friend's apartment, or simply under conditions that reflect a relatively planned experience. Even the pattern of "going steady," so typical of previous generations, is changing — partly because young people are not interested in copying adult patterns of sexual behavior. As a result, many young people are beginning to learn something that has taken most adults years to appreciate: that sexuality is far more fulfilling and complete when it is freely chosen by the two involved, planned consciously, and surrounded with all those elements which can add to the experience. And far from detracting from the supposedly desirable effect of spontaneous sexual release, this makes sex into something more personal and rewarding for those involved.

A third and perhaps even more serious misconception of adults is the notion that too much sexuality before marriage, too many experiences of sexual intercourse, may well deprive marriage of its greatest power, namely, the heightened pleasure of sexual love within the boundaries of marriage. The assumption which has long accompanied this belief was that sex is an explosive instinctual drive which must be constrained within certain socially acceptable limits lest it cause the individual to become a victim of endless internal demands for release. Unfortunately, the morality of Western civilization has added to this fear, thus turning the sexual act into a guilt-associated experience. Women have had to think of sex as being condoned only by the marriage vows and the rationalized purpose of having children, while both men and women have often felt unconscious guilt as the emotion which most tends to enhance the sexual experience. Indeed, guilt has long played a very important role in the significance of the sexual act. That is why periodic sex with the "other woman" or "other man" has made the marriage bed seem less appealing to many adults over the years. Overcoming one's resistance to the taboos has been for many adults a prime emotional feeling in sex. But without the taboos, as in the case of marriage itself, many men and women feel they have lost something they had during their earlier courtship. What they have lost, in fact, is the guilt, the excitement, and the daring they once felt as they broke down their mutual guilt.

As a result of this guilt-oriented attitude toward sexuality, too much becomes invested in and expected of marriage itself, as if it was supposed to compensate for one's desires for pre- and extra-marital experiences. Of course, it has never worked that way. Few marriages can overcome the fact that men and women remain individuals, quite capable and willing to have extramarital involvements. In fact, the prohibitions about extramarital affairs tend to make such experiences seem far more important, exciting, and rewarding than they actually are. This is why those young people who have been emotionally and mentally free to have as much sexual and emotional experimentation as they feel they need are usually far more capable of entering marriage on the basis of choice than those who have escaped into marriage to avoid confrontation with society's taboos. It still remains true that escape from any set of emotions only delays having to deal with them later on. And for a man or woman to discover only after they are married and have children that they have never really permitted themselves to experience deep emotions and physical involvement with others on a sexual basis comes as quite a shock. All the illusions, beliefs, and assumptions about marital fidelity cannot make that feeling of having cheated oneself diminish one iota.

As a rule, therefore, it must be recognized that it is not the actions but the attitudes of young people which set them apart from adults. Nevertheless, in some circles, especially among the affluent upper middle class, there seems to be evolving a new attitude among a few parents toward their teen-agers which is unique. A kind of quiet identification by parents with their children is beginning to take place. Recognizing that their own children may well be more emotionally prepared to experiment with life than they have been, these parents secretly compare their own wishes for experimentation with those of their teenagers. Stories are told of mothers sharing their contraceptive pills with their teen-age daughters, or at least finding a physician who is willing to prescribe them. And the subject of sexuality is discussed openly and freely under the general assumption that no one has the right to invade the lives of others.

Underneath this innovation in some homes (and there is no way of knowing how common this kind of parent-child relationship is) lies the discovery that most adults have cheated themselves as teen-agers and young adults and are now determined to live their lives in the same kind of freedom they see in the younger generation. In this sense, youth has taken the lead in providing society with a much healthier attitude toward sex. But young people are still experimenting and learning, and that is the area in which to observe some of the factors that characterize the meaning which sex seems to hold for so many youngsters today.

Without a doubt, the phenomenon of narcissism in childhood, later confirmed in early teens, plays a most important role in the evolution of newer attitudes toward sex. For any youngster who believes that he or she is autonomous and self-directing in the things which really matter in his or her life, it follows quite naturally that sexuality would be one area where self-expression is primary. Not surprisingly, young people insist that sexuality is not really a matter for society to determine; it is something at the very heart of one's most private self. Nothing could be more typical of the narcissistic ego than such an assumption. In fact, it characterizes the whole dynamics of sexuality among the young far more than most adults appreciate.

For the narcissistic ego, the world is an extension of one's own body and emotions. This is what the myth of Orpheus sought to convey. Being in union with nature, Orpheus sought to control the world with his music and love. Typical of the Greek mentality, however, he was finally destroyed because the world was not prepared to accept his reality, even as Christ was killed by the representatives of "reality" in his day. Nevertheless, the real power of the Orphic and Christ-like people is in their radical openness to the world around them. Whether or not they are suffering from an illusion about reality, they still have an impact on others that more "realistic" ways of relating to the world cannot have. And whether or not most adults appreciate this fact, the attitudes of many youngsters today are far more like that of Orpheus than is recognized.

This means that young people are not relating to the world of others in terms of the traditional attitudes of male aggression and female submission, but more like children in love with themselves. But now this kind of self-love is not exclusive of others. In fact, it openly includes a much wider range of others than we have heretofore seen. In the lyric of a rock and roll hit, a girl rejects her suitor because he is capable of loving only her. She sees his love as possessive and selfish, whereas she is "traveling to the tune of a different drum." For as we have pointed out, a confirmed state of primary narcissism does not tend to lead to selfishness in individuals, it only tends to make one's relationship with others and the world itself far more trusting and honest. Of course, when the world of others does not respond willingly and openly, the pain which is felt is far more intense. This then leads the individual either to withdraw his erotic and emotional feelings or else to affirm the right to extend his or her feelings all the more. And the person whose narcissism has received enough love and support does not easily withdraw. He feels that his love and emotions are the only true forces in the world to "turn others on" to himself.

The relationship between two narcissistically oriented young people ultimately produces some very interesting consequences. Oftentimes, two people love each other by each permitting the other to have access to his narcissistic world. In this sense, there is no surrender or giving up of the self; there is only confirmation of the self by having had someone else added to one's universe — not like so many credits to one's ability to make love but, quite to the contrary, populating one's universe with others who love and share that which means the most to one. Surprisingly, those who possess such narcissistic feelings do not experience love as having lost or given up a part of one's self; they tend to feel it as a new affirmation of the self.

What confuses many adults is that this appears to be complete egotism and even a kind of mutual admiration. It doesn't seem to be love as it has always been understood. And yet, it is love. In fact, it is a kind of love that is highly fulfilling and rewarding. It has all the characteristics of sharing, trust, openness, and feeling, while at the same time it appreciates the individuality of each person. If you come into my universe, you do so because I want you there. Otherwise you cannot get in. But even more important, you exist in my universe, even as I exist in yours, freely and willingly.

The single most revolutionary aspect of this type of narcissistic love is the type of freedom it demands from both partners. Such people exist in one another's world only because the other wants them to be there. In no case can this ever mean that the other person loses any part of himself to that relationship. One is always free to have many other people live within his or her world at the same time. Of course, the more important one becomes to another, the more that relationship takes on the characteristics of conjugal love. But at the same time, this does not diminish the importance of others as loved objects as well. For a natural hierarchy can readily be developed which makes some people more important and more loved than others, but it does not mean that one must surrender his or her involvements with many people for that love to be there.

Ultimately, this means that marriage and family will no longer serve as barriers to deeply personal involvements with others. Marriage no longer becomes based upon anything more than a kind of situational ethic, or what some have called "monogamy with one person at a time." Doubtless this type of relationship has been taking place for centuries. But never before has it been established as a principle of freedom based upon both the man's and the woman's wishes to remain open to the world of others. Whether or not the young people who adhere to such a principle will be able to tolerate the pain of seeing their loved ones involved with others has yet to be tested on a sufficient scale for us to assert that the young have already proved the maturity and superiority of their type of freedom. But it is clear that this attitude obviously stands in judgment against the conventional attitudes toward sex, emotional freedom, and personal involvements which have characterized the lives of so many adults: the guilt that is felt when one finds himself in the arms of another, the titillation of daring thoughts and wishes, and the shock and anger felt when a stranger offers his or her affection.

In any case, it is obvious that many young people are trying to eroticize the world around them. Rather than taking the more functional approach to sex and love, this more narcissistic style provides a fresh and exciting alternative. At its very core it is an attitude which starts with the self and ends with the self, and there are few illusions about the freedom of one's partner. Independence is the *sine qua non* of the relationship. But instead of this serving as a continual basis for selfishness and possessive demands, it means that the two are together only as long as they want it that way. Thus, when one finally makes a commitment to be with someone he or she loves, it is a commitment made in freedom and inherently presupposes that each has chosen the other.

Of course, it is very easy to idealize such an attitude as this and to assume that most young people have fully achieved it. But such is not the case. We are simply pointing out that the kinds of sexuality and feelings of love which follow from lives which have been narcissistically confirmed are essentially different from lives which have been based upon delay of gratification, guilt about sex, repression of narcissism, and the related emotions of competitiveness, aggression, possessiveness, and self-doubt. Too many adults know how these latter emotions can turn them into fearful, hurting, and suspicious individuals. And too many young people know that loving and trusting others, no matter how painful it may be, can bring to them feelings that they cannot find in the adults around them.

Fortunately, a growing number of young people have not accepted the adult evaluation about life's inevitabilities, and we are beginning to discover that sex is not necessarily so frightening and chaotic as once was believed. Nudity, premarital sex, extramarital sex, varieties on the whole sexual theme have finally begun to shake up the arts, religious values, political assumptions, social practices, and personal beliefs. But far more important, we are finally beginning to discover that one's own body exists for the pleasures that experimentation, creativity, and involvement can bring. The old rituals are changing, and we are beginning to feel, if only by identification with an adolescence we never really had, a certain amount of freedom to reexamine the boundary lines we once so quickly placed around our lives. For this, we cannot help but thank the younger generation.

Unfortunately, the young cannot fully share their own feelings and attitudes with parents who are defensive and repressive about sex. Traditionally, in those families which have avoided mutual honesty in matters of sexuality, the sons and daughters have had to leave the home in order to find themselves. They could not share the joy or the pain they felt in their first encounters with sex. In those few homes, however, where it is possible for the young to trust adults and parents, a kind of mutual growing and sharing can and does take place. It really depends on what the parents want from their relationship with their maturing young people. But for those parents and adults who are unable to have that kind of a relationship, the following characteristics may well be typical of their own children's feelings, values, and behavior.

1. There is a primary willingness on the part of large numbers of teen-agers to find out for themselves what sexual experiences can

mean. Essentially, their sexual drives are linked with narcissistic ego drives, which means that sex is only secondary to their need to test themselves and ultimately define themselves as men and women.

2. For an ever-increasing number of girls and young women, sex is being discovered as pleasurable. This means that women's motivations about sex are no longer limited to desires for marriage, babies, and security. One simple sociological fact makes this clear. For the past two decades, prostitution houses surrounding college campuses have all but disappeared. The local girls, coeds, and female students at nearby campuses have finally displaced the professionals.

3. The growing availability of contraceptive devices has made the sexual act a matter of choice for countless girls and women. But since choice itself plays such a great role in the thinking of both young men and women, choice can well mean "no," as well as "yes." There is no reason to assume that "the pill" has led the young to become promiscuous. They are only more free to make up their own minds.

4. Because sexuality means much more than genital sexuality for large numbers of young people, the entire youth culture itself serves as a kind of stimulus as well as a kind of deferral for genital sex. There is just as much reason to believe that the openness about sexual matters in music, dress, conversations, and attitudes leads to deferral of sexual acts as that it serves as a kind of "foreplay" for the sexual act.

5. And in the last analysis, since sexuality means much more than simple genital sex, adults must understand that sex among the young involves more of the total feelings, values, and attitudes than simply having genital experiences. The young are trying to eroticize the world around them, to make it into an organic or whole experience. Many of them are not even interested in genital sex as a goal. They want everything to feel sexual, physical, and pleasurable.

8

DRESS: PUTTING ON HISTORY

Characteristic of the vague generalizations adults make regarding the young today is the claim that the new and different styles of dress and self-expression are nothing more than old-fashioned "peer-group" or "herd-instinct" wishes to belong. Adults remember the "flappers" and later the "bobby-soxers" and the adolescent longings to be a part of their own generation's world. Consequently, they conclude that what the young today feel must be similar to the emotions they once experienced so deeply. Actually, the phenomenon of group psychology is, as we have said earlier, far more characteristic of those individuals who are products of classic Oedipal-type small-town groups than of those whose lives have been dominated by continued affluence, technological mass culture, and the resulting reorientation to external reality. The reasons for this are quite simple.

Small-town group psychology (which also applies to ethnic groups in large cities) is patterned after the family Oedipal dynamics. Consequently, when youngsters in the past reached their teen years, adolescent rebellion and peer-group pressures served as an interim period of testing before the young finally assumed more adultlike traits and characteristics. The competitive and peer-group pressures of the twenties and thirties were logical extensions of traditional forces within the home, dictating that the young struggle to find themselves within their own age groups, thus providing them with emotional security beyond the limits of the home. Historically, this has been the role of such groups as the Scouts, competitive sports teams, fraternities, and clubs. In turn, this is why society at large eventually became a kind of surrogate home environment, giving young people an unbroken set of experiences predicated upon their primary relationships within the home. Adolescence was a phase in life naturally given to one's need to test the reality principles of the world — first in the home, then within one's own age group, and finally in the world of one's adult peer group.

Most adults have little trouble remembering how this transition from childhood to adolescence and finally to adulthood worked for them. But they do have difficulty in understanding how the changes of the past two and a half decades have altered the experience of their own children. Most of the influential psychological factors which have evolved in recent years have turned out quite differently from those of the past. Instead of adolescence continuing to be that brief period between childhood and adulthood wherein the young tentatively test the standards of adult reality, it has tended to become a "life-style" or subculture of its own, standing dramatically in contrast to the so-called adult culture. And for this very reason, most of the elements which now characterize that youthful subculture are elements of behavior which will eventually alter the very nature of the adult culture itself. In other words, many young people are saying not that they want to remain adolescents only to hold on to their childhoods but that they want to change the factors which determine the meaning and style we now accept as definitive for adulthood. Their various styles of dress, language, and custom are not periodic examples of peer-group rebellion. They are the developing styles which the young seem bent on carrying into adulthood. The impact of a developing primary narcissism among so many youngsters has taken over the motivational dynamic which used to be the function of the group. And what we are witnessing today in the styles of dress and self-expression among the young is a much truer kind of individualism than we have ever known in this country, with the possible exception of the individualism of the frontier pioneers.

In the language of Marshall McLuhan, this television-oriented generation is "putting on history." They are not simply falling into place, having thus inherited the styles which have been handed down to them by the previous generation. To understand this better it is helpful to make a clear distinction between copying the styles of historical periods and making a "caricature" of them. To the group-conscious individual, it is important to copy what is prescribed by the group (i.e., the business suit, the uniform, etc.). But to the narcissistic individual, "putting on" the images of the past is a sign of freedom from that past as well as a conscious identification with selected aspects of the past. For example, a teen-ager wearing an Eisenhower jacket together with Levis, sandals and beads is poking fun at the father figure of the Second World War. Related to this, the so-called granny look, which honors the old-fashioned simple woman of the frontier, portrays her as a real swinger, who underneath is a sexual being. (Oftentimes a girl wears little or nothing underneath her "granny" dress.) Once again, history is "put on" for the purpose of identifying with certain desirable elements of the past, while at the same time ridiculing what is perceived as undesirable.

In this sense, adults do not seem to appreciate fully that the role of dress among the young has become a medium for self-expression. Each youngster is a walking picture of history, interpreted by himself as he wishes it to be. History is no longer a linear process whereby styles change under certain clearly understood pressures. Instead, history has become a "morality play" — a series of vignettes or episodes available to the narcissistic ego in the present time, as though he were a playwright or movie director giving direction to his own living theater, in which he is the chief actor. If he chooses a pair of sandals, he is playing the part of the prophet, the Jesus figure. If he wears beads, he is worshipping the elements of the universe, like an American Indian or an Oriental mystic. If he lets his hair grow to endless lengths, he is showing his own distinctiveness. Uncut hair grows at its own pace and under its own biological limits. His Levis identify him with the poor, the dirt farmers of "Tobacco Road" and "Of Mice and Men" as well as the black people of the Mississippi delta, while his large hat, boots, thick belt, and heavy jacket stand to mimic the Western villain, a kind of modern motorized cowboy. Indeed, history for these youngsters is a disconnected series of mental pictures, each available to the narcissist's playful jest.

Not all young people dress or act like what we now call "hippies," but this ought not delude anyone into thinking that hippies are atypical of their generation. Actually, there are many youngsters who periodically "put on" a pseudohippie exterior as only one part of their overall "life-styles." They are often called "plastic hippies" because they can only identify with their more autonomous peers on certain occasions, as, for example, on Friday nights when they break away from their homes and venture into the city. As a rule, these "plastic hippies" are younger teen-agers who see in their older peers a freedom and a self-expression which they desire for themselves.

The hippie culture itself is obviously only one aspect of the narcissistic-type individualized group. As such, it cannot be seen as a standard-setting part of the larger youth culture. In fact, most of the influences upon such aspects of the youth culture as dress stem from forces outside the youth movement itself, quite apart from the peer-group identification. And two of these outside forces parallel the same struggle within which young people find themselves today. These two forces are the revolutions in black consciousness in the ghetto and among women throughout the country. The black male and the white female have become a new force for change — both are deeply committed to the principle of self-determination. And their impact on the youth movement, partly overlapping it, is almost incalculable.

To understand how the black culture has influenced the young people, it is important to realize that the Afro-American culture and modern affluent upper-middle-class society have certain things in common. At the heart of this peculiar comparison is the fact that both the blacks and the upper middle class live in matriarchal environments. Mother is the strongest member of both communities, especially in terms of who relates to the youngsters. And where this is the case, the psychology of woman tends to override the psychology of traditional Western paternalism. However, since there is still the remnant of a paternal role remaining within the white affluent culture, the full impact of mother is muted, whereas in the black culture mother has always had a dominant influence.

Within the black ghetto, most young men (in traditional African style) are supported and loved as the playful, erotic, and aggressive members of the community. Not that this plays down the role of the black female. She is also a highly erotic, playful, and strong figure, but she is inevitably influenced by the role of becoming the provider and central figure in the family. Her man, however, traditionally follows the naturalistic styles of the animal kingdom. He wears colorful clothes, initiates sexual play, expresses his feelings openly (soul) and provides the woman with as much pleasure as he expects her to provide him. Most whites have traditionally interpreted this phenomenon as the black man being castrated by the stronger black woman, and because of the social and economic conditions imposed by the white man's world this has more than a shadow of truth. But to assume that the playful, erotic, and aggressive black male is less of a man than the white, rational, hardworking, middle-class male is nothing but racism. Whites have assumed that the blacks do not have a fully developed culture. They do, but it is quite different from the white man's.

Growing up within the white ghettos of modern upper-middle-class suburbia in recent years, however, has provided many young men with if not similar at least parallel experiences to those in the black ghetto. A white youngster often finds that his desires to inherit the adult male world of work, participation, and involvement are thwarted, an experience not unlike that of the black male unable to find a job. Obviously, however, the effects of this shared condition are extremely different. One returns to a continued affluence while the other experiences deeper frustration and pain-filled poverty. The white youngster lives out an adolescence, even through college, wherein he is not really needed by the society. And since he feels the desire to participate, to make himself heard, he finds this experience extremely frustrating as well. Consequently, he adopts the world of matriarchy (mother being the adult he finds it easier to relate to) and begins to play out the desired role of his own personal choice. In so doing, he discovers the black male as an ally against the white adult male's world. He has become a similar victim to the domination of a system governed by faceless white men. He finds in the black male an existing culture of freedom, self-affirmation, and an honest expression of his deepest feelings. And as the black male dresses to show his feelings, the young white male encounters a new and exciting image of what it means to be a man. Thus, the more the young white man divorces himself from the white man's world of institutionalization and regimentation, the more colors, style, and self-expression take on the characteristics of freedom from the adult white man's control.

Of course, the white mother does not quite know how to deal with her son as he takes on these varieties of self-expression. A part of it seems delightful, even more pleasurable than the ways his father relates to her. Yet another aspect of it seems threatening. But with the father out of the picture much of the time, the mother tends to let the son carry out his life-style. In a sense, the son has won the Oedipal conflict without even having struggled with the father. Insofar as the mother enjoys seeing her son express himself, she does not stand in his way and possibly even gives her own quiet support.

If we turn to the revolution in dress which the young women are bringing about, we find something else happening, which in turn supports the young white males. For example, if a mother sees in her daughter or other young girls a kind of self-expression or erotic playfulness that she wishes she possessed, then it is more than possible that she identifies with the younger girls. In this regard, the impact which the mini skirt has had on countless women in their thirties and forties is quite remarkable. There is one thing about the mini skirt which style-consciousness cannot explain. Either a woman wants her legs, and perhaps more, to be seen, or she doesn't. And if she does, then she is saying something about herself, about the way she wishes to relate to the world around her. And peer pressures can only have a reinforcing and secondary effect on the decision to wear clothes that are as erotically oriented as the mini skirt. Consequently, where this attitude is shared by women who are themselves parents, it cannot help but have an effect on their children. It teaches them that mother is, and wants to be, erotically appreciated.

The open expression of eroticism in modern styles of dress, however, is an invention of the young. This is partly why the traditional style-setters of clothes are finding themselves in something of a turmoil. New styles must not violate the younger generation's wish to be self-expressive, nor must it deny the eroticism which has become so natural and common. On the other hand, however, the designer's own feeling of self-expression and antiregimentation causes him to experiment with the human form and has created a revolution of opportunity for the creators of clothes. The styles are endless and open to complete variety. What this means, therefore, is that the older attitude of having to have a particular dress or style of clothing is being replaced by the creators and manufacturers of styles following the demands of the younger generation.

The present debate over the invasion of the midi-type dress as the dominant style of this year only shows how frantic the manufacturers and designers have become in their attempt to regain control of the public fashion-consciousness. Never before have the manipulators of design (more material means more money for the business) been put in such a position of "dictating" style. The "closed system" of textile industry–designer–manufacturers–department and specialty stores stands

as a giant monopoly against the growing number of individualistic younger women. And were it nor for the many remaining
"repressed" and group-conscious women who depend upon
someone else to define style, such a blatant attempt at control
would immediately collapse. As it is, the midi will still probably
fail, but not instantly. Economics may dictate the desire of industry to have predictable markets, but young people basically
ignore all such attempts to manipulate their choices. The reverse effect has now been established. The young know all too
well how powerful they are as a symbol of independence and
personal freedom. And eventually the fashion business will discover that planned markets and controlled taste do not make
much sense to a growing population of narcissistically motivated young people. Diversity and personal choice are here to
stay.

The reason behind this innovation and liberation from style-
consciousness has very little to do with economics. The young
are not trying to put anyone out of business. It simply means
that the younger generation is demanding that a new set of
rules be established, rules which reflect the value of personal
choice and self-expression. And according to those new rules,
anything goes, including the midi. Nudity, functionality, creativity, and individuality set the range of options — even for
men. The business executive who is afraid to wear anything
but white shirts has been frozen into his own mechanical
world of business. The group- or social-conscious male who
fears his own eroticism must now either accept himself or be
willing to remain invisible behind the uniform which the system demands; while the man who longs to let his feelings be
shown finally has a world wherein he can take the risk and be
in style at the same time.

To get a clear picture of what this can mean from now on,
one must think of the individual as having a bird's-eye view of
history, as though he were not a part of linear history. From
this transcendent vantage point, the individual then adopts various symbolic styles from the past and "puts on history" as
though it were a collage or syncretistic picture of history. In so

doing, the man who wears an Edwardian suit is playing with history within his own person. Like the child during the thirties and forties watching the serials on Saturday and going home and dressing up like the hero, so the adult today can dress up and play. And thus, showing that history no longer has power over him, he can make history his servant, even his wardrobe. His choice is as great as history or as functional as his need. There is no one style which can capture the needs of man or woman and thus dictate what is acceptable. Narcissism then, determines the meaning of style and reinforces the feelings that one can make reality do for him what he wants it to.

Typical of narcissism in modern dress is the eroticism which characterizes so much of the behavior of youngsters today. For rather than clothes serving the older purposes of covering the human form, allowing the stylist to experiment with only that which the society would tolerate, today's revolution in dress is predicated upon the assumption that the naked body can hardly be improved upon. And as McLuhan has pointed out, clothing is really little more than an extension of the skin. Of course, no interpretation of dress could better define the dynamics of narcissism than this. For narcissism means that external reality is perceived as an extension of the self, or the body. That's the infant's world-view, and it's the way the confirmed narcissistic ego perceives things. Consequently, clothes cease to be barriers between individuals and the world of others, and they become the medium for the body to communicate itself directly to the world. In other words, the individual narcissist, male or female, is continuously "taking" to those around him in a language of movement, shape, color, and form which says that he is open to the world of others, not hidden behind the norms of society as dictated by the antierotic models of traditional dress.

Obviously, there is something else being communicated here which only the most norm-conscious individuals cannot perceive. And that is that it is no longer possible to look at any one younger person and see the whole younger generation. Many adults tend to think that they can see a kind of peer-group consciousness among the young. As one parent put it, "they all look alike." But the truth of the matter is that they do not. In fact, the variety which characterizes the youngsters today means that we are confronted with radical individualists, not conformers. When one lets his hair grow, or when one's feet are black with dirt, or one's body smells with the aroma of human flesh, there is no way on earth to claim that these people are copying one another. There are no two sets of feet, bodies, or heads of hair that look exactly alike. The young are saying that the true standards of fashion are determined by the feelings, choices, and desires of the individual, not by the priorities of business, ethnic groups, social class, or region. It is their freedom which strikes us as so contagious among them. And for the individual, no matter what age, if this is what he likes, he has the whole world to pick from in expressing his "lifestyle."

9

POLITICS: ALL POWER
TO THE PEOPLE

As confusing and illegitimate as it may sound to most adults, the fact remains that this society *does not* provide our younger citizens with any viable political options. Typified by the institutions of business, labor, the universities, and the professions, this society is governed by adults, most of whom share a remarkably similar world-view. It is a system of power and decision-making which they have inherited from the past. And it is a "closed system," rooted in all the values which trouble the youth deeply. It is competitive, economically determined, hierarchical, and ritualistic. And the often used definition of our governmental structure as "representative and democratic" strikes the young as propagandistic and hypocritical. Consequently, to understand the politics of these young people today, one must begin with these basic differences in values and perspectives.

Most adults continue to use their own frames of reference to judge what they witness among the young, and that is where their perception of the young breaks down. For example, it is quite common for adults to place a very high priority on the role of "leadership" within the political and governmental process. Knowing full well that modern bureaucracies deplete the power and effectiveness of leaders by qualifying, filtering, and managing the information with which they make their decisions, adults continue to assume that leadership is the secret to power and change. The young people, however, do not want leaders, nor do they accept the traditional role of leadership as most adults understand it. For example, many of those youngsters who supported Eugene McCarthy in the 1968 primaries remained suspicious of him throughout the campaign. They knew that he, too, came from the same political process as the Kennedys, Lyndon Johnson, Hubert Humphrey, and Richard Nixon. Consequently, McCarthy didn't really have a constituency at all. He had thousands, perhaps hundreds of thousands of young people who were seeking to use him, hoping that they might change the very system of which he had been such an integral part. The older political psychology whereby the issues and platforms are determined by party leadership had been reversed. "The people," as the youngsters put it, were dictating from the streets the platform and policies which they demanded should govern the elections. But like everything else, the political system was closed to such threatening challenges. As the press had predicted, the party system elected its men.

Of course, the variety of interpretations given by the young of what they actually experienced in Chicago that summer of 1968, and later on in the November election of Richard Nixon, is greatly determined by their own personal memories. This is as true for those in the streets as for those who watched it on television. Adults saw the political process shaken but remaining intact. But countless young people saw Chicago as a major watershed in their experience of our political system. The education they had received about the American political ritual severely depressed many of them. They saw with their own eyes the futility of trying to stop the machine which places the biggest, strongest, and smartest on top. And another myth about the "free society" and liberalism came crumbling down. Perhaps they had to experience it, to learn how powerful their adversary really is, to confirm what their own radicals had been saying — namely, that it is the system and not the individual participants which matters.

One of the major reasons why the young had become suspicious of "leadership" was heavily conditioned by their own television orientation to the mass culture. Adults who watch television tend to forget that the deception and lying they witness on the television screen strikes the young far more seriously than it does them. Children naturally expect honesty from adults, and when they discover that they have been lied to, it is very hard for them to muster the trust they once felt so deeply. In fact, since the deception is so deeply ingrained in the public fiber of our mass culture, the young discover very early that very little of what one sees and hears can be believed. That is the true origin of the phrase "never trust anyone over thirty." And it explains why the young listen to rock musicians as authorities on such subjects as war, drugs, and morality, rather than to political leaders, doctors, and clergymen.

Perhaps discovering all this too late, many commercial advertisers, politicians, and representatives of the adult establishment have recently tried to use more subtle techniques in their attempts to capture the trust of the young. Borrowing the language of the young, they hope to communicate the illusion that the young are now being heard and taken seriously. But without seriously questioning the political system, such a trick as this cannot help but deepen the suspicion the young feel. And without a new generation to give fresh blood to the tribal ritual, the older manipulators of political power are finding their basis of support growing smaller. Smaller in the sense that fewer of the young can be relied upon to feed the system's inherent need for continued control of the culture.

What some of the brighter founders of SDS discovered in the mid-sixties has now become a popular assumption among many young people. Our political, economic, and social system is deeply rooted in a general suspicion of the public at large. No institutional leader, whether he be a corporate executive dealing with his employees or stockholders, a college president facing his students, a politician trying to cope with his con-

stituency, or the President of the United States addressing the
public, can tell the truth. It is a *sine qua non* of institutional
life that power is information, and shared information is the
loss of power. One manages, rules, or leads his constituency by
illusions, half-truths, and deception. Such concepts as "government by the people and government for the people" are political illusions, which if ever taken seriously cause liberals to en-
vision mass murders and social chaos, and conservatives to see
images of communism and surrender to the "enemy." Consequently, when the SDS pamphlets used to be signed at the bottom "the people" or "all power to the people," the young
radicals were making a cryptic statement about the nature of
politics and government in this "democracy." They also knew
that they themselves did not represent the Midwestern farmer,
or the New York taxi driver, or the white racist in the deep
South. Such people already had their representatives in the Department of Agriculture, the Teamsters Union, and the Southern Senators who headed up all the significant committees in
Congress. What these young radicals were saying was that
everyone, in spite of such pressure groups and special interests,
is still a victim of a system which rewards the acceptable citizen
and excludes the unacceptable. Citizenship is no guarantee of
democratic participation in this system.

In other words, the issue these radicals have been raising has
to do with the nature of the society and how its political system reflects that society. Consequently, when adults ask,
"What will the young produce to replace the old political
system?" they do not fully understand that it is the society and
not just the political system which is under attack. And given
the nature of this technological mass culture, it is too difficult
to predict what the young will bring about, politically speaking, in the next few years. Obviously, if party politics continue
as they have in the past, especially as they manifested themselves in the two conventions in Chicago and Miami, one can
expect greater alienation of the young. For example, the one
history lesson which the 1968 Democratic convention taught
the young was the mechanics of the traditional system of pa-

tronage, play-acting, and ritualistic showmanship of the thirties. Mayor Daley's Chicago was the perfect location for such a lesson. It had all the characteristics of the past, like an old movie on television, a "Last Hurrah." Perhaps that is why the ubiquitous television camera seemed so embarrassing. In a mass culture, such an antiquated bit of political ritual looks comical and ridiculous, especially to the young. That is why the introduction of issues from the masses of youth in the streets had little to do with the party priorities, and why those issues met with such swift resistance. Such a political process is too typical of the classic Oedipal psychology of the past for it to relate to young people. And until now, there never has been a social or cultural change great enough to break this ancient pattern.

But there is one behavior trait or, better yet, "biologically determined mode of being" which perfectly suits the highly technological, urbanized, and complex social environment we have finally evolved. And while it adapts to the society's mass culture dynamics, it violently resists the older political rituals and practices which hang over from the past. Clearly, this mode is the type of narcissistic individualism which so readily characterizes the behavior of today's youth. And as we have already shown, it is a new mode of being, not typified by the older definitions of narcissism which Freudians and other early-twentieth-century intellectuals have labeled as "infantile fantasy," incapable of adaptation to the "real world." The young narcissist today has far more internal resources for adaptation and survival than does the group-conscious adult. For example, the youngster who seeks the city as a dwelling place instead of the bucolic suburban environment is revealing that his own narcissistic world is more spacious and rewarding than the "real-estate"-oriented world of most middle-class adults. As a narcissist, his world begins with his own mind and body, and it can include the city or the rural setting as the context in which he lives. Unlike those who feel caged in the city, these youngsters look upon the airways as arteries of the city, as their own personal avenues which carry them into and out of the city.

The story of what is already happening to our large urban

communities perfectly reflects how significant this newer behavioral and psychic evolution can be for the future. In one sense, it is the story of two classes, i.e., the upper middle class and the lower middle class. A great many young people who were reared in the affluent suburbs now move to the cities, partly to attend an urban college, partly to escape their homes, and partly to be "where the action is." And if seventy percent of the population in this country live on one percent of the landmass, as demographers tell us, then it is safe to say that a great many youngsters live in urban surroundings. And as the blacks have inherited the central cities, feeding into urban life their own culture, the young upper-middle-class white youths find such a setting greatly to their liking, while the lower-middle-class youths move to the surrounding suburbs, confused by what they have left behind and deeply troubled. The urban rich, although troubled by the blacks as well, often find the influx of youth stimulating and exciting. And in such places as New York's Manhattan, the impact of the youth, politically and socially is incalculable.

However, since traditional politics have long been identified with job-oriented working-class adults, such an evolutionary shift as this is somewhat disorienting to the lower-middle-class working man. The old Protestant work ethic, coupled with the ethnic vote, has finally begun to be challenged. For example, the reason Mayor Lindsay has remained in power is precisely because he divorced himself from the traditional party machines. He relied upon the very rich, the blacks, and the young. And he defeated the working-class party politics of the past. There is no historical model by which to compare such a political event as this. And although the blacks overwhelmingly gave him the election, the role played by young people was extremely crucial. Obviously, Lindsay was not considered by the young radicals as a political option. But as the blacks understood full well, the alternatives were absurd.

Encountering the blacks and the youth as a serious social and political threat, however, many working-class people have begun to look like Southern conservatives. Indeed, the parallel between many Midwesterners, deep South Protestants, and lower-middle-class workers in the large urban-suburban areas is truly remarkable. The old coalition of liberal Democrats pulling together the unions, the blacks, the farmers, and the intellectuals has been dismantled, while the conservative working-class vote, once heavily Democratic, now finds itself without a party, except for its consistent support of candidates who preach a hard-line reactionism. In other words, politics in our urban areas can no longer be considered predictable. And that may well be true for the nation as a whole.

To appreciate how this has come about in recent years, and how it affects the youth, one must understand some of the changes which a few Labor Department statistics easily reveal. For example, when the Democratic party first captured the overwhelming support of the unions in the twenties and thirties, it must be remembered that labor was of a special kind. It was "production"-type labor, in which men and women suffered great burdens and had little hope of exercising a political voice. The nation was in the throes of an industrial recovery, and the goal of production (especially during the war) characterized the great moral contribution of the workingman. Today, however, the nature of labor has changed enormously. In fact, there are only twenty-eight million Americans who are involved in the production of "goods," both agricultural and manufactured, while forty-six million people provide the services. Increasingly, most of what is produced comes from beyond our large cities, while the vast majority of services are located within the cities. This means that work is rapidly becoming service-dominated and not production-dominated. The most crippling strikes today are not in plants and factories. They are among teachers, firemen, policemen, and sanitation workers. In other words, the service sector controls the union role once so heavily limited to the production-type unions. Thus, no longer can work be defined as something produced. Work now is defined as one man's service to another, usually managed through the local political and governmental controls. The issues are not management versus labor any longer, they are labor versus government.

One of the chief "fallouts" of this peculiar shift in the nature of work is the effect it has on the meaning of work to the individual. Without a doubt, most public services are dominated by men and women who continue to think of their work in the classic work-ethic sense of production. To these people, morality is circumscribed by the work-income rationalization of "an honest day's work for an honest dollar." Unfortunately, they do not realize that the fastest growing segment of the service industry is the clerical workers. Seventeen percent of the entire work force is composed of those in clerical positions, and when we add to this the fact that more women have entered the labor force in the past twenty-five years than men, we get another image of how the labor force has changed. Characteristic of this growing part of the work force is the rapid turnover in jobs. There is an "ad hoc" character to much labor in this country today. And a great deal of it typifies work in our cities. In other words, it is impossible to claim that most workers today actually belong to the institutions for which they work, except that the greatest employer of them all is the federal government. Coupled with the service-type jobs in the cities, where workers labor for the local governments, the overwhelming fact is that the vast majority of Americans work for the public sector. And the political significance of that fact is inescapable.

Most young people, on the other hand, readily accept the concept of selling one's services instead of belonging to the system. It gives them the personal freedom to do with their lives what they like. This is especially true of the upper-middle-class youth, who only work part-time anyway. The lower-middle-class youth, who normally take jobs instead of attending college, are naturally more conservative than their more affluent peers, but they do take notice of the freedom which their peers demand, and it seems to be quite contagious. We have yet, however, to see how effective this influence will be in the future.

Socially, and ultimately politically, the narcissism of the affluent youth is affecting the meaning of work. Increasingly, the young see work not as a moral condition which defines the nature of man but as a means to an end. In this sense, there are very large numbers of young people who work for government and industry but who do not consider themselves as a part of government or industry. To whatever degree their narcissism dictates personal goals of gratification and satisfaction, to that same degree are they motivated to work. The criticism that most affluent youngsters are parasites on the economy totally misses the point. In a mass culture such as ours, where much work is fabricated in order to justify a salary, where employment by the government has had to replace the diminishing need for workers in production-type industries, it is impossible to define what kind of work is parasitic and what kind is productive. In fact, it would be far more meaningful to say that young people who work only when they have the need to do so have made a remarkable adaptation to the economic scene in urban America. Not only do they not have to belong, through jobs and salaries, to the governmental and industrial system, the system really doesn't need them. "Doing your thing" is fast becoming a significant way of coping with the job scene, as everyone knows who has changed jobs more than a few times in his life.

The question of a parasitic drain on the economy must not be dropped, however, because far too many adults, having been conditioned by the older morality of work, react negatively to the wrong sources of political and economic difficulty. Rising school budgets and the growing need for greater welfare assistance are not parasitic in nature. But since such economic and political issues as these involve young people and the poor minorities, job-oriented adults tend to assume that these are major limitations on the economy. Actually, the greatest parasite in the political and economic sphere is the federal government itself. But since most Americans are hired by the government, and most adults find it very hard to criticize their government seriously, the question is begged.

A few more Labor Department statistics, however, show how misplaced this fear and hostility toward the poor and the youth have become. And these statistics also paint a new picture of the national political structure, which itself reveals a fundamental change in the social scene. For example, in the 1970 national census, experts were amazed to discover how the population had seemed to shift dramatically to the eastern, western, and southern boundaries of the country. From Boston through Florida to Texas and up throughout the state of California, the demographic picture of the nation was startling. But had one compared this population picture with certain economic and employment figures, the consequences of this change might have proved to be even more remarkable. It is no accident that these regions of the country should now become so populated. One out of every six jobs and one out of every five dollars are generated in just three states — Florida, Texas, and California — the direct and indirect results of the space industries or the military-industrial complex. In fact, one out of every three engineers lives and works in California alone. And these people work for the government. Economically, an enormous part of this work and production cannot be labeled as anything but parasitic. The addition to the national economy of such labor goes no further than the next year, that is, only in terms of the salaries of those paid by the government and its industries. The actual production of a gigantic portion of their labor is into nonconsumable hardware and nonproductive services. Consequently, if hard-working Americans want to know where their tax dollars are going, let them get it straight. They are not going to the poor and the blacks, nor to the youth who do not work for the system. They are going to the governmental system itself. And since that system hires most working people, who is going to bite the hand that feeds them?

In effect, what all of this means is that we have succeeded so well in the area of traditional production of goods that we have been able to create a completely useless sector in the national economy. And every historical economic theory has been violated in the process. Government industry now has to invent ways to spend the federal treasury (the C5A, the supersonic jet, the ABM, etc.). And since there exists a manpower force of scientists, technicians, and managers perpetuating this process, almost half the federal treasury cannot be pumped back into the growth needs of the economy. That is the true meaning of a parasitic drain on the economy. The young people who learn how to "do their thing" in such an economy as this are political only insofar as they remain free from the constraints which inhibit criticism of such a system. The real political effects of their freedom from immediate involvement in the system cannot help but have greater impact as more of them come upon the scene.

Some political analysts, however, have recently remarked that the young cannot expect to have a direct effect on the political system because the voting age average remains somewhere over forty years of age. And even if the eighteen-year-olds get the vote throughout the country, the balance will not change drastically. But what these experts overlook is the fact that nearly half the population now is twenty-five years of age and younger and a third of the population is fifteen years old and under. In terms of education, a traditionally important criterion for political analysis, there are some fifty-eight million Americans between the ages of three and thirty-four who attend school full time. And more than seven million of these citizens are in college. If one thinks that young people will not have a direct impact on the political system, he had better look again.

In the past, another barometer of political significance was manpower shortages. Ironically, we do have a manpower shortage of a type. We need more people with technical skills. We can't get our cars or television sets or plumbing fixed when we need it. And the union resistance to solving this problem is inexcusable. But characteristic of our adopted goals in the fifties, and our usual lack of foresight (not to mention racism), we have continued to let this segment of the economy dwindle. Thus, when we break down the real manpower figures which the Labor Department presents each year, we find that as of 1969 the "generation gap" can be measured in actual manpower terms. Those from sixteen to twenty-four years of age comprise forty-seven percent of the national manpower, while those forty-four years old and over make up forty-one percent. Once again, the parent generation and the youth stand on opposite ends of the spectrum. Those between the ages of twenty-five and thirty-four make up only thirteen percent, and the Depression babies between the ages of thirty-five and forty-four are overemployed. Statistically, they don't exist. They comprise what the Labor Department measures as minus one percent. To put it bluntly, there is no one in the middle of this manpower age range to fill the top jobs when the older generation steps down. The youngsters are all that is left!

Now for those who wonder how widespread this upper-middle-class environment is, from which the Woodstock generation comes, let them look at one final set of Labor Department figures. In 1969, for the first time in history there were more professionals than all skilled labor combined. Similarly, there has been a shift to white-collar from blue-collar workers ever since 1952. Today's parent generation is an educated generation. The average worker has more than a high school degree, and the average professional has spent seventeen years in school, or the equivalent of a Master's degree! We are, in fact, a society of middle-aged managers and professionals rearing an enormous generation of young aristocrats, as Paul Goodman calls them. And we have provided most of them with the option of not having to earn a living in the traditional manner. Consequently, since much of our political system has been based upon the manageability of a job-conscious voting public, handing out political favors to those who can deliver the votes, this new structure of manpower ought to tell us something about the future effectiveness of our existing political system.

Doubtless, the less the young are involved in the political-economic process, the more visible becomes the self-sustaining character of the adult establishment. When a senior Southern Senator who is chairman of the Armed Services Committee is given an award at a military-industrial banquet, the immorality of it all immediately strikes the young. Or when the President receives a religious heritage award by a foundation which is supported by one of his most munificent campaign contributors it seems a bit ridiculous. Power suddenly becomes naked in a mass culture, where the banality of such absurd rituals takes place in the public eye. And the young, who have automatically received all the traditional economic rewards of the system by reason of their middle-class existence, do not look upon such power and self-congratulation with much sympathy. What the politicians don't understand is that economic rewards, when sustained for a long enough period inevitably lead to self-determined and self-motivated citizens, not predictable and faithful voters.

How long the government-based political system can be maintained is a real question to consider. Today's parents have unwittingly constructed an automatically functioning system composed of all those who presently benefit and participate in this governmental superstructure. In part, that is why Richard Nixon wasn't worried about not getting the traditional support of the large industrial states in the East. The new America, created by government's contracting prowess, wields the power now. It is locked into the very fabric of the government's existing priorities and programs. At the same time, this new constituency is not really a political party force at all. It is a fabrication of the economic system which the government has created over the years. It is conservative only insofar as it supports the continuation of similar policies. Consequently, it is not so much whether one works for or supports the government which determines one's political loyalties. It is whether or not one feels one "belongs" to the governmental empire. And if the parents who belong to this empire cannot free themselves politically, perhaps their children can. Political loyalties today are far too tenuous for one to assume a smooth continuation of the same old process indefinitely.

For such reasons as these, therefore, it is particularly pointless for the adults to dwell upon the radical fringes of the
youth movement. For every time the establishment seeks to
repress the radicals, it creates more of them. SDS learned long
before the adult establishment did that repression is their best
instrument for gaining support. Most youngsters, however,
couldn't care less about the violent, Marxist-type radicals. The
real revolution has no leaders, unless the press and the adults
insist on creating them. The true roots of the revolution are to
be found in a society which has taught its young the values of
democracy and then set them free to demand that the system
function accordingly. The revolution stems from a growing
generation of narcissistically oriented individuals who demand
the freedom to "do their thing" and who ironically are free to
practice such an ethic. The revolution is not led by young
New York Jewish radicals, picking up the flag of socialism
their parents dropped. It is universal and it reaches into the
homes of conservative Midwestern parents, Southern racists,
and establishment liberals.

The concept of "street theater" which Abbie Hoffman and
his codefendants sought to describe to Judge Julius Hoffman in
the trial of the Chicago Seven, was not politics in the conventional sense of the word. It was political and social ridicule, the
drama of our absurd political and social situation acted out. To
call it "conspiracy" is to label it with a term which can only be
translated as political repression. It is a blind lashing out at
youth in general, seeking to find the heart of the movement but
only blundering and misunderstanding what is truly happening
politically.

Once again, the young understand this mass culture better
than most adults. It makes no difference to them on which side
of the television screen one sits. It is a society of total involvement, as McLuhan pointed out. The Woodstock generation is
everywhere. And when the young take to the streets or hold
their festivals or collect in their communes, they are acting out
their roles in this artificial culture, seeking to legitimize themselves as human beings with human emotions. They know that

the political consequences of their actions are determined by the effect they have on society. They do not want to take over the political system, they simply want to embarrass, startle, and disturb the older generation into a realization that they are what's happening to the world.

Such behavior probably will never be mobilized into an alternative political force. It runs counter to the dynamics of their own narcissism and presupposes a kind of group psychology which is quite foreign to most of them. They are all radicals and revolutionaries, but not in the sense that the Attorney General's Office would define. They are radicals because there is no way they can "fit into" the existing social and political system without altering it drastically. They are revolutionaries because their behavior is already beginning to change the very fabric of values which govern this society. It is not their politics but their freedom from the system that threatens us. That's what they mean when they say "all power to the people."

10

DRUGS: HOLY
COMMUNION WITH
CHEMISTRY

Without a doubt, the widespread and increasing use of drugs has caused more alarm among adults than any other activity of the younger generation. In many ways the open use of marijuana, and in a growing number of cases the experimentation with stronger or "harder" drugs, has fomented a reaction among adults which puzzles young people more than it frightens them. For if one is candid about the degree to which all manner of drugs are readily available to everyone, or even more commonly, how often adults themselves rely upon the variety of drugs which induce highs and lows, depressions and mania, compensation and escape, one cannot help but recognize the fact that drugs are an everyday part of our lives. The young have grown up in a culture which has an enormously high dependency upon drugs of all types. And to the question which is often asked: "Historically, how unique is this pattern of drug use today?" the answer is that it is not very unique at all. The real question has to do with the meaning of drug use and the role which drugs play in determining human emotions.

Any psychologist knows that every civilization has always relied upon a variety of religiously condoned means by which the individual can be brought into the cultic life of the race or tribe. In many cases drugs themselves were used to elicit particular emotions and spiritual experiences, which would in turn reinforce the individual's wish to belong to or participate in the mystic body of the group. And even in those cultures, such as our own Puritan ancestors, the psychobiological effects of certain religions and authoritative pressures could readily induce similar effects, even when the actual use of external drugs was avoided or was unknown. The truth of the matter is, man is a composite of chemicals, all functioning together in such a way as to result in a wide variety of emotions, experiences, and behavior.

From a clinical point of view, even psychiatrists, pathologists, and pharmacologists are not certain as to what constitutes a "normal" chemical balance within any given human being. This is one of the reasons why many psychiatrists have recently raised serious questions about such things as the origin of psychosis, homosexuality, characterological defects, and related forms of "pathology." In fact, there does seem to be some evidence that many so-called pathological defects are the result of chemical factors in the hereditary line of the individual, in his genetic structure, or even within his own hormone balance. For example, it might just be possible that certain homosexuals are individuals with a different hormone balance than most other people who have a "normal" ratio of male and female hormones. It also might be possible that many psychotics are individuals with a different chemical balance or genetic structure in their systems. And recently, experts in the field of public health have reminded us that health, food, and dietary practices among the poor can result in serious cases of brain deficiency among the very young. In fact, it is possible that many defective character traits are related to dietary, chemical, and genetic deficiencies. In any event, it is clear that we do not have all the information we need to know what the real differences are between health and pathology.

At the heart of the problem lies an ancient philosophical dilemma concerning the definition of man himself. Where does the individual end and the rest of the universe begin? What are the true boundaries between the individual and the biosphere from which he comes? And the truth of the matter is, we don't really know the answer. We know that each individual has a definite link with his own genetic past, his so-called family tree. He even has a link with the future in his own children, who carry the genes and chromosomes which mother and father pass on. But beyond this we do not know how to understand the psychological aspects of the individual's relationship with the world around him. How much is man a part of the biosphere, and how much is he a solitary individual, unique and without an identical pattern?

Konrad Lorenz has spent years studying the problems of aggression, patterns of behavior, and related phenomena in lower forms of life; and he implies in his book *On Aggression* that the laws which seem to govern animal life probably have some effect on man himself, especially when it comes to instinctual or biological patterns which directly link the human race with the lower forms of life. Some of the facts are quite clear: man does have a patterning relationship to the laws which govern all life forms. There is such a thing as the individual fish, monkey, or dog, but it is probably also true that identity for such lifeforms is strongly determined by the individual animal's membership within his species. Consequently, when we speak of the psychology of a fish, monkey, or dog, it is obvious that we are talking about a phenomenon which involves the individual's membership within his species.

And yet, far from all this being taken as an argument for historical or biological determinism in the human species, there is something else far more important at stake here. The argument which is presently taking place between the "determinists" and the "environmentalists" only clouds the picture. The real problem is, how does genetic predisposition become altered by environmental pressures, and how is environmental influence diminished by genetic determinism? In other words, is it possible for a pattern of genetic factors to be changed by an environment which introduces to the individual organism a

new set of experiences? Can genetic patterns be made powerless by a set of experiences which change the historical continuity of human adaptation? And on the other hand, is it possible for certain genetic factors to affect the way in which the
individual copes or reacts to his environment?

One of the subjects which this debate has centered around is
the problem of aggression. Some anthropologists have taken
the view that aggression is a biologically determined characteristic of the human organism. It explains man's proclivity for
war and bloodshed. But other anthropologists have insisted that
such arguments ignore other factors of influence, namely, that
man has not always been an aggressive creature and that man is
a highly adaptable being, capable of reorienting himself to totally unique and different experiences. Unfortunately, the historical determinists overlook the fact that each individual
human organism can adapt to vast ranges of environmental
change.

Assuming, as most geneticists do, that the human species has
a wide variety of genetic patterns which ultimately can determine the behavior of individuals, then it follows that each individual human being can and will adapt to the environment he
finds himself within, and thus become affected by the genetic
pattern most suited to that environment. If war, scarcity, deprivation, and fear characterize his environment, obviously
patterns of aggression can more easily come into play. If, however, security, plenty, gratification, and contentment dominate
the individual's life, then aggression may well be turned into
playfulness, eroticism, and experimentation. In any case, there
are no behaviorists, determinists, or environmentalists who
know how to generalize on such matters as these, because the
human environment has become so complex. Obviously, the
real danger lies in the assumption that one pattern exists within
our environment to the exclusion of another. In other words, a
scientist working for the Pentagon can make an argument for
man's natural aggression, rationalizing the mobilization of manpower to fight wars, by asserting man's basic aggression as a
biological fact of existence. Similarly, if another scientist seeks

to argue that war has become insane and self-destructive, all he needs to do is assert that man also has a genetic pattern of peacefulness and adaptability which makes it possible for aggression to be put to more creative uses. In both cases, science is used for political or propaganda purposes.

In our society young people, are growing up in one environment, while the rest of the world continues to live in another. And if aggression is suitable and consistent with the everyday reality of other people's lives, it does not follow that it must be as prevalent in the lives of those who have known nothing but gratification, security, and narcissistic self-expression. In fact, it is more than possible that young people, especially those from affluent surroundings, have become oriented to reality by being environmentally influenced by patterns which are different from those of most other human beings. This is where the phenomenon of confirmed infantile narcissism comes into play. Let us stay with the nature of aggression for a moment, to see how narcissism affects the nature of aggression, as opposed to the way repressed narcissism affects aggressive behavior.

For the secure and loved child, aggression is nothing more than mental or psychic energy flowing out from the individual narcissistic ego, seeking to expand the cathexis of the self to the external world. Out of that security, the child seeks to discover and derive an order from his universe in order to expand his narcissistic-ego boundary lines. But instead of discovering that external reality is hostile, ungratifying, and punishing, the narcissistic child learns that it can be an even greater source of pleasure and fulfillment of the self. His desire, therefore, to play with or examine that reality is thus greatly heightened, especially if he receives direct gratification from developing the necessary skills to make that reality do what he wants it to. What this means, therefore, is that his normal aggression is increasingly turned into ego-oriented abilities to affect external reality. And as a result, his narcissistic view of the external world is reinforced. He actually sees reality as belonging to him, not to others who take it away from him or deprive him of it.

The more conventional child has a much different introduction to external reality, and usually at a very early age. For as soon as the society of scarcity (the predominant reality for most human beings) begins to invade this child's narcissistic world, he resists by expressing his aggression, hostility, and fear. Most civilizations of the world are prepared to cope with this type of reaction. Instead of simply rejecting the child's aggression, they ritualize, manage, and adapt it for the purposes of maintaining the social order. Aggression is thus condoned under certain prescribed modes, and the individual child is taught the skills of sublimation, namely, work, performance, war, marital fidelity, submission to authority, and group behavior patterns. As a result, this latter child comes to view reality in the terms dictated by his tribe, culture, or society. It is not his universe, it is his group's universe. And his aggression is no longer his own, it has been captured by his group. Thus, since his aggression is not only condoned by his group or society but indeed reinforced (teaching him the values of competition, loyalty, overexaggerated definitions of male and female identity, and similar notions), such a child begins to feel that his entire security is dependent upon the definitions of selfhood which the group or society dictates. He has thus become aggressive, because the society requires it. And when his aggression is turned against the society, he is considered sick, antisocial, and/or immature, i.e., fixated at the infantile stage of narcissism and having a highly unsocial perspective toward reality. But when one represses such narcissism, he is considered an asset to the society.

Very similar to this problem of aggression in these two types of early childhood development is the role of drug use. To the socially conscious individual, the one who has his emotional security rooted in the society to which he belongs, drug use may or may not be considered acceptable, depending upon the norms of the culture. In our society, only certain drugs are condoned by social norms. These include alcohol, cigarettes, coffee and tea, plus a wide list of prescribed medications for the relief of certain symptoms. At the very heart of most of these socially approved uses of drugs is the notion that they serve to "benefit" or slightly alter the individual's feelings. They are used to relax, deaden certain emotions, heighten others, or alter the "normal" patterns of feelings which accompany our everyday activities. And yet, beneath all these uses of drugs is the old Puritanical assumption that man must not inject into his system any "foreign" substance that might interfere with his normal functioning. This is why those religious sects which are particularly "American" in their value structure, such as the Mormons, Seventh Day Adventists, and other fundamentalist groups, adhere to the strictest prohibitions against all drug use. As a rule, they do not accept the fact that man himself is a chemically structured being, as are all life forms. Consequently, it is forbidden to interfere with God's creation.

But to assume that these religions of total abstinence do not rely upon the "spiritually"-induced results of prayer, meditation, conversion, belief, and even abstinence itself is to forget that man's chemistry can be altered by many means. If this were not the case, psychosomatic medicine would not exist. The mind can alter the chemical structure of the body, and vice versa. Ironically, this is what Billy Graham was saying to a group of students at Berkeley a few years ago when he told them that Jesus was a better "trip" than LSD. Obviously, Dr. Graham was not trying to assert that Christ was a drug with the same effects as hard drugs. Behind his homiletical trick was the same attempt to replace drugs with religion that the Salvation Army has been using with alcoholics for years. And yet, Billy Graham was much closer to the truth than he realized. Religious behavior has had a druglike effect on believers for countless centuries. One does not have to partake of the "sacred mushroom" or the Oriental opiate in order to achieve the beatific vision. It can be done with prolonged abstinence, denial of honest emotions, repression of erotic feelings, ritualized behavior, and all the practices which usually characterize the fanatic's life. What we tend to forget in this society is that we have inherited Dr. Graham's morality, or better yet, that he represents the modern version of the Puritanical ethic. As a culture, we have never reached the point where we could consciously condone the use of drugs in order to achieve a "spiritual" result.

This country has a history of drug use and misuse going back well into the nineteenth century when millions of our older citizens became "hooked" on the tonics and treatments of the friendly local vendor. Opium addiction was very common among these citizens, since it was the one drug which seemed to satisfy the needs of older or lonely people, whom society had denied the more basic pleasures of sex and eroticism. The spinster aunt who seemed a bit "out of it" or peculiar, was still loved and tolerated. But she was a real-life addict. Fortunately, however, society was still simple enough for such behavior to be accepted — the side effects could be submerged under the tightly female family structure. Today, the story is quite different. The demise of the large family and the growth of our artificial mass culture mean that we have to "invent" social institutions to handle what the society used to absorb rather easily. Widespread use of alcohol among adults today — our first problem created by the loss of traditional family-oriented communities — was followed by other drug misuse such as sleeping pills, tranquilizers, and pep pills. And it was into this kind of drug culture most of our children have been born.

In a sense, drug use has developed in this country for the specific purpose of alleviating the burden of our Puritanical consciences. And the more hectic the pace of our lives has grown, the more we have searched for means to relieve ourselves of this burden. In fact, it was the adult generation of today which introduced the ubiquitous use of drugs. What the kids have done is to take our drug culture seriously and to seek ways whereby drugs can induce better "highs" and more meaningful experiences. If we have to have a reason for the increasing use of drugs among the young, nothing could better serve to give us an answer than the behavior of most adults. Unfortunately, however, that doesn't really tell us very much about the role which drugs play in the lives of the young. But since most of the young people, outside the ghetto, who have gone beyond experimenting with drugs come from our more affluent homes, we must turn to the phenomenon of narcissism once again. Most white young people who come from lower-class working homes never really get much beyond experimentation with drugs. It is the narcissistically oriented youth from affluent America that have taken the greatest steps into the unknown of drug use.

All that we have said up to this point is a preface to what must now be said about the drug culture among the young today. For even as sex, dress, music, and dance are forms of narcissistic behavior, drug use is about the most narcissistic activity available. For if one can appreciate that the chief characteristic of narcissism is nondifferentiation of the self from the world, then it is clear that drugs serve as perfect instruments to heighten the narcissistic view of reality. But this is also why it is very important to understand that nondifferentiation of the self from external reality leads one to believe that ego boundary lines are entirely relative. They can be as great as the universe or as limited as the skin on one's body. In fact, many young people have often reported that their "trips" gave them feelings of becoming one with the universe, meeting God, or becoming swallowed up in the womb of the earth. In any case, what most of these young people were searching for was an experience which could confirm their own narcissistic wish to "be" the center of the universe.

Significantly, most hippies have begun to develop a series of interpretations of reality which strongly conform to the narcissistic view of the self. God is called an "energy force," while emotions such as selfishness, possessiveness, sentimentality, and romance are called "ego trips." The juxtaposition of such concepts as these is really quite interesting. On the one hand, God is turned into a life force which serves to cement the universe together through particular mystic or psychic experiences, while "ego trips" are those emotions in civilized man that prohibit the individual from attaining union with the true laws of

God. Consequently, one must surrender his "ego" or self and seek to join the realm of God's Being. And any sets of emotions or thoughts which inhibit such an attempt are considered "hangups."

The truly peculiar aspect of this particular attitude toward the spiritual life is that it completely reverses the traditional experience of "surrender to God's will." In the past, denial of the self has been meaningful only within a culture of poverty, where the group's requirements for individual submission to authority were reinforced by the religious values which denied the individual any selfhood apart from the sacred group. In the narcissistic world, however, one begins with the assumption that he is already at union with God and that it has been society which has caused him to become alienated from God. Therefore, he tends to interpret the word "ego" as self-assertion, defensiveness, and aggression, meaning those emotions which society seeks to elicit for society's ends. The truth of the matter is, however, that most hippies are almost total narcissists, oriented to the universe as though they were themselves indistinguishable from the rest of the biosphere. Consequently, they do not really deny their ego feelings, as they claim. Instead, they confirm them by seeking to reach an even greater union with God and nature.

In the mind of the small child, the way by which this narcissism is nurtured is through the use of magical thinking. He wishes for the universe to meet his needs simply through his making demands upon it. He cries for mother's milk and usually gets the attention he demands. He seeks comfort and gratification, and if the nature of the external world is beneficial, he usually receives what he seeks. In the traditional culture of poverty, however, the infant soon learns that reality will not always meet his needs. Consequently, he looks to the leaders of his group to meet his needs, and eventually turns to religion as the magic whereby he can maintain his narcissistic attitude. He then uses prayer and believes that there is a direct connection between himself and the forces in the universe which can eventually meet his needs. And if external reality continues to frustrate him, then religion takes on even more significance as a primary source of compensation for his unmet needs. Inevitably, the reality of scarcity teaches the traditional child that he cannot have all that he desires. Religion must therefore meet the needs the real world cannot.

In the culture of affluence, the exact opposite tends to occur. Rather than external reality denying the individual child's needs, he finds higher and higher levels of gratification. As a result, his narcissistic ego expands and becomes strengthened. And this is where the role of drugs comes into play. For as soon as the narcissistic youngster discovers that the real world is not what he had come to believe it was in his earlier childhood, and that there are people trying to manipulate his life, his choices, his destiny, and his values, he turns to the nonsanctioned means of narcissistic "liberation" which drugs, especially hallucinogenic drugs, can give him. He thus strives to achieve a direct union with God and the higher laws of God, and maintains his narcissism in spite of the demands which the real world places upon him. Significantly, there are a great many religious values and beliefs which reinforce his narcissistic interpretation of ultimate reality. And most of these are Oriental beliefs, teaching surrender of the socially determined self to the disciplines of the spirit, ultimately seeking union with the true forces of the universe. One finds such concepts in the books *I Ching,* the *Bhagavad Gita,* and any number of source books which teach the arts of meditation and discipline as well as the "secrets" of the universe.

What obviously puzzles a great many adults about this growing interest among the young in Oriental religion and mysticism is their blatant admission that only religious experiences can help man achieve what he needs and longs for in this life. To a great many sophisticated adults, this seems to be a kind of regression into the primitive past, rather than a normal advance into the postreligious values of today. What most adults do not seem to understand is that religion in this country has come a very long way from what the young mean when they use the designation "religious." As we tried to point out in the chapter on Puritan secularism, our religious heritage is far more secularist than religious, whereas Oriental religions teach a meaning to life that secularism cannot even begin to communicate. The basis for this interest in Oriental religion is not conversion to the Oriental culture. Only those Oriental values and practices which enhance the narcissistic view of reality are sought. And if we add to this the fact that most of those youngsters who conscientiously pursue the meaning of Oriental mysticism are also highly self-actualizing individuals, then it becomes apparent that what they are seeking is an extension of our own secularism. For secularism is the logical extension of Protestantism, while mysticism, self-development, fulfillment, and harmony with the forces of ultimate being are the logical extension of secularism. If we return to Maslow's needs-hierarchy for a moment, we can get some idea how this transition takes place. On the survival end of the spectrum we find the most primitive of religions, namely, animism. The next step toward a security-based religion leads to the tribalized cults of family and clan, while the belonging stage begins to abstract the group life and thus develops organized religion, wherein the concept of "membership" takes on great significance. The next stage appeals to the individual member and teaches him that his salvation (esteem or self-understanding) is rooted in his direct relationship with God, while the final stage teaches that organized religion is unnecessary and that it is totally up to the individual to develop himself, to become in tune with the powers of the universe. In abstract form the scale looks like this:

Survival	Security	Belonging	Esteem	Self-Actualization
Animism	Tribalism	Organized Religion Roman Catholicism	Personalism Protestantism	Narcissism and Mysticism

Obviously, there is a certain amount of overlapping in this process. And one can also find various aspects of other stages within any one particular stage. For example, Catholicism has a certain amount of animism, especially in those cultures where the Church developed a syncretistic approach to worship as in Latin America, for example. And Protestantism has definite links with the Catholic past. Narcissistic mysticism, however, can be found only in the singular individual who has been reared to believe that the universe revolves around him. He can easily adopt the symbols of any other religion, i.e., the cross of Christ, the amulet of animism, the rituals of mysticism, and the self-disciplines of Kindo or Buddhism. But he cannot return to the total world-view of any previous stage as though it were his own. He can only borrow elements from the past in order to add to his interpretations of the spiritual life. But then, this is what makes his view of the spiritual life so narcissistic: it has no sense of historical continuity. Christ, Buddha, Gandhi, and whoever happens to fit into the realm of wise men or prophets are all contemporaries in a world of eternity. They all say the same things.

Consequently, as the narcissistically oriented young hippie seeks to achieve the same visions of truth as those have done in the past, he relies upon drugs to aid him in the process. As a result, it becomes clear that such a person does not conceive of drug use as unnatural or antisocial. He only takes it, along with the rest of modern technology, as a means to achieve the same age-old goal of union with God. In fact, there are many young people who have taken drugs for "spiritual" purposes who have since given them up for more meditative means of achieving the same ends. But in any case, the use or nonuse of drugs can be understood as options. They are not necessarily "escape mechanisms" used to avoid the painful realities the rest of us must face. They are seen as natural or technological by-products of nature which can serve to reinforce the narcissistic ego's view of reality.

And yet, it remains quite obvious that the hippie culture does not encompass the entire younger generation. Nor is it true that all young people use drugs for "spiritual" ends. There is far more experimentation with drugs than there is a complete adoption of drugs as a part of one's total "life-style." What are we to conclude from this fact? Is drug use a means of escape from reality for everyone else? Is it an attempt to reach certain feeling levels which normal consciousness cannot achieve? Or is it simply normal adolescent curiosity about the forbidden?

Whatever drug experimentation may mean for most young people, it must be made clear that most youngsters never go much beyond marijuana or maybe a single experience of some other drug. But in any case, there is an enormous difference between the motivation for taking drugs in the ghetto and taking them in the more comfortable surroundings of modern suburbia. By and large, most young blacks and poor whites who take drugs do so in order to anesthetize themselves against the everyday horrors of ghetto existence. It may begin as experimentation. But anyone who works in narcotic rehabilitation centers in our large cities will insist that the lure of drugs is directly linked with the desire to escape from reality.

In our more affluent communities, however, the role of drugs cannot be so easily designated. This is because many of the values which the hippies and radicals have passed on to their younger brothers and sisters often seem far more viable and exciting than the values adults tend to espouse. As a result, drugs take on for many high school and even junior high school youngsters a romantic significance which is linked to a very deep desire to discover for oneself the wide variety of emotions and experiences that can come to the narcissistic youngster. In fact, this is probably how the youth culture tends to grow. The older adolescents set some of the patterns for self-expression and discovery, while the younger ones begin through the normal channels of copying their older peers. After a while, however, the younger adolescents come into their own and then use drugs for their own personal ends. This means that they have joined the youth culture, but since joining the youth culture also demands that they express or disclose themselves, it doesn't tend to have the traditional characteristics of group behavior. One joins the youth culture in order to become liberated from the suburban culture of one's parents. But what it means to belong to the youth culture, remains something for the individual youngster to define for himself.

Obviously, a certain amount of experimentation with drugs stems from a curiosity about that which is forbidden. But it is very naïve of parents to assume that this is the major motivation for taking drugs. The fact is that drug use is condoned by the very culture which means the most to young people, namely, the youth culture. It determines too many important values, attitudes, and choices as compared to what the adult world offers. And at the very heart of the youth culture is the one value which agrees with the predisposition of youngsters anyway, namely, use the world that is available to you to express yourself. Use its technology, its plenty, its pleasures, and its choices. In other words, do with the affluence what your parents can only partly do. Use it, play with it, become creative with it, and ultimately find meaning beyond it all.

Youngsters who experiment with such drugs as "pot" are trying to develop their own rituals, life-styles, and behavior patterns which can enhance the meaning and pleasures of life. To insist automatically that they are doing nothing more than avoiding the realities of the world is to overlook the fact that they do not actually want to cope with those realities, nor do they feel the need to do so. One does not grow up in a world where he can get almost anything he desires and then suddenly become socially performance-oriented. He tends to continue to believe that the world is available to him and that those who are trying to manage things for him are illegitimate beings. Only a society which continues to be permissive about the individual's use of his or her own body and mind is considered a viable society. To such a person; anything short of that kind of world borders on fascism.

Obviously, when one experiences the feelings which a high

on pot or LSD can give, he isn't likely to want to return to the limited rewards of social conformity. He has instead begun to approach feelings which carry him far beyond the normal awareness, perspectives, and attitudes of social existence. He has found a confirmation of his basic narcissistic point of view, and he cannot easily give that up if the rewards are anything less. It would be foolish, however, to assume that there is no "escape" value in the uses of drugs for young people. For in many ways, their desires for "sanctuary" in a world that imposes enormous demands and limitations upon those who are approaching adulthood is quite logical. It's like hanging on to their narcissism through the use of drugs, dance, sex, dress, and a host of related matters while they confront the fact that adulthood continues to await them.

The true irony, however, is that adulthood is no longer the reward for a faithful, obedient, and normal childhood. We have reversed the process. And by giving the children of affluent America the rewards of the land, we then make them pay for it when they become adults. Instead of the traditional process of delayed gratification, repressed narcissism, conformity, competition ultimately leading to the pleasures of adulthood, i.e., sex in marriage, money, property, position, recognition and responsibility for the self, we have reared a generation which has all these factors readily available to them and which isn't about to pay for them in some kind of conformity to the society's demands.

Beneath this irony lies the question of whether or not it is possible for the next generation to become adults while continuing to maintain a high degree of narcissism as their perspective toward life. Actually, much of the answer to this question will rest with the ability of the existing adult generation to cope with the increasing effects of narcissistic values and behavior on the society as a whole. If, for example, the present fear and repression which characterizes so many adults' attitudes toward drug use can be changed, and such things as marijuana and LSD can be studied, and perhaps legalized, then it is

possible that certain forms of narcissistic behavior can be accepted, and the process of transition from childhood to adulthood will be ameliorated. Whatever happens, however, the
responsibility of the adult world is quite clear. We must find
out what the effects of drug use are, if for no other reason than
providing the younger generation with better information
about the possible consequences of further drug use. No civilization can long last with the complex use of permissiveness and
repression, as is the case in our culture. Either we become a
society committed to greater personal freedoms for the individual, placing the responsibility for whatever happens to the
individual solely upon his own shoulders, or we return to some
Puritanical society with all of the powers of guilt, deprivation,
and repression.

The responsibility which this places upon the adult community may well prove to be the greatest single service adults can
offer to the young. To date, youngsters remain highly suspicious of adult "wisdom" regarding drug use. Kids listen to
"rock" musicians instead of physicians and authorities; they are
convinced adults would rather hand out propaganda than facts.
But the time has come when morality, no matter how well in-
tentioned, must be replaced with facts. And adults are going to
have to accept those facts as well. If scientists tell us that marijuana is less harmful than alcohol and cigarettes, and that there
are no serious side effects, then adults will have to accept the
consequences of such data. If, however, it is clearly proven
that LSD, speed, and related artificial drugs produce serious
side effects, or that heroin does not cause addiction after one or
two uses, then such facts will have to become common knowledge. The time has come when the "conspiracy of silence"
cannot only not be tolerated any longer, but must be rejected
once and for all.

In any case, we cannot tolerate as a society the illusions and
fears upon which so much past morality has been based. Our
children are too sophisticated. In this light, it is our responsibility first of all to insist upon the facts, then insist that the facts

be made public, and finally teach our children that our greatest respect is for the truth. Obviously that means that we shall have to summon more courage than we have yet shown. But, in the final analysis, we really don't have much choice.

11

MUSIC AND DANCE: THE RITUALS OF NARCISSISM

There have been three distinct sources of influence upon the present rock and roll styles, all of which converged during the late fifties and early sixties. The first was the new country style of people like Elvis Presley, with his distinctively male gyrations. The second came from the black culture, or what has become known as "soul music." And the third came from the message-laden songs of "folk music," typical of Pete Seeger and Peter, Paul, and Mary. Most of today's young people, especially those in college, joke about the music and dance styles of the late fifties and early sixties, as though they characterized ancient history. What has actually happened is that the three sources of influence have finally merged into one erotically oriented cultural force. Instead of the lone singer performing sexual antics before a passive crowd, the listeners have taken his role away from him. The songs which are sung are filled with completely explicit erotic meanings, couched in a message for the youngsters to appreciate, while in the dance styles, which have been almost totally created by the blacks, the male and the female participate in what amounts to ritualized lovemaking.

By and large, most young people have lived with their own

newer styles of music and dance long enough for them to look upon the big band era, the jitterbug, the shag, and even the twist as musical forms from another period in history. This is why it is not rare anymore to see a young couple experimenting with some of these older styles at a dance or musical festival. Like the clothes from the past, they are showing that they can take from the past what they want without having to be identified with it.

As a general rule, however, there really are no particular steps today which dictate the proper manner of dancing for the individual or the individual couple. "Doing your thing" has great significance for modern rock and roll dancing. And this oftentimes becomes quite disconcerting to the adults who would like to be "with it" and keep up to date in the proper styles of dance. Most young people, however, are not interested in such peer-group attitudes. They let the music and a few basic steps and movements determine what they will do on the dance floor. This is because they are not really dancing in the traditional sense of ballroom dancing. If anything serves as a kind of model for the newer forms of dance, it is the African and American Indian rituals of nature — i.e., fertility, hunting, and religious rites. But since even these examples are not directly related to the styles of modern dance and music, the fact remains that there really aren't any hard and fast rules or norms.

And yet at the very heart of rock and roll dancing lies the narcissistic dynamics of the lone individual, standing face to face with his or her partner, making movements symbolic of the act of sexual intercourse. Of course, not all youngsters are conscious of participating in a kind of symbolic coitus. Many of them tend to see themselves as expressing themselves, not simply seeking to elicit sexual advances from their partners. The fact that the old "bump and grind" movements which used to be characteristic of the gyrations of an exotic dancer or stripper have been adopted by most younger people today points up how physically erotic the dances are, but it does not necessarily mean that anything conscious or intentional is being communicated. It may or it may not, depending upon the attitudes and desires of the individuals involved.

In a sense, what young people are communicating by such gestures is the belief that they can experience almost any erotic feelings, and make erotic gestures, without having to surrender to the biological end of sexual intercourse. Choice remains at the very heart of their lives, and the actions thus become a means of testing and playfulness, all without having to suffer the supposed consequences of moral surrender to instinctual desires. Because many of them feel a certain degree of freedom in choosing what ultimate actions they wish to experience, the traditional "domino theory" of morality does not apply to their lives. Dancing does not inevitably lead to drinking or to sex with someone under the effects of alcoholic stupor. One takes that step only when and if one wants to. In a sense, dancing and music today are a kind of continual foreplay, not leading to sexual surrender to one's instincts but rather turning life into a kind of ritualized erotic play.

Many parents unfortunately project their own feelings into the young subculture and conclude that if they were to participate in these erotic actions, they would eventually fall prey to their own internal chaotic wishes. And yet, the younger generation is actually demonstrating that the feelings, movements, and normal gestures of the human body are not inevitably under some deep dark forces of the unconscious. They are simply the uses of the body which ultimately remain under the control of the individual himself.

For example, a very popular movement of the body in rock and roll dancing involves gyrating the pelvis so as to simulate the specific action of sexual intercourse. Whether or not any given youngster is conscious of making explicit sexual movements, there is something else happening which ought not be overlooked. In modern studies about the significance of body language and body movements, some investigators have discovered that the inability to express feelings of a sexual nature — namely, by a constraining of the pelvic region — is a typical syndrome of the sexually repressed. In fact, most adults tend to believe that free and open movements of the pelvic region are directly related to explicit wishes for sexual activity. But all that the uninhibited movements of the pelvis mean is that the individual feels relatively free to express that part of himself which is sexual. It does not mean that he is inevitably willing or anxious for any particular sexual involvement to follow. Indeed, expressions of body ego are directly related to the narcissism of the individual. If a young man or woman feels happy and content with his or her own body, then he or she is liable to express feelings which can be directly related to body language. And whereas so many of the physical expressions of rock and roll dancing are explicit, the older gyrations of dance seemed to deny and even disguise erotic and sexual feelings.

Comedians used to joke in the early sixties about the new styles of dance in which the couples did not touch one another. The standard approach was: "I don't see why parents worry about these modern dances. Personally, I would worry when they stop dancing." This relates directly to the fears of adults: namely, that too much is being communicated between couples in rock and roll dancing, inevitably leading to feelings and actions after the tribal ritual is over, which must involve the completion of the act which the dance initiated. Older adults realize that traditional ballroom dancing served to communicate its own limitations. One could touch, even hug one's partner while not really saying anything more about one's intentions, whereas in rock and roll style, the end always seems to be an invitation to sexual union.

It would be foolish to assume that sexual union is being ignored by the young people who participate in rock and roll dancing. To claim that they are not conscious of it, or that they have no interest, is tantamount to saying that they are anesthetized. The major innovation in the feelings and actions of most young people in their various styles of dance is based upon the open admission that sexuality is a part of life. They want to have sexual experiences. Girls want it as well as boys. They feel it is normal and completely healthy. They do not want dancing to serve as a specialized but limited act of touch-

ing. It is as though they are imitating the primitive cultures of
the world, in which the phenomenon of foreplay is turned into
a highly complex and prolonged experience. For the repressed
individual, foreplay is too much a barrier to sexual relief. Many
adult males consider helping the woman achieve complete
pleasure as a necessary burden to be tolerated. And a lot of
women go through life never having experienced a completely
fulfilling sexual involvement. This is due not so much to any
lack of knowledge about male and female psychology but to
the manner by which sexuality is understood in society. Our
civilization has lived for so long with the notion that sex should
be surrounded by restrictions as to person, place, and time that
we have tended to repress or leave undeveloped all the emotions which arise during the day previous to our accepted encounters in the evening.

This means that men and women go through the day with
blinders on, trying to avoid feelings of eroticism and thus
building up within themselves giant barriers to gratification,
which must then be overcome when the socially acceptable
partner is available; whereas, in those primitive cultures where
eroticism is condoned, even encouraged by the traditionally established patterns of erotic play among men and women, the
day is turned into a kind of extended foreplay leading one to
prepare himself for union with his partner in the evening.

Obviously, rock and roll dance and music are far more akin
to this primitive pattern than to our own Western tradition.
This is why the mini skirt, the language, the dance, the drugs,
and the music are all rapidly becoming parts of a prolonged
foreplay, rather than what so many adults fear — namely, a
heightening of erotic desires which inevitably lead to blind
emotional involvements. It simply must be understood that the
freedom of choice about sexual activity makes for an entirely
different type of human being than the one whose repressed
feelings either explode in antisocial actions or cause insurmountable barriers to gratification when the permitted occasions are at hand. For example, a young girl who prepares to go
out on a date and who knows in her own head what she wants

on that date can experience the prolonged event of erotic play as a normal and exciting aspect of the evening's relationship. She does not have to feel as though the dancing were some compensation for more genital wishes. She can choose what she wants, develop a mental economy, and achieve her desired end. But in no case is it inevitable that she must go to bed with her date because she has been seduced by the sounds, movements, and feelings of the dance.

It does not follow that all girls and boys today are more conscious and healthy about their erotic and sexual desires than were their parents a generation ago. But the emotional, intellectual, and social climate of the younger generation's subculture is different. For instead of the culture presenting classic situations and experiences of ritualized repression, the young today find enormous support from their peers in discovering their own independence and self-expression. The degree of honesty about feelings, desires, fears, and needs characteristic of the younger generation is quite remarkable when compared to previous generations, making the young today far more mature than most adults were when they were the same age.

Conventional definitions of maturity usually have to do with adjusting to the business, political, and economic realities of society, rather than coping with feelings, desires, and needs. For this reason, many adults tend to listen to the music of the younger generation, observe their dances and various cultural styles, and conclude that they are not prepared for mature roles in society. Happily, how one fits into society is only one aspect of maturity. In fact, one can easily have the external attitudes and patterns of behavior to join the adult world without possessing emotional stability. In fact, there is substantial reason to question the so-called maturity of the older generation, particularly in the area of feelings and behavior. As we have said earlier, as long as the traditional values and attitudes of adults are molded by group pressures to belong, it follows that childish emotions of dependency, competition, and loyalty will take the place of more mature feelings of independence, self-assurance, and emotional autonomy.

If we take a look at the music of the younger generation, we get a stark picture of people trying to wrestle with some of those emotions which can only be characterized as mature. Of course, there is the inevitable context of adolescence setting the stage for the lyrics. But far more common than not, the emotions, thoughts, and needs which are sung about reflect a concern with the problems in life which really count the most. For example, some of the songs by the Beatles, the Rolling Stones, Bob Dylan, Janis Joplin, James Brown, and Aretha Franklin deal with subjects which involve the most complicated and difficult sets of emotions known to man. When Dylan sings "Lay, Lady, Lay," he is expressing in warm human terms how a man feels trying to communicate to a woman that life is real and present. To many adults, the lyrics seem to reflect the age-old attempts of the male to seduce the female, but young people know differently. For rather than the traditional attempts to communicate false emotion and related examples of simple seduction, Dylan reveals that the best relationship a couple can have is one based on the conscious choice of the two people involved. He tells the girl what he wants, what he can do for her, and tries to help her make her decision.

And yet, even beyond most of these very concrete "love" songs, the social message songs from "Hair" tell young people what feelings, issues, and problems really matter the most. The lyrics of one song from "Hair" portray the essential cruelty of modern life: "It's easy to be cold, easy to be proud, easy to say no." And in the song which the Youngbloods have made famous, "Get Together": "You can make mountains ring, or make angels cry. . . . come on people now, smile on your brother, everybody get together, try to love one another right now. . . . you hold the key to love and fear. . . ." What is being communicated to the young in such lyrics goes beyond the traditional moral demands of Church authorities. They are the self-explaining values of simple humanity, the discoveries which people make about life when they are free to face it like it is. Interestingly, the songs do not shrink from expressing the warning that life and love include pain, fear, loneliness, and death.

Of course, the influence of the black culture on rock and roll music is unmistakable. And in many respects, the black man has provided the very soul of honesty which characterizes most of the most popular tunes. Significantly, however, it is no longer possible to tell, simply by listening, whether or not the singers are black or white. It doesn't make any difference any longer. The phenomenon of letting one's deepest emotions come forth in sounds of pain, joy, delight, and even simulated feelings of sexual climax are far too honest and human for the young to be categorized racially. This is very clear in the style of singing which Janis Joplin represented. Her voice was almost harsh, very deep, and filled with the most basic feelings of erotic love, rejection, hostility, and deep pain. For the uninitiated adult, her voice could easily be mistaken for that of a black gospel singer wailing the joys and heartaches of the ghetto. Young people find these sounds of emotion more honest and far more communicative than traditional ballads. When pain is felt, it is expressed in sounds. And since this has long been the style of black music, the distinction between the feelings, desires, and styles of the younger people and the blacks is all but irrelevant.

Of course, a major contribution which the blacks have made to the younger generation is the rhythmic beat of the drum. The drum is probably the oldest instrument of music and dance known to man. And this means that the essential styles of music and dance which characterize this particular type of musical instrument follow the dictates of tribalistic ritual. The drum teaches the body the logical movements consistent with the emotions of love, hate, joy, and eroticism. The drum, in other words, is a nonintellectual instrument of body-oriented movement and emotion. It cannot be replicated by any other instrument, except perhaps the electric organ and the electric guitar, which, incidentally, are often played to sound very much like the drum.

In response to this drum-dominated type of music, one's body movements speak, like the drum itself, in a nonverbal language. There is no way possible to express the same feelings in words. It is direct, intuitive, and completely emotional. As a result, the music and dance which express this very basic sound cannot easily be communicated to those who have yet to permit themselves to have such feelings and experience such movements. In fact, it might even be called "therapeutic" under certain circumstances. The individual is provided with the freedom to express himself, in a deeply emotional way that immediately involves his whole person, body, mind, and spirit. Typical of such tribalistic rituals in certain primitive cultures, and even in a few experimental therapies which emphasize dance, erotic sex-expression, and related body movements, the therapeutic release or gratification is immediate and substantial.

It is interesting to note, however, that while this nonverbal communication of beat and body movement takes place on one level, the other extreme of a message-laden set of lyrics almost always accompanies the music. The entertainers, while providing the basic sounds for narcissistic self-expression, also provide words and meanings that orient the listeners to the essential value-questions. But rather than leading the individual to divorce his narcissism from his head, it tends to unite the two in such a way as to enable the individual to experience the intellectual meaning of the lyrics as both thoughts and feelings. Consequently, the language of love is understood in both physical and intellectual ways, one always reinforcing the other. And as a rule, the same thing is true for all messages which the lyrics communicate. And as a result, there tends to develop a feeling for the meanings of the songs which express such thoughts and values as those that characterize the beliefs and attitudes of the younger generation.

This phenomenon is difficult for adults to understand and appreciate, because adults tend to divorce feelings from meanings more than is necessary. The assumption is that feelings are untrustworthy and misleading, while ideas are rational, functional, and meaningful. Adults would rather listen to the words of songs and derive whatever significance they can while feeling the music as a separate phenomenon altogether. And the endless extensions of this very attitude are almost typical of the ways adults tend to look at the world around them. They listen to ideas, lectures, sermons, and speeches while using music as background sound to add something to the setting. The young, on the other hand, find more meaning in the words of songs when the sounds, beat, and movements of the music give life and energy to such meanings. But then, this reflects the difference between a narcissistic view of reality and a repressed narcissism. The narcissist seeks an organic unity of the world within his own body and emotions, while the repressed narcissist seeks to divorce himself from reality in order to master it intellectually, at a distance. The narcissist does not tend to detach the world from himself or his emotions — the two remain an extension of one another; while most adults fragment reality into a series of facts, events, and realities, each demanding a different reaction, and each requiring a separate thought, feeling, or emotion.

12

THE UNIVERSITY:
SANCTUARY OR
SOCIETY?

Is the university, or the "multiversity" as Clark Kerr calls it, a sanctuary from society for affluent youth, or is it the real world where basic issues, problems, and dilemmas in society are both fermented and attacked? Obviously, any answer depends heavily upon one's perspective. If you are a research professor working under contract from industry or the military-industrial complex, the latter makes more sense. But if you do not want to be bothered by those within or on the outside of the university who raise questions about your work, then the first answer makes more sense. If you are a member of SDS trying to attack or uncover the various ways by which the modern university is involved with political and governmental pressures and priorities, it is ridiculous to call the university a sanctuary. But on the other hand, if police have invaded the campus in order to "bust" or expel radicals and their associates from certain buildings, then the cry of sanctuary sounds quite logical. Thus, whatever the circumstances, the meaning of higher education is far from clear.

In many respects, the problem is an old one, going back to seventeenth-century New England. The first universities to be built in this country were specifically organized for the aristocracy. At Harvard, Yale, Columbia, and Princeton, the young men who attended were the sons of society's leaders. They were considered not "kids," as adults call them today, but young gentlemen. Indeed, they were gentlemen. And the society from which they came all but totally determined the nature of the curriculum, the types of fraternal organizations which existed, and the norms for conduct.

Administrators and alumni assumed that young men often indulge in activities outside the bounds of gentlemanly conduct, and it was quite common for deans and other administrators to intercede on behalf of students who had fought with local young men who frequented the same bars and whorehouses that surrounded the campuses. Not a few great men in this country once had some official of the university intervene on their behalf in some serious confrontation with the law or social custom. One did not expect society to exact the same price for disruptive behavior from the children of the aristocracy as might be exacted from those on the outside of this "ivory-covered" sanctuary.

When the Land Grant Act was passed in the latter part of the nineteenth century and farmers were given a chance to educate themselves in order to better cultivate the lands of the great Midwest, a new model for higher education came into being. For the first time, the lower classes had a chance to become college-educated and, hopefully, enter the ranks of leadership in society. Unfortunately, all the benefits which normally surrounded the Ivy League universities did not readily apply to these newer institutions. By this time state universities and Church-related colleges had begun to flourish, but apart from the models provided by Harvard and Yale, or large urban institutions like the University of Chicago, there was no model for these newer universities. Since the nation had great needs for talent in engineering, law, medicine, agriculture, and science, the requirements of the nation determined the nature of the curriculum. There simply was no social model, however, like that of the wealthy class to provide a transportable culture to the growing campuses. Functionalism ultimately determined the life of the university, and the average student had one goal in mind: to get his degree and then a good job.

Of course, students still had all the normal adolescent tendencies to get drunk, find promiscuous women, fight, and destroy property on occasion. But outside the high culture of the New England colleges, it was not nearly so clear that the university had a responsibility to protect the children of the common citizenry. Of course, many deans, professors, and administrators felt a paternal desire to help students who found themselves in conflict with the "town." In fact, the phrase "town and gown" referred to a double standard whereby the educated few were protected from the working classes of society. Nevertheless, it remained true that college students in the large universities of the land were not understood to be in the same class as those who attended the prestigious colleges in the East. As a rule, therefore, the concept of sanctuary did not apply as fully to the colleges and universities outside the Ivy League.

It has not been until the last few years that the aristocratic image of the Ivy League schools has been seriously tarnished. When the police finally came onto the campuses of Columbia and Harvard, it became clear that the old "town and gown" morality was no longer relevant. There couldn't have been any better examples of aristocratic colleges, oriented to the traditions of gentlemanly custom, suddenly being forced into the twentieth century of the common man. These were no longer sanctuaries for young gentleman. Try as they might, deans and presidents could not think of students like Mark Rudd as gentlemen. They were revolutionaries. And although they may have come from the upper middle class, they had all the marks of the common citizen. Consequently, their behavior was not to be excused. Their rhetoric was taken with the deepest seriousness, and their intentions were seen to be completely conspiratorial; their values and attitudes were nothing but deplorable.

To add to this strange shift in custom and practice, many deans and administrators were "liberal" academics, deeply committed to the concept of the university as a sanctuary for "free" ideas and the endless search for truth. But the manner by which many of them have tended to interpret their ideas has left a great deal to be desired. It is ironic that an administrator should call "sanctuary" when he has, himself, participated in the process whereby the university has been sold to the highest bidders in government and industry. The "invasion" by government and industry into the very heart of university life — namely, determining what must be taught, researched, and studied — was the true beginning of the end of the concept of sanctuary.

The very first issue which turned the University of California at Berkeley into a public riot was the problem of raising funds *on campus* for the civil rights workers in the South. Students asked, if the university can accept money from government and industry, and in turn provide knowledge, skills, and information to those interest groups, why were they not permitted to use the university for meeting the needs of the blacks? The students clearly saw that the university was not a sanctuary. It was a part of something the students recognized as the "system," namely, the complex interlocking network of governmental, business, military, and educational institutions. Administrators sat on boards of directors of an endless list of corporations, governmental agencies, and foundations. And to many students, it seemed that such a system of mutual self-interest had nothing at all to do with the notion that the university was a sanctuary.

At Columbia University, this fact came home very quickly to many students in the mid-sixties, when one of the college's favorite deans, then vice president of the university, made a series of pleas for the concept of the university as a sanctuary for free ideas. Being an old civil libertarian, sanctuary had a very special meaning for him. He remembered the early fifties, and the specter of Senator Joseph McCarthy hung over his head like a cloud. He and many of his dearest friends and colleagues had once been burned by the fanatical finger of political paranoia, and he wasn't going to let it happen again. He saw

the image of the thirties coming into focus again, and he remembered how painful it was for the socialists and communists, many of whom held the most honorable intentions. Consequently, sanctuary was a sacred concept for him. It meant
that government had no right to attack the university for its
free and open exchange of ideas. Nor should men in government, who were actually professors and scholars on loan from
the university, be subject to the political punishments which
once fell upon them. Without intellectual sanctuary, the university as an institution of honest learning was ultimately
doomed.

Unfortunately, this particular dean could not see that his
participation in a modern university forced him to be inextri-
cably bound to the endless interests and pressures which the
system exerted upon the so-called sanctuaries of free and open
learning. But many students could see it. And they knew that
the concept of sanctuary had to take on a new and different
meaning. They did not long for the "good old days" of aristocracy, privilege, and position. They demanded that the university become the context, free from outside pressures of all
types, of society's teacher and reformer. But some of them
began to realize that such a change would never come about.
The modern university had become too important to the government, the military, and the business world. And such institutions weren't going to surrender it to the likes of SDS, the
Black Panthers, or any such groups which made their goals and
intentions so demonstrably clear.

For the individual student who was pursued by his local
draft board, sought for the purpose of giving his life to a pointless war in Asia, the meaning of sanctuary took on a new and
vital significance. There simply had to be some places in this
world that were free from the controls of the establishment.
And so they tried them all: churches were made available to
them, university buildings of all types, and if need be, perhaps
even another country. Indeed, it is personal sanctuary they
have been seeking. But it has been very hard to find.

Significantly, the contrast between the large state universities and the older Ivy League colleges came into focus once again. Only it was not Harvard and Columbia students calling for sanctuary. It was those in the Midwestern universities for whom sanctuary was a new and sacred concept. The radicals at Columbia and Harvard expected the police to come onto the campus. In fact, they wanted them to do so in order to make clear that the university was more interested in maintaining its property and its status quo position than it was in dealing with the real issues of the day.

Of course, the real irony was that those who attended the very institutions which initiated the concept of sanctuary were the very ones who refused it ultimately, while those who attended the state and city colleges and universities had to rediscover the concept and to fit it into an entirely unique context. The aristocratic schools were forced into the society's midst when large numbers of students were repelled by the notion of privilege, while the state universities found growing numbers of students seeking to turn the university into a sanctuary from the society's pressures and demands.

Because of the resulting confusion, most adults do not understand what the students really mean when they speak of sanctuary. Obviously, it no longer remains what a few paternalistic deans once thought it was. On the contrary, it means that the young want an institution which can be their own, one that is not subject to the bureaucratic forces, priorities, and pressures that make government and business what they are today. They want an institution which can be subject to their ideas, beliefs, and judgments, one that can ultimately have an effect on the larger society and finally begin to create the kind of society they feel is viable. Unfortunately, a great many students have become convinced that the modern university is beyond repair. It is too deeply buried in the rest of the system and therefore cannot really become what the young feel they need. Thus, many young men and women have "dropped out" of formal education and are saying to the rest of the world, "There is no sanctuary."

But quite apart from the subject of sanctuary as the major

issue of strategy for most young people (and there is serious doubt now as to how important it is), the psychology and morality behind the subject are far more important. For it really doesn't matter any longer how often the problem is or is not raised. The real issues have to do with the fact that a great many young people do not feel that the world they live in can readily be called their own. And for someone who has been raised to be narcissistically oriented to the universe around him, there can be no greater blow to his world-view. This is why those radicals who have finally taken violence seriously and who plot and plan their next guerrilla attack are convinced that they are living in an alien country. It is why Che, Mao, Ho, and others have become their cultural heroes — not because these young radicals are communists but because they see such men as those who ultimately have been able to stand against the American establishment and flaunt their values and beliefs in our faces. The young people do not turn such men into better "father figures," as some writers and critics have insisted. Rather, they tend to identify with them. Such is their narcissism. For to many young men and women, the boundary lines of age, nationality, race, and culture are meaningless. The world has no true adults for them. There are only so many adolescents who give their loyalties to the tribe or clan that is most suitable or near at hand. The true adults are citizens of the world, because they are also narcissistically oriented to the world. And psychologically, that is the real significance of what it means to be a radical. But it is also why such young radicals can never become real communists or follow any other ideology. These ideologies are nineteenth-century concepts, suited to the world of work, organization, leadership, party loyalty, and personal denial. Most young people today haven't the slightest interest in any of these values. And whether they know it or not, they will never be able to build a world predicated upon such outmoded beliefs. In this sense, the radicals are a most unfortunate lot. And intuitively, most of their peers, in and out of college, feel that the radicals simply don't have it any more.

Consequently, what has finally begun to happen is that the problem of sanctuary has become a deeply personal issue. It is not whether or not the university can become "their" institution (and let us not think for one moment that the push to make it so will decrease). Rather, the problem has become a matter for the individual to interpret for himself. How can the singular person find sanctuary for himself? And since the greatest thing most young people have going for them is a strong narcissistic ego, many of them can live out their lives in a new kind of privacy that most adults cannot fully appreciate. Consequently, for those who would like to understand better the common thread which links university disruption to the other elements of generational change, it must be remembered that the narcissism which affects the dress, language, music, values, and behavior of the young strongly influences their attitudes as students. For most young men and women soon discover that once they are in the colleges and universities, society tends to see them as older children. This is because most American adults have the unfortunate tendency to view attendance at school as an adolescent phenomenon. Adulthood has to do with having a job, getting married, and rearing a family. But to a growing number of young adults, such standards are totally meaningless. And as a consequence, many of them see themselves not divorced from the real marks of adulthood but definitely estranged from the so-called adult world. This invariably leads many of them to question what their roles in society can be. And since modern university life provides many of them with a context for testing such questions, they use the university as a sanctuary from the world their parents and other adults live in. But far from this meaning that the university is a haven for the young to prepare themselves for adulthood, it has become an environment where one can experiment with living out the kind of life he thinks he wants for himself.

This latter fact explains much of the motivation of the young today to think of themselves as a subculture. And instead of the university being what it was for most of their parents, namely, an introduction to the real world of adulthood, many young people see it as only one part of a new world which is all their own. This is why a young man can call himself a student even though he may not be enrolled at any particular university. He simply does not understand the bureaucratic assumption that enrollment or matriculation is what really constitutes studenthood. Many call themselves students because that is the life-style which provides the most options in life. They can go to class when they want to, change their major interests, even change schools, and perhaps drop out altogether if they decide to get a job for a while.

This new kind of life-style remarkably reflects the nature of higher education in this country today. In most of our larger urban communities, one can find a long list of colleges, universities, and specialty schools which all but make these cities into university complexes themselves. For example, it is very difficult to understand why a city like New York continues to have so many educational institutions which are independent from one another. Many young people prefer to ignore these distinctions, and a growing number of them treat New York as though the whole city were their campus. The same thing is happening in the Boston area, Chicago, Los Angeles, and San Francisco, and even in Dallas, Atlanta, and St. Louis. The young have begun to take over our cities, and they are rapidly turning them into their own educational sanctuaries.

The narcissistically oriented young people thus are beginning to find communities which are perfectly suited to their narcissistically determined life-styles. Instead of readily surrendering to the requirements, regimentation, and rules which normally constitute university life, they have begun to turn our cities into an educational experience. They may or may not bother to work for a certain degree within a given college or university. But the freedom to go beyond the boundary lines of any given curriculum is greatly enhanced by the fact that they use the whole city as their learning context. If they can't get a particular course at one school, they easily take it at another. And if the course they want isn't being taught any-

where, they set up a school among themselves and find someone to teach it.

Of course, one truly remarkable aspect of this developing
life-style is the effect it has on our cities, as well as on our
colleges and universities. For example, a great many young
people go to school in New York, Chicago, Boston, and San
Francisco not because they simply want to attend particular
schools but because they want to live in these cities. Intuitively, they know that the kind of education they want will
not be packaged at any given college but rather will be available to them throughout the city. Consequently, they tend to
adopt the problems, benefits, opportunities, and options that
the city makes readily available to them. And nothing could
suit their narcissistic egos better. Instead of being institutionalized, they are using institutions for their own purposes.

Unfortunately, this approach brings with it a whole new set
of problems to solve. For example, if a youngster does not readily join the "community" of a given university, then he must
find one he can join. And this is partly what the development
of "communes" in and around our cities is all about. They are
newer forms of social life in which the young can have all the
benefits of close and intimate relationships, but which also provide most of the sophisticated aspects of modern urban life.
They have sexual involvements, therapy, educational benefits,
and a whole range of experiences which teach them the skills of
interpersonal communication. Also, there is usually a highly
developed "underground" of information, services, job opportunities, and an entire network of associations which make the
once-alien environment of the lonely crowd into a personalized
community. Obviously, however, none of these aspects of
community have solved all the problems which the lone individual confronts when he chooses to live in the city. In many
of the communes there are serious problems of health, finance,
and simple organization. But when you place hundreds of
thousands of narcissists into communities, it is quite predictable
that they will have serious problems to solve, particularly since
most of them have totally rejected the established group pat-

terns of the adult world. In any case, it will simply have to be accepted that education today is no longer a degree-acquiring preparation for normal adulthood. Higher education has fast become a process of learning which is inextricable from living. It no longer makes sense to speak of education in terms of colleges and universities. This lack of clear definition, organization, and even geographical boundaries makes the concept of sanctuary even more difficult to apply. But no matter how difficult the concept is, students still require some kind of sanctuary if they are going to have enough time and freedom to test their new ways and ideas.

13

VIOLENCE AND NARCISSISM

Practically every Western culture is firmly grounded in the phenomenon of repressed narcissism and unconscious violence. Every psychologist, anthropologist, and psychiatrist knows this simple fact of life. And in a cryptic way, this is precisely what Stokely Carmichael meant when he said: "Violence is as American as apple pie." He was not simply condemning the white man's world, he was saying that everything we know as progress in this country, and in Europe as well, is rooted in the highly developed control of inherent human aggression. But he was also saying that it has been an aggression which only the white man has permitted himself to possess. In other people it is animal behavior, lust, or weakness.

But if, as Konrad Lorenz's popular interpreters insist, man is a creature of natural aggression, then what can we say about aggression in the narcissistic youth of today? Are they any different from the rest of their species? Isn't the disruptive behavior on college campuses and on the streets of our cities a typical example of youthful aggressive behavior? On the one hand, aggression is a natural biological aspect of human existence. But on the other hand, aggression takes whatever form society dictates. It is not true that aggression must inevitably mean violence, war, killing, and murder. For aggression is nothing more than the mental and physical energy which serves to meet the needs, flee from the dangers, fight the enemies, and master the environment which man is forever faced with. Why aggression turns into hatred, rage, violence, and destruction is a purely secondary matter, primarily based upon the patterns of human adaptation to the environments in which men find themselves.

We have already addressed ourselves to this problem in the chapter on drugs and have pointed out that there is a real difference between the behavior of the "civilized" repressed individual and that of the narcissist. The repressed human being is one who has been thrown into a world predetermined for him by the groups, pressures, values, and forces which ultimately define the boundary lines of reality. But the narcissist has strangely avoided this radical process of initiation, and thus has assumed that reality is something quite different from the way most of the rest of us experience it. To him it is a world that is available, indeed, a world that is vital to his own being and ultimately under the controls of his own wishes, desires, and needs. When the repressed individual encounters aggression, he responds with aggression. He understands that the world is composed of aggressive forces, all of which cause the individual to draw his boundary lines clearly and take his stand. But when the narcissist is confronted with aggression, he is first confused, then frightened, and finally aroused. His aggression has been so eroticized, since it serves his physical and emotional needs, that it takes time for him to discover that someone may be trying to harm him. Although this may appear like weakness to the normal aggressive being, it really means that the narcissist has to turn his aggression away from its normal eroticized mode of expression into an instrument of survival — a shift, incidentally, which comes with difficulty for most narcissists. It tends to violate their whole conception of and orientation toward reality.

Most adults are confused and angered at the violence involving college-age students that they see on television and hear and read about in the public media. It seems that the young have been pampered, and that violent acts such as the sit-ins, occupations of university buildings, and street riots are infantile forms of rage. Ironically, they are partly correct in this judgment. It is rage which has never before been tempered by the values, morality, and pressures which conventional civilization once imposed on everyone. But to call it infantile rage does not automatically mean that it is any less legitimate. For so many of these young people, their awareness of the true nature of society didn't develop until they were in their mid-teens. And the contradiction they witnessed has become too much for most of them.

But rather than approach the problem from this relatively generalized perspective, let's examine it from a more contextual point of view. First of all, how widespread is the violence among the young? Second, has the Vietnam War caused or simply aroused the violent emotions of the young? And what is the nature of violence which the young have discovered in the society? Unfortunately, no amount of statistics can even begin to answer any of these questions. For one must appreciate the fact that violence among the young is a purely relative matter. Most youngsters are not violent at all. And the few who seem to be involved in every demonstration, disruption, or act of violence are themselves prone to drop the tactic at any given moment. While a large number can be involved in violent acts, only an extremely small number are *consistently* violent. Obviously, I have no way to document this. I only know that those who seek violent acts of confrontation comprise a very small number. The rest, who participate on certain occasions, usually become violent when the situation seems to demand it — when the police begin to arouse the crowd or threats are leveled by the authorities against them.

The classic example of this phenomenon can be found among the hippies who often join demonstrations and tend to symbolize acts of utter rejection of society's norms for behavior. On many occasions, the police have brutalized hippies because they seemed to represent all that the police, as a social class, fear and hate. Unfortunately, this has caused many hippies to express a violence they might never have shown otherwise. Over the last few years, however, many police departments have sought to make distinctions between hippies and radicals. And some police are becoming fairly sophisticated about the variety of differences in the youth culture. They are beginning to realize, for example, that there are distinct groups and individuals who have violence as their major intention, and that most of the rest of those who participate in demonstrations are merely seeking to express their protest. The more this kind of understanding can grow and prevail, the more difficult it will be for certain sects within SDS and related groups to mobilize violent actions involving thousands of people. This is why the blacks have become very sophisticated about their use and threats of use of violence. They know how much can be lost, and they consciously move with the greatest caution. The vast majority of white youngsters are just beginning to realize the same thing, and the most violent radicals are increasingly left to themselves.

When we come to the problem of what role the Vietnam War has played in arousing violence among the young, the answer cannot help but be that it has been the major source of conflict. But this does not mean what it seems to. It is not so much the fact that we are in a war that provokes such violent reaction as it is the kind of war that ultimately matters. Far too much information exists as to how the war began, what pressure groups helped to initiate it, what forms of military and industrial planning made it inevitable, and what bureaucratic and party government does to keep it alive, even when the majority of Americans want it to end. For young people it is a classic war of imperialism versus nationalism, the strong against the weak, the powerful against the poor, the Western against the Asian. And this strikes directly at youthful narcissism.

What most adults cannot understand about the values and attitudes of so many young people stems from their inability, once again, to appreciate the nature of narcissism. For any youngster who has been reared to experience the world as an extension of his own mind and body for whom Vietnam is only another neighbor, the historical demarcation lines between tribe and clan, governments and people, make no sense whatsoever. To kill Vietnamese people is just as bad as killing one's next-door neighbor. But rather than this being just a belief or a naïve assumption, it is a very clear perception for the young. Almost none of the older conditioning factors of racial or ethnic distinction matter to the narcissistic youth of today. Of course, they recognize differences between people, but it is also true that they can just as easily feel alienated from people of their own ethnic or racial groups as they can from foreigners. The major difference for them, however, is that they can also more readily identify with differences among people than most adults can. And wherever the society seeks to force conformity, likeness, and commonality of traits, values, and beliefs, they tend to react immediately, because such regimentation is a direct attack upon their own narcissistic worlds. Someone is trying to manipulate their reality for them, and narcissistic egos cannot tolerate that.

For example, when the television camera focuses on a youth carrying a Viet Cong flag, many adults immediately assume that the youngster is a traitor. But the truth of the matter is, he is trying to bring the enemy close to home, hoping that some adults might begin to realize that the enemy is human, a neighbor, for whom it is just as horrible to die as for one's next-door neighbor. This is also why some young people have taken up drama in the streets. They act out the realities of death, love, sex, and fear, hoping that they can reach the unconscious narcissism of adults and "turn them on" to a different perception of reality, namely, one that makes the world real, present, and totally involving. In this way, the young have discovered a great deal about the way the adult world is structured, as well as the ways in which adults orient themselves to those structures. And much of what they have learned is that our society is built upon the control of human aggression.

Many of those in their late twenties and early thirties, however, learned this fact (and how to cope with it) in the early sixties while working with the civil rights movement. They soon discovered that the police in the deep South were extremely violent men with heavy overtones of guilt-oriented morality. A Southern cop or sheriff would welcome violence, for it gave him an excuse to lash out and destroy the enemy. But when he was confronted with smiles, gentle emotions, and courtesy, he almost always — at least at first — backed up and showed bewilderment. Had it not been for this phenomenon, it is not likely that Martin Luther King's appeal for nonviolence would have succeeded as it did in the South. But when the students who worked in Alabama, Mississippi, Georgia, and South Carolina returned to the North and West to apply their lessons to the scene there, they found a different kind of reaction. Aggression had become institutionalized over the many years of industrialization and liberal bureaucratization. Suddenly, the whole society seemed to change before their eyes. What had been seen as liberal and well-intentioned became economically, politically, and bureaucratically dominated. Actually, nothing had really changed. Only the perception of reality had changed dramatically for many youngsters. They had begun to discover something about their society which completely disoriented many of them. And it took a long time for most of them to discover finally that their perception was not faulty at all. Indeed, it was quite correct.

That perception was that this society, which likes to think of itself as peaceful and committed to the principles of freedom, has a very deep layer of repressed and controlled violence which invariably serves the interests of those who hold the greatest power. Like some gigantic obsessive-compulsive neurotic, this nation is haunted with violent thoughts, feelings, and fantasies, forever being bombarded from within by aggressive drives, but continually covering them with a complex structure of rituals, institutional loyalties and values which only serve to make the unconscious aggression all the more threatening. In fact, so close to the truth is this diagnosis of our nation's character that a great many adults are beginning to express the fear that the young will eventually and unwittingly bring forth a kind of violence which will ultimately throw us, as a nation, into utter confusion and destruction. These adults do not fear the violence of the young so much as the violence of many calm, peace-loving citizens. And that is because they know their own adult generation quite well. They can visualize parents completely rejecting their own sons and daughters, willingly giving them over to the militant forces of "law and order." They can see the nation fighting in the streets, families being torn apart, and brutality becoming the rule of the day. And that is why they often express their deepest longings for the younger generation to be "rational" and tolerant of the values and attitudes of the adult generation. They know what the consequences can be.

But do the young themselves understand how violent this nation really is? Unfortunately, many of them know it all too well. Of course, not all of them have had personal experiences — many have been mere bystanders and observers. Most have never really been confronted with violent realities, but they have seen them on television. And they have learned to equate them with the violence in Vietnam, the aggression of ghetto discrimination, and the meaningless demands of the draft. In fact, almost everywhere they turn they find men's energies (another form of aggression) being co-opted for institutional, governmental, and bureaucratic ends that often have nothing whatsoever to do with the real needs of human beings. And the saddest consequence is that a growing number of youngsters believe they might not ever grow up and have an effect on society. To wait for an appropriate time when they become "adults" means, all too often, getting sucked into the system and ultimately made powerless like most of the adults they know. And so they learn how to use their youth, their naïveté, and yes, even their aggression to challenge the world as it is presently structured. Many of them obviously feel completely hopeless about having a substantial effect, but some keep on trying. A few use aggressive violence, either out of simple frustration or as a conscious tactic to remind the American people that violence is the very energy which makes our system function.

Without a doubt, the one characteristic of most adults (especially those who hold responsibilities within major institutions) which reinforces the frustration and hopelessness of the young is the common belief that there are no alternatives to our present way of functioning. Creativity, innovation, and experimentation are not permitted to alter the existing goals, policies, and practices of the gigantic institutions which normally determine the nation's destiny. And if one wants to talk about the "gap" which exists between the generations, then this one fact alone represents a difference of perspective between the young and the old which is all but insurmountable. The young do not understand why basic changes in priorities, policies, and practices cannot be made, while the older generation cannot understand what is so wrong with the way things are. Not that adults are ignorant of the real problems and dilemmas which face us, but they simply cannot perceive how it would be possible for any substantial changes to take place without ultimately disrupting the very fabric of the system which has carried us this far. And yet, for most young people, maintenance of the system is the least of their concerns. The violent ones really do want to destroy it. The rest want it changed, but they do not see how it will be possible as long as most adults continue to express helplessness and powerlessness in the face of the obvious obstacles.

If anything frustrates the narcissism of the young, it is this very problem. They simply cannot accept the fact that "their world" cannot be made into something better. And when they encounter the repressed narcissism of so many adults, all that buried energy to revitalize life, they become completely confused. They don't understand why adults must bury their feelings about injustice, why they become concerned about lesser matters, and why they continue building the walls of financial, political, and institutional security around themselves. Narcissists, as a rule, have very few walls to protect themselves. They are vulnerable to attack but open to change. But they cannot understand people who place mental and emotional security above the freedom to experiment with life. And for all those adults who think that this attitude will eventually pass away as the young take on the responsibilities of adulthood, they had better take a good look at the nature of narcissism once again. *If it isn't repressed in the first few years of life, it is almost impossible for it to be repressed later on;* because narcissism is not simply an infantile fantasy-oriented ego, incapable of developing useful skills, solving complex problems, and dealing with the major issues which threaten human survival on this planet. Surprisingly, it is precisely the narcissistically confirmed ego which longs to tackle such problems. They love their world, and they are not afraid of it. They know that they can make things work the way they want them to if only adults will stand by them and work with them to attack creatively whatever problems must be solved.

But a society of adults, predicated upon the inevitable repression of narcissism and aggression, is really a society of repressed and angry children, deeply afraid of the world and extremely cautious in their manner of dealing with that world. And when such a society is confronted with a generation of conscious and confirmed narcissists, the anxiety, fear, and dread which many adults feel is all but overwhelming. They have visions of a return to the jungle, of total vulnerability, and images of standing, like the Empire of Rome, on the brink of complete destruction. Consequently, they react with all their self-righteous rage, they take comfort in their "law and order" values, and they even find themselves feeling a bit secure that the system is more powerful than all the youth in the world combined. And the gap between the generations stretches even wider.

Fortunately, for those adults who understand what is already beginning to happen to us as a nation, there is also much reason to take comfort in the persistence of the younger generation. They witness in the young definite signs of behavior and value changes which have been long overdue. And not being threatened by such innovations, these adults tend to welcome them all the more.

Some adults are beginning to perceive in the behavior and values of the young a type of "life-style," emotional freedom, and personal independence which can and will help us out of our institutionalized and bureaucratized patterns. Someone has to pay the price of confronting the system as it stands, and it is obvious that most adults are not willing to pay that much. This leaves them alone and often endangered by the very system which presently supports them. The younger generation does not have the same kind of emotional, financial, or "spiritual" investment in the existing system. Typical of most narcissists, they see the system as composed of power-hungry, frightened, and essentially angry men and women who are basically afraid to discover anything about themselves. And for those adults who know this is true, it is something of an apocalyptical event to find an entire generation which is not predisposed to maintain such an inauthentic way of life for another few decades.

What price the young are willing and able to pay, however, is another question. There are many ways to challenge this society's structure and values, and the young are not incapable of discovering new and different methods of confrontation. This is why adults who really think about it are not disturbed by the problem of adolescent violence. Violence, like pornography, is more of a problem for adults than it is for young people. As we pointed out earlier, one doesn't surrender his adolescence to militarism, institutionalization, and bureaucratization (as has been the case with the vast majority of adults over forty) and not feel a deeply frustrated, unresolved adolescent rage. It is too easy to assume that reality must always be like that and therefore to avoid asking the question: "Have I really permitted myself to test reality and find out who I am?" The young are doing it. So what really constitutes adulthood after all? And who is more prone to violence? One thing is certain: If violence ultimately destroys this society, it will be the violence of institutionalized rage, aimed at all those who threaten the very tenuous security upon which this country rests.

14

CONCLUSIONS ON THE
THEME OF NARCISSISM

Perhaps the only truly threatening aspect of the rapidly changing patterns of behavior and values among the younger generation is that it is so difficult to predict or anticipate what the next two decades will bring. No industrialized civilization has ever reared a generation of people conditioned to perceive reality from a narcissistic point of view. Somehow the values, politics, behavior patterns, and attitudes of every older generation have always been allowed to pass on without much transformation to succeeding generations. Although there have been dramatic changes and innovations in the last one hundred years, none of them have converged rapidly enough for any single generation not to accommodate itself, oriented to the past from which it came and prepared to adjust to the future which seemed relatively consistent with past experience. The adaptations from rural to urban, from ethnic ghettos to pluralism, from world war to corporate life, and from lower-class to middle- and upper-middle-class patterns of life have all taken place with an amazing facility. Values have changed, but not so much as to disorient the entire nation. Working patterns have been altered enormously, but work remains as an established part of most adults' lives. And technology has moved us from an agricultural society to an industrial society and now is thrusting us into what some are calling a "postindustrial" age. And all of this has occurred within less than one hundred years.

But as any futurist or planner understands, many of the changes which have been taking place within the past twenty-five years have been increasing at a geometrical rate of innovation. A simple graph or chart of change for almost any single aspect of our society shows how our technology, economics, life-styles, institutions, and even our values, have been changing on an exponential curve. The faster things change, in other words, the more innovations there are for the society to adjust to. We are suffering from a kind of "overload" of information, innovation, and invention. And the more our business institutions, politics, universities, churches, and simply people are confronted with a burdening overload of change, the more difficult it is to predict what the immediate future will bring. Even the most ambitious futurists, who try to take all the options and possibilities seriously, cannot possibly chart a "surprise-free" map for the nation. If predictions could be limited to simple matters of mathematical probability, it still would be highly dangerous to assume that economics, technology, and science will follow a scale of anticipated developments. But even if we assume that such an approach to the future is viable under certain limitations, it is impossible to program information about human behavior. About the only thing one can assume is that the changes which have occurred in recent years in terms of behavior and values have something to do with the direction we seem to be taking. And whereas most of history as we know it has been a linear process of consistent moral and psychological repression of primary narcissism, the last two decades have been moving us in a new direction away from this ancient pattern. More and more, young people are growing up under the conditions of a narcissistically confirmed world-view which stands in direct opposition to the world-view Western man has evolved over the last two thousand years.

If we add to this startling phenomenon several statistics which reflect how "youth-oriented" our society is becoming, we can begin to guess what some of the behavioral changes we are witnessing today will mean for tomorrow. For example, as we mentioned earlier, one-third of our entire population is fifteen years of age or younger, while nearly half the population is twenty-five years of age or less. There are more than seven million students in higher education, and more than fifty-eight million people from age three to thirty-four attend school. On the other end of the scale, the blue-collar segment of society is proportionately declining, while those in the so-called white-collar professions are on the increase. The educational median or number of years in school for that growing segment of professional and managerial workers is seventeen years, or the equivalent of a Master's degree. Also, the single largest group of men and women available for work are those between the ages of sixteen and twenty-four who make up forty-seven percent of the nation's manpower, while those who manage the society and are over forty-five make up forty-one percent of the manpower. At the same time, over seventy percent of the entire population of the country lives and works on *one* percent of the landmass.

In other words, we are an urban civilization dominated by two very large classes, the youth and the managerial-professional class. And since most of those who make up the management class of society are living longer and retaining their positions of control and professional decision-making power, the other class — youth — is confronted with increasing difficulty in trying to inherit enough of that power to feel that a smooth transition of control is possible. Thus, we are fast becoming a society composed of two distinct cultures, one in power which is highly educated and skilled in maintaining our existing institutional priorities and another which is rapidly seeking to create its own set of options, life-styles, and values, often in clear contrast with those who manage things. In this sense, the generation gap is really a culture gap, and there doesn't seem to be any reason to assume that the youth culture will be assimilated into the adult world of institutional responsibility fast enough for a more serious culture conflict to be avoided.

Those adults, therefore, who hope against hope that the next generation will finally adopt the values and behavior patterns of previous generations will have to accept the fact that such a stabilizing transition from youth generation to adult generation is all but impossible. There is no reason whatsoever to assume that the present conditions which cause our conflict will pass away in the near future. If anything, they cannot help but become worse. Therefore, it is best that we try and speculate what some of the continuing problems will be during the next two or more decades. And although there will be many events, innovations, and changes which we cannot anticipate, there are some things we can safely assume will become commonplace problems for us all to cope with.

1. Major institutions without values, under the domination of technology and "systems-type" reasoning, will produce a serious crisis in the realm of priorities, meaning, and purpose for the entire country. A kind of Marxist attitude, which claims that action precedes values and ultimately determines values, will provoke the prime philosophical and religious issue for the majority of Americans.

2. With the growing effects of a narcissistically oriented younger generation, it will become impossible to control human behavior through the conventional means of education, politics, and economic pressure. Either drastic steps will be taken, involving the use of technological, military, and police-type tactics for the direct control of the masses, or else a far greater acceptance of what is now considered antisocial or deviant behavior will come into being as a means of avoiding total alienation of the young.

3. Assuming that our political, educational, and business institutions cannot afford to confront larger numbers of more alienated young people, greater freedoms in the area of personal choice will be demanded and granted, thus forcing greater amounts of individuality and autonomy to be tolerated in our social and institutional lives.

4. Inevitably, this country will evolve a "benevolent fascism" as a political, business, and educational model for management. The vast majority of citizens will insist that the "technocrats" who govern do so by exercising their technological skills and not their political values, thus co-opting the individual's commitment and energy through *ad hoc* or periodic service to the rest of society. Traditional motivations of money, power, and prestige will no longer serve to capture the talents and skills of the citizenry. Only options which coincide with the individual's choice will serve to provide the manpower the nation will need to keep its economic infrastructure intact.

5. Among the innovations in behavior and values which will ultimately alter our present industrial values and behavior patterns will be those which encourage total experimentation. Consequently, a very wide variety of life-styles will exist alongside one another without there being any serious threat to social order. Thus, many laws will have to be passed which guarantee the individual total freedom over the ways in which he experiments with his own body and mind. Thus, a new kind of legal structure will evolve which seeks to protect the individual from the ability of the technocrats to manipulate the choices of individuals as consumers, voters, employees, and individuals.

6. In the next two decades, most large institutions of government, business, education, and related managements will seek to govern through a constant process of "feedback control." The degree to which this can serve the society as a viable process of information management will depend greatly upon the ability of existing technocratic managements to understand feedback in terms of "service" to the public, as opposed to manipulation of the public interest. By and large, however, it is this very process which presently causes so much conflict between those who manage and those who are managed. A very high degree of sophistication and sympathy between these two groups, one for the other, will have to develop very soon or there will be such a profound alienation of one group from the other that a complete collapse of the society will become inevitable.

The most pronounced evidence which leads one to assume that problems such as these will confront us in the next few decades stems from the contagious effects of narcissism. Those who assume that narcissism is only a characteristic of the very few or the very sick fall prey to the belief that society cannot tolerate narcissism as a way of perceiving the world around us. In the past, narcissism could not possibly become conscious and effective in determining the life-styles, because the values and attitudes of most citizens were primarily due to the pervasive effects of scarcity economics, limited technology, and traditional morality. Only the artists, inventors, and philosophers could be tolerated as narcissists. Ironically, it has been precisely such men and women as these who have had the greatest effects on our civilization. For like most narcissists, they saw the world organically and holistically. They did not see it as determined by establishment or civilized norms. And that is why they provided us with insights that changed the world.

Also ironically, today's younger generation is fast becoming a kind of "research and development" department for the entire nation. And as fast as young people develop new styles, values, and attitudes, the faster our social, political, business, and education institutions seek to incorporate them. This has happened most visibly in the "marketplace," but it is also beginning to happen in government, industry, and our universities. No matter how skilled these institutions become in turning such innovations into "feedback," they cannot cope with the contagious effects of narcissism among those within the younger generation. In spite of the fact that this society doesn't really leave any options or alternatives for the younger generation to accept in order to adopt the values and attitudes of the older generation (far too many young people are prohibited from joining the adult world of work, decision making, and power), the fact remains that the narcissistic world-view, which teaches the individual that he is autonomous, self-directing, and lives at the center of his own narcissistic universe, fast becomes infinitely more attractive and appealing. If we add to this the fact that our economic and technological levels of sophistication make narcissism a much more viable way of perceiving reality, then it becomes clear that repression of narcissism cannot possibly be imposed fast enough to thwart the development of greater numbers of narcissistic young people. For narcissism is something far deeper than an ideal of freedom or a belief about autonomy. It is a biologically and emotionally determined point of view which, if not checked at a very early stage in life, tends to be reinforced and grow stronger with every year of development.

Of course, it remains true that psychology still leaves room for defining certain types of psychopathology of a narcissistic nature as neurotic or even psychotic. Anyone who sees the world around him in such a way as to feel himself totally threatened by other people's freedom cannot possibly be called healthy. His narcissism remains locked into the perspective of a frightened infant. The person who must always assert himself in the face of criticism and self-doubt is also considered a narcissistic individual. Certainly, the most extreme case of narcissism of a pathological type is the catatonic schizophrenic. He is so threatened by external reality that he totally withdraws into a world all his own. But narcissism, as such, is not pathological under all conditions. The real problem has to do with whether or not the infantile world-view of the narcissistic ego can become confirmed, strengthened, and perpetuated into later life, thus teaching the individual that he can have some effect on the world around him and receive a certain amount of reward or gain from that world. Under normal conditions in the past, such a process of development was not possible for the masses of people. Only the rich and the aristocratic were capable of such attitudes. And that is why so many working-class people, even to this day, consider the effects of affluence to be dangerous. It spoils the young and teaches them of an unreal world. But it is no longer possible to make such easy judgments when, in fact, a large proportion of the population has become oriented to reality in much the same way as aristocrats of the past. Ironically, most of our better theories about child rearing, education, and self-development parallel the experiences of our upper-middle-class young people rather than of those who experience severe repression at an early age. Consequently, narcissism becomes its own standard of health. And those who continue to suffer under the older "reality principle" of work, submission to authority, and repressed aggression seem increasingly to suffer from socially conditioned neuroses. They acquire obsessive-compulsive traits, they feel unnecessary guilt and shame, they become overly competitive and aggressive, and they tend to develop weak ego-structures when it comes to assuming responsibility and decision-making power. So the question of whether or not narcissism is a pathological condition must now be qualified by the newer "reality principle" of a world wherein the child can and does develop a strong narcissistic-ego structure which, ironically, is confirmed by external reality, rather than simply being repressed. Thus, as narcissism tends to become the dynamics for perceiving external reality, the more it tends to affect external reality. And that is what ultimately turns it into a social, political, and educational force. Thus, if we now turn to the six problems which will probably characterize the next two decades of social change, perhaps we can see how the problem of narcissism fits into the picture.

1. Without a doubt, many of our largest and most powerful institutions are beginning to develop what amounts to a "value-free" approach to problem-solving. It characterizes our governmental, industrial, and educational ways of planning and managing society. Although there are a great many examples of this phenomenon, let us take the role of the military-industrial complex as a case in point. For not only is this a subject of increasing interest and concern to the younger generation, it is precisely the type of problem which describes the moral and philosophical dilemma we are facing as a nation. Significantly, many of those who belong to the various sects of the New Left have done their homework on Marx, Mao, and other communist ideologists. And one of the ideas which Marx sought to elaborate was the notion that ideology must always be evolved from experience. In the words of Sartre: "Existence precedes essence." Obviously, if one examines the rhetoric and strategy of the North Vietnamese, the Chinese, the Russians, and the Castro-type communists of Latin America, it becomes clear that ideology is actually secondary to strategy, and strategy is developed from practice and experience. To many young radicals in this

country, this has come to mean that strategy must always be geared to provide encounters, experiences, and confrontations which, in turn, force people to derive what values and meanings they can after the fact. Ironically, this is precisely the same type of strategy which is beginning to take hold in the Pentagon. For the more investments are made in the creation of certain types of military "hardware" and alternative plans for action, the more that hardware and those plans tend to determine what rationalizations must be developed to give meaning to their use and application. Consequently, the war in Vietnam was initially carried on for experimental purposes. And there was nothing in this process which could be labeled "winning" such a war. For that is not really the purpose of such action. Originally, the purpose was to force the North Vietnamese to go through a "cost-benefit analysis" of the war and to conclude that it would be far too costly for the war to continue. Unfortunately for the planners, the meaning of "cost" is a purely relative one, and Ho Chi Minh was motivated by an entirely different set of cost-benefit assumptions.

If we also take a look at the process whereby certain technological innovations are introduced into the Pentagon decision-making structure, we find that this strategy is continuing. If a large industrial firm seeks to sell a certain piece of military hardware, it soon becomes clear that strategy and policy are developed only after the contract is let, the hardware produced, and the Pentagon has tested the product. After the test, normally, a new strategy tends to evolve, which then determines what policy is needed for "deployment" of the new hardware. This has been true of the so-called Safeguard missile (except that it cannot be tested), the rapid-transit Navy vessel for moving men and supplies around the world on immediate notice, and the endless list of other tactical devices used in fighting "wars of intervention." By and large, the general public is completely ignorant of this process, and most planners in the Pentagon know this fact quite well. Consequently, when one seeks to discover where the element of control comes into play in this approach to governmental and military planning, it becomes frighteningly clear that no one is really in control at all. In Congress, for example, there are four men who control the budget of the military, and three of them are old-time Southern Congressmen. The one who carries the most weight in the Congress is the chairman of the House's military appropriations committee. All these men, and especially the chairman of the House's committee, are ignorant of the implications of this newer type of systems planning in the military. They are old-fashioned ideologists who continue to think in terms of previous wars and conflicts. Consequently, they not only fight for more money for the military, they sometimes give more than is requested. And since the economic benefits of a large military establishment, coupled with a rich and rewarding industrial complex, spend enormous sums of money in the states from which these Congressmen come, the process comes full circle. The military planners have a secure system, blessed by irrelevant patriotism in the forms of Congressional support, all while endless experimentation is unknowingly encouraged. Thus, if we ask why many young people today are becoming hardened by the experiences of confronting this system, and if we ask why they seem to become so committed to destroying the system, then we must ask: "Whose behavior is the most chaotic and anarchistic — those whose narcissism is frustrated by a gigantic system of military and industrial expansionism and experimentation, leading to unpredictable results, or those very institutions themselves?

2. If we ask the question: "What will the phenomenon of narcissism mean in terms of our social norms, predictable attitudes, and beliefs, not to mention behavior which is difficult to manage and control?" it becomes clear that we are already on a course of reaction which would lead one to conclude that repression, prosecution, and even technologically oriented controls will be applied, even as they are now. At the same time, however, there is some evidence that many institutions are not as ready to demand conformity among the young as would seem to be the case at first glance. Our universities are recognizing the justice of many youthful demands, the government is slowly responding to the criticism and effectiveness of the youth movement, and a great many executives in the business world are reevaluating many of their own values and attitudes toward the younger generation. Of course, this does not mean that society is readily accommodating itself to the narcissism of the young. But it does mean that many of the "positive" aspects of the younger generation's effect on society are being felt quite strongly. Perhaps one sees it most vividly in the arts and drama, as well as in the impact in music, dance, dress, and related factors of cultural change.

Doubtless, one of the elements of influence which eventually will alter many of our present institutional reactions to the narcissism of the young is the role played by the parents of the young in seeking to protect their children from the effects of a repressive society. We are already beginning to see some effect in that a growing number of parents of the most radical and "way out" young people do not want the government or the universities to prosecute or punish their children for such things as drug use, demonstrations, sexual acts, draft evasion, and antipolitical actions. Too many affluent and influential parents are learning that some of the youthful protesters are quite right in their rejection of higher education as it is presently structured. And they are coming to agree with their youngsters that the military-industrial complex is getting out of hand while the country suffers from profound social ills. When it comes to such matters as narcissism, however, most parents are confused by their children. They understand the moral demands, but they cannot comprehend the psychology which tends to reject society out of hand. And, unfortunately, not all young people are articulate enough to help their parents understand them better.

Exactly how far the society can go with repression is not very clear. Obviously, repression seems to add greater force to the young people's alienation and rejection of the society. And there are quite a few young people who seem quite willing to take the punishment while continuing to maintain their attitudes and values. But to assume that the society itself can indefinitely control through suppression the narcissism of the young is to see this society as far more consistent, logical, and self-conscious than is actually the case. We are not a nation with viable and universal values. We are fast becoming a nation without direction, goals, or meaningful priorities. And any time such a vacuum exists for too long, any set of values which comes along at the right time can easily have a profound influence. And since all of us are narcissists to one degree or another, it is highly likely that the young will continue to provide the society with its basic value questions, its newer norms, and its alternative life-styles.

3. In the most profound sense, the real question the younger generation has posed for this country is whether or not democracy is possible. Can the people govern themselves without a government

which seeks to manipulate everything for institutional ends? Obviously, there are not too many adults who have asked this question. There are, however, a great many adults who have expressed their frustration and powerlessness in regard to the bureaucratic nature of governmental control. Taxes are too high, governmental expenditures seem endless, and no one seems to be in control of the entire process. And yet, in spite of all these problems, most adults appear to be willing to believe that someone really is in control, since it is too frightening to believe otherwise. But for a fast-growing number of young people, it is quite clear that controls exist only when individual citizens dare to challenge the system as it stands. And what usually tends to happen on occasions like these is that someone in the bureaucracy takes it upon himself to enforce what he believes is the meaning of the law. It may be a member of a draft board, an individual policeman, a dean in the university hierarchy, or a Senator who feels that some particular new legislation must be enacted. But until an individual citizen or a particular group of citizens challenge some aspect of the system, these representatives of the system normally remain quiet. Consequently, one is forced to ask how changes actually do occur within the system, and it becomes immediately clear that there are no internal forces within the system to effect basic and relevant changes. Change must come from outside the system. A great many young people have finally concluded that only in the individual's personal liberation from the system is there any hope of ultimately changing the system. Indeed, so pervasive is this assumption among those in the younger generation that it is becoming a strategy for confronting things as they are. It is the political and social meaning which lies behind the phrase "do your own thing."

Without a doubt, the more this society confronts countless young people seeking to "do their thing," the more difficult it will be to enforce what the singular bureaucrat assumes is the meaning of the law, the relevance of existing norms, and the purpose of certain policies. A continual process of "feedback control" will have to come into being as a means of continuously determining where the system stands in relation to greater levels of individuality, choice, and personal autonomy. In this sense, the true meaning of democracy will probably come directly from the people, especially those who will not wait for the system to define it for them. But between now and then, a great many people are going to suffer from the inability of the system to keep up with them.

4. It doesn't take a crystal ball to see that the ultimate consequences of this growing confrontation between relatively autonomous individuals and bureaucratized institutions will finally result in the creation of what amounts to a "benevolent fascism" in the system. We have already begun to evolve many of the characteristics of such a system. Essentially, the major factors of influence which can and will bring this kind of system into being stem from two existing forces already at work. On the one hand, we find more individuals demanding and receiving a degree of liberation from the once all-pervasive values of loyalty, belief, and acceptance of the system. Today, too many people on the inside as well as the outside of the system, no longer "believe" in the system. On the other hand, it would be foolish to assume that those who presently manage the system are completely ignorant of this phenomenon. Many of them even share some of the values of individuality, personal choice, and autonomy. The question then arises as to how the system can be maintained while it continues to grant more and more individuals greater personal freedom. Because it is rapidly becoming clear that the very few (the technocrats) are ultimately taking over the responsibility for determining the system's direction, large numbers of individuals, especially in the younger generation, are dropping out of the traditional race to compete for positions of power within the system. In other words, we are fast evolving a system which is comprised of the very few, highly trained technocrats who ultimately make policies about the system's direction, while the majority of citizens continue to express their demands for personal freedom and comprise an enormous force which cannot easily be managed.

Ironically, the more the systems approach to problem-solving is applied by these technocrats, the more it will be possible for methods of co-opting talent and skills from the citizenry to be applied in the place of ideological or value-laden methods of motivation. Instead of seeking the energies of the young to be captured by traditional appeals of loyalty, competition, and related group dynamics, the appeals will have to be through rewards, opportunities, and challenges. Of course, the big "hangup" today which surrounds the systems approach is the fact that it is used to reinforce existing conventional values, priorities, and practices. But as soon as these irrelevant values and practices are challenged and altered by the next generation's refusal to support them, the systems approach can readily be applied to solve more relevant and pressing problems.

The real paradox in this process of evolution in the systems approach will probably lie in the refusal of millions of young people to support the system. But the more this tends to happen, the more the systems approach will be forced to take this disaffection seriously. Once again, however, the alternatives to this type of change are too frightening. We are going to have either a real fascism or a benevolent one.

The forces which work against a real fascistic state's occurring are subtle indeed, but very real. The Puritan secularism of most adults tends toward both fascism and violence at the same time. On the one hand, there is a very real wish among adults for freedom from the constraints of Victorian morality. This leads to benevolence and tolerance of individual style. But fascism rises to the surface when personal freedom seems to threaten the structure of power, especially as it seeks to maintain institutional power and controls. And since the young are easily characterized by their demands for personal freedom, the constraints adults wish to impose on the young come in the form of institutional limitations, not simply personal controls.

At the same time, however, the narcissistic freedom of the young has become so contagious a force in society that adults find themselves having to accept, indeed even adopt, many of the innovations which the young introduce as elements of a new life-style. To manage this innovation the institutional system is forced to treat such changes as "feedback" and to learn how to continue the management of the society. Inevitably, the adult establishment is influenced by the behavior of the young and forced to treat new forms of behavior as "feedback" instead of simply rejecting them out of hand. Fascism remains because the controls are still in the hands of the Puritan secularists, but it is forced to become benevolent because the kids prove to be a subtle but influential force on the way policy and programs get established. Consequently, the more "feedback"-conscious institutional management becomes, the more impact the young will have in altering the management decisions about institutional policy and actions.

5. In order for this process of "benevolent fascism" to take place, there will have to develop one very essential innovation which will guarantee the individual a means whereby he can be protected from the power of the technocrats to misinterpret his freedom or his tolerance of bureaucratic manipulation. And that very essential innovation will be a kind of Ralph Nader-type approach to law and the public interest. Until the most recent years, this country did not really have a legal structure to deal with this problem. The laws which were once written to protect the rights and privileges of the individual were ultimately applied to institutions rather than individuals — this is what the industrial age has done to our legal system. If an individual could identify himself with an institution, then he could be protected by the laws which reinforced the institution's self-interest; but if the individual found himself alone, then he usually would have to suffer at the hands of superior forces under the domination of institutions. The attempts by the Supreme Court in recent years to recognize this problem only show how commonplace it has been for such a long time. It is ironic that most "conservatives" have interpreted this attitude in the court as "liberal," when in fact it is really a very old conservative value judgment. The problem, unfortunately, is due to the fact that most conservatives have locked themselves into an institutional, social, and political structure of self-interest, while those individuals who have not benefited from such protection have only had the courts to guarantee them their freedom from institutional controls.

The Supreme Court, however, cannot possibly meet the needs of the rapidly increasing numbers of individuals who have divorced themselves from institutional protection. A new body of legally skilled and trained servants of the public interest will have to be developed in order to provide the general public with all the information, protection, and awareness of the internal workings of the system. It is not, nor has it ever been, a trustworthy system. But if the variety of life-styles which presently have developed around us are to be protected from institutional, governmental, and bureaucratic reaction, then a true guarantee of individual liberties will have to be created very soon. Those who do not believe that the younger generation is willing to pay the price, to achieve a transformation of the system such as this are blind to the nature of the youth revolution. Experimentation with life-styles is not about to disappear in the foreseeable future. It is the only way the next generation can find itself and finally develop the values and attitudes which can enable man to survive on this planet.

6. Of course, the biggest question mark we face regarding the ability of the system to change and to serve the needs and interests of the general public will greatly depend upon the degree of sophistication which can be acquired by those who manage the existing technostructure. At the present time, much of our problem stems from the fact that most technocrats believe that institutional self-interest is the only reality which determines how things get done. One works for the government, business, or the university and assumes that these institutions are geared primarily to serve themselves and secondarily to serve the public interest. In fact, it has traditionally been interpreted that serving the public is directly related to serving the institution. Consequently, society has grown up around the interlocking institutional process of mutual self-seeking, only secondarily meeting the needs of the public. In fact, many great thinkers and social critics in the past have insisted that this was the only way society could intelligently be ordered.

But a large number of individuals who do not believe in this type of reality principle, especially since the vast majority of them are bright and concerned young people, will not continue to believe that the company always comes first. The question is whether or not many of these large and powerful institutions can understand that the society itself is increasingly dependent upon their technocrats' reading the needs and problems of the public correctly. The great irony is that the younger generation has now become a new force in the national economy, an experimenting and risk-taking class of individuals who can provide the technostructure with much more creative and viable markets, options for management, ideas for invention, and a virtual wellspring of new talent and skill. For technocrats to turn their backs on these factors of influence and potential contribution to the system is the blindest and worst form of self-interest. But to assume that they will do so is even more foolish, since the system is not really geared to perpetuate itself by irrelevant ideologies. The one factor in the entire system which can work to its own benefit is the fact that it is highly conscious of pressure and profit-and-loss accounting, and ultimately makes pragmatic judgments to keep it alive. And if the generational conflict does not diminish over the next few years, then one can assume

that the system will be forced to take the younger generation's behavior and values into serious consideration. It's the only way the
system can survive.

If we can assume that these are some of the issues with which
the society must deal in the coming two decades, then what
can be said of the behavior and values of the next generation of
young people? There is very little reason to believe that the
generations yet to come will ever return to the values and attitudes of today's adult generation. If we do not destroy ourselves in the next few years, then the levels of affluence and the
technological sophistication which will be required to live in
this society cannot help but reinforce the narcissism of the vast
majority of youngsters yet unborn. Society will not continue
to possess enough lower-middle-class and traditionally motivated youngsters to feed into the system of production, repressed aggression, and institutionalized values.

We must rapidly take into consideration the manner by
which we do make projections and plans about the future. And
one of the most serious flaws in our present systems of planning is that we do not take behavioral change and human values
enough into consideration. We tend to use mathematical and
abstract methods for prediction and elaborate our projections
on the basis of what factors of change we have understood in
the past. But this is the most dangerous oversight we could
imagine. If there is any one factor of change which is rising
with the exponential curve of innovation, it is the behavioral
and value change which accompanies all the other innovations.
This means, in the most direct way, that the phenomenon of
narcissism, far from being a mere innovation in a time of un-
certainty and change, is probably the dominant future nature
of man. It was Aristotle who stated that "man is most man
when he is at play." Another way to express the same thing is
to say that human nature is most productive, creative and inventive when the conditions of existence are supportive and
beneficial. In a sense, Western civilization has been living in an
interim period between the dawn of human civilization and the

revelation of utopia. For over two thousand years we have been taught to wait and work for the Kingdom of God. We have polarized heaven and hell, good and evil, pleasure and pain, and time and eternity. We have not been willing to accept the fact that man himself might well introduce the elements of change which can bring in the utopian age which the prophets and eschatologists claimed they saw. But how we anticipate that future, more than ever before in human history, plays a role in whether or not we shall ever achieve it.

INDEX